Metro

Student Book & Workbook

3

with Online Homework and ON THE MOVE Smartphone Activities

James Styring & Nicholas Tims
Alexandra Paramour • Aírton Pozo de Mattos

OXFORD
UNIVERSITY PRESS

Contents

Listening	Speaking	Watch	Writing
• Fears and phobias *15* • Speaking in public *18*	• Sharing problems *20*	▶ Happiness in Mexico *22*	• A story about a memorable experience **Good writers tip:** using adverbs of manner *101*
• Home rules *25* • Restorative justice *28*	• Asking for and giving permission *30*	▶ Rules at home and at school *32*	• School rules **Good writers tip:** using expressions of purpose *102*

Welcome to Metro

Transportation

1 Look at the pictures. Complete the sentences with the words. Use the simple past of the verbs.

fly / plane   ride / motorcycle   sail / ferry   take / bus   take / subway   ~~take / train~~

Last week, …

 1 we __took a train__ to my cousins' house.

 2 we _____ in a _____ to my grandparents' house.

 3 I _____ on my brother's _____ last weekend.

 4 I _____ a _____ to the beach.

 5 we _____ on a _____ around New York.

 6 we _____ the _____ to the theme park.

Travel adjectives

2 Look at the pictures in exercise 1 again. Complete the sentences with the adjectives.

comfortable   crowded   delicious
historic   modern   noisy   ~~quiet~~

1 **Mark:** It was really q_uiet_ and the seats were really c_____.

2 **Gloria:** They gave us lunch and it was d_____!

3 **Callum:** It was fun, but it's really n_____!

4 **Jenna:** The bus was really c_____ and we couldn't find anywhere to sit.

5 **Ethan:** It's the best way to see the Statue of Liberty and other h_____ buildings.

6 **Sofia:** The station is really m_____.

Money verbs and shopping nouns

3 Complete the conversations with the pairs of words.

borrow / counter   ~~can't afford / sale~~   pay / receipt
spent / change   wasting / bargain

1 **A** Look, there's a _sale_ on at the store.
  B Sorry. I _can't afford_ anything at the moment.

2 **A** Excuse me. Did you _____ for that hat?
  B Yes, I did. Here's the _____.

3 **A** This is a _____. It's only $10!
  B You're _____ your money. Good headphones are more expensive than $10.

4 **A** Can I _____ $5 to buy these pens?
  B Sure. I can give you the money when we get to the _____.

5 **A** Did you remember to get your _____?
  B There wasn't any. I _____ exactly $20 and gave the assistant a $20 bill.

Present progressive for plans

4 Complete the questions and answers with the verbs.

> do / not work   get back / meet   ~~go away / see~~
> hang out / go   take / not swim   travel / not take

1 A <u>Are</u> we <u>going away</u> this weekend?

  B Yes, we<u>'re seeing</u> your cousins.

2 A What _____ we _____ this weekend?

  B I don't know. Dad _____ so we can all go out together.

3 A _____ everyone _____ at the mall on Saturday?

  B No! I_____ to a comics exhibition.

4 A How _____ you _____ to Jack's house tonight?

  B I_____ the subway. It's too hot.

5 A What time _____ you _____ on Sunday?

  B About lunchtime. My brother _____ us at the airport at 10 a.m.

6 A _____ anyone _____ their phone to the beach?

  B I am. And I_____, so you can leave yours with me.

Comparative adjectives

5 Complete the conversation with the comparative form of the adjectives. Add *than* if necessary.

A Do you want to hang out on Saturday?

B Sunday's ¹ <u>better than</u> (good) Saturday for me.

A OK. What about going to the beach?

B Sure. South Beach? It's ² _____ (quiet) the others.

A OK. How are we going to get there?

B The subway is ³ _____ (fast) the bus.

A Yes, but the bus is ⁴ _____ (cheap). And it's ⁵ _____ (hot) on the subway.

B OK. Let's meet at your house and take the bus.

B South Beach is ⁶ _____ (popular) I thought.

A Yes. It's ⁷ _____ (crowded) last time.

B But I'm ⁸ _____ (upset) about the weather.

B Yeah, it's ⁹ _____ (bad) it was at home.

A We could go back and sunbathe on your balcony …

B I guess it's ¹⁰ _____ (comfortable) here, too …

A Come on. Let's go!

Indefinite pronouns

6 Complete the words with *-one*, *-thing*, or *-where*.

1 There's no<u>thing</u> to do near here.

2 I want to go some_____ hot.

3 Are you taking any_____ to eat later?

4 No _____ wants to go swimming.

5 Every_____'s taking the subway to the mall.

6 Some_____ in this salad is delicious!

Your turn

7 Look at the pairs of pictures. Write as many sentences as possible in your notebook to compare the pictures.

1 the moon / the sun   2 pizza / pasta

3 cats / dogs   4 South America / Asia

8 In pairs, take turns reading your sentences. Which person has the most original sentences for each pair?

> The sun is older than the moon!

2 Working lives

Jobs

1 Complete the sentences with the words.

> architect   chef   doctor   journalist
> nurses   salesperson   ~~software developer~~

3 Arcadia High School cafeteria is growing and we need another _____. Contact the principal at AHS.

4 Upton Soccer Team needs a new club building. Do you know a good local _____?

HELP WANTED

1 We have the ideas, but we need a talented **software developer**. Are you good at Java? Contact The App Agency.

2 We need a _____ for local news and sports reporting. Bay Area, evenings. Apply here.

5 San Merino Health Center is looking for two _____ and a _____ to join our busy team. Details here.

6 Have you ever worked as a _____? At St. Quentin Mall we need confident, hard-working people to join the toy department. Contact us!

Safety online

2 Complete the labels. Use one word of each color.

> antivirus   click   different   ~~information~~   install
> links   on   passwords   ~~personal~~   ~~share~~   software   use

Staying safe at work

1   share personal
    information

2   _____
    _____

3   _____

4   _____
    _____

Crime

3 Complete the text with the words.

> arrest   break   ~~catch~~   commit
> investigate   rob   steal

Working Lives
Officer Doyle

I'm a police officer and my job is to ¹ **catch** any criminals who ² _____ crimes in my neighborhood. Often the same people ³ _____ into homes and ⁴ _____ things, or they ⁵ _____ people. But although we know most of the criminals in the area, we have to ⁶ _____ carefully and collect evidence before we can ⁷ _____ anyone.

Personality adjectives

4 Match the opposite adjectives.

1 confident   a anxious
2 easygoing   b cheerful
3 lazy   c hard-working
4 miserable   d rude
5 polite   e shy

5 Which five personality characteristics in exercise 4 would be helpful in a job?

1   confident   4   _____
2   _____   5   _____
3   _____

have to / don't have to

6 Complete the text with the correct form of *have to*.

GILES McPURDEY

DENTIST

Q Is it hard to be a dentist?

A It's not easy to become a dentist. But being a dentist is fun!

Q ¹ <u>Do</u> you <u>have to study</u> (study ?) a lot to become a dentist?

A Yes, we ² _____. Dentists ³ _____ (study ✓) the same college courses as doctors, and we ⁴ _____ (pass ✓) a lot of exams. More than most doctors!

Q ⁵ _____ you _____ (work ?) long hours?

A No, I ⁶ _____. I only ⁷ _____ (work ✓) from 8 a.m. to 6 p.m. I ⁸ _____ (take ✗) my work home in the evenings, and I ⁹ _____ (work ✗) on the weekend. I have better working hours than most professionals. My wife's a lawyer. She ¹⁰ _____ (start ✗) work until 9 a.m., but she ¹¹ _____ (work ✓) most evenings.

(not) as ... as, too / not ... enough

7 Choose the correct words.

1 I'm not going to be a scientist.
   I **'m too good** / **'m not good enough** at physics.

2 Sara's brother is a chef, but Sara can't cook very well.
   Sara's food **isn't as delicious as** / **is as delicious as** her brother's.

3 My dad's office is in a historic building. My mom works in a modern office.
   My dad's office **isn't as new as** / **is as new as** my mom's.

4 You can't drive a car yet, you're only 15.
   You **are too old** / **aren't old enough** to drive a car.

5 I don't want to work in the market because it's noisy.
   The market **is too quiet** / **isn't quiet enough** for me.

6 My cousin David looks younger than me, but actually we're both 17.
   David **looks as old as** / **doesn't look as old as** me, but actually he **is as old as** / **isn't as old as** me.

Superlative adjectives

8 Look at the chart and complete the sentences with the superlative form of the adjectives.

	Sam, architect	Marc, chef	Zoey, taxi driver
high or low salary?	$$$$$	$$$	$
interesting or boring?	☺☺☺☺☺	☺☺☺☺	☺☺
easy or hard?	❄❄❄❄	❄❄❄	❄
long or short hours?	⏳⏳⏳	⏳⏳⏳⏳	⏳⏳⏳⏳⏳
safe or dangerous?	⚠	⚠ ⚠	⚠ ⚠ ⚠

1 Marc has a high salary, but Sam has <u>the highest salary</u>.

2 Marc's job is interesting, but Sam has _____ job.

3 Being an architect is _____ job. Architects have to study for six years. Driving a taxi is _____ job.

4 Sam and Marc work long hours, but Zoey works _____ hours. Sam works _____ hours.

5 Being a chef is quite safe, but designing buildings is _____ job. Driving a taxi is _____.

can / can't for rules

9 Copy and complete the chart with information about the rules in your home. Use the ideas below or your own ideas.

> cook meals   do homework every day
> play computer games before breakfast
> use devices in our bedrooms   wash the dishes
> watch TV until midnight

We can	We can't	We have to	We don't have to
use devices after dinner	be rude		

 **Your turn**

10 In pairs, compare your rules.

> We don't have to cook meals.

> Oh, in my house we have to cook meals.

3 Get active

Sports and adventure sports

1 Read the definition of *bucket list*. Then complete the bucket list with *do*, *go*, or *play*, and the sports.

> bungee jump   karate   rafting   sailing   ~~scuba diving~~
> skateboarding   sky diving   snowboarding   surfing
> tennis   track and field   volleyball

> **bucket list** *noun* /'bʌkɪt lɪst/
> a list of things that you want to do during your lifetime
> *I've never gone rafting, but it's on my bucket list.*

My bucket list

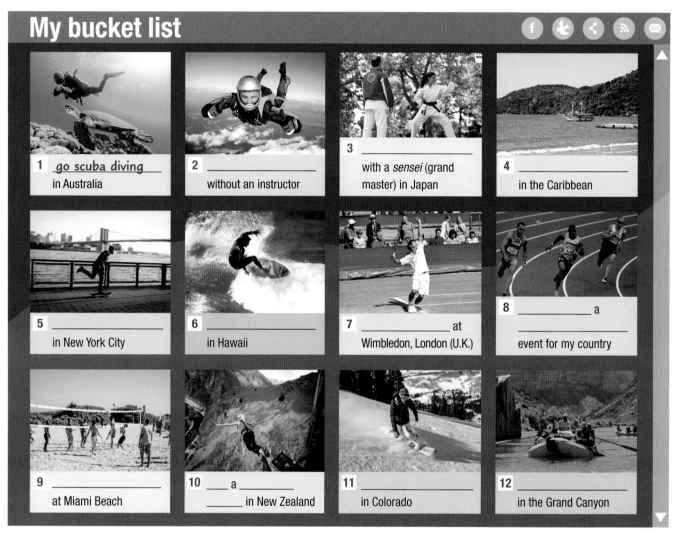

1 _go scuba diving_ in Australia

2 _____ without an instructor

3 _____ with a *sensei* (grand master) in Japan

4 _____ in the Caribbean

5 _____ in New York City

6 _____ in Hawaii

7 _____ at Wimbledon, London (U.K.)

8 _____ a _____ event for my country

9 _____ at Miami Beach

10 ___ a _____ in New Zealand

11 _____ in Colorado

12 _____ in the Grand Canyon

Sports verbs and feelings

2 Complete the text with the words.

> caught   ~~disappointed~~   kicked   lost   proud
> scored   shot   surprised   were winning   worried

I was ¹<u>disappointed</u> with United today. We ²_____ 4–2 against City, but then in the last ten minutes of the game City ³_____ three goals! In the end, we ⁴_____ 5–4. I was really ⁵_____ at their new center forward, Jaime Martin. He ⁶_____ the ball over 40 meters a few times, and each time the ball reached the penalty area. He ⁷_____ at the goal three times from the center circle. Our goal keeper ⁸_____ the first two balls, but the third was a goal. Jaime Martin should be ⁹_____ of that goal. Now I'm ¹⁰_____ about our game against City next month!

be going to

3 Complete the news story with the *be going to* form of the verbs.

> go   help   ~~play~~   not play   stay
> teach   not think   travel   win

Marina Marinova
¹ is going to play her last international tennis game on Saturday. After that game, she ² _____ on vacation with her family. They ³ _____ on an island in the Caribbean for a few months. She said: "I ⁴ _____ this last game of my career. Then, we ⁵ _____ for a while. I ⁶ _____ about tennis at all! When I get back, I ⁷ _____ in international games. I ⁸ _____ at a tennis academy in Cannes, France. I ⁹ _____ young players prepare for international games."

4 Complete the questions and answers with *be going to* about Marina Marinova.

1 When _is Marina Marinova going to play her_
   _last game_____?
   _She's going to play her last game_____ on Saturday.

2 Where is she _____?
   _____ to the Caribbean.

3 _____ with her family?
   Yes, _____.

4 Where _____?
   _____ at a tennis
   academy.

5 _____ help older tennis
   players?
   No, _____.

 **Your turn**

5 Make lists of your plans and intentions.

this weekend	go to the market with Mom, ...
this term	
this year	
when I'm an adult	

6 In pairs, compare your lists. Use *be going to*.

Past progressive

7 Write affirmative and negative past progressive sentences.

1 Evan / sunbathe / swim
   Evan was sunbathing. He wasn't swimming.

2 Bella / fly / run
   _____

3 Carter / do parkour / ride a bike
   _____
   _____

4 Daisy / kick the ball / throwing it
   _____
   _____

8 Write past progressive questions about the pictures. Answer the questions.

1 What / Bella and Daisy both / wear?
   What were Bella and Daisy both wearing?
   They were wearing shorts and T-shirts.

2 What / Evan / read?
   _____
   _____

3 What / Daisy and Bella / play?
   _____
   _____

4 Who / jump?
   _____

5 Who / not exercise?
   _____
   _____

6 What / Evan and Carter both / wear?
   _____
   _____

It's the weekend

Weekend plans and phrasal verbs: movement

1 Complete the sentences with the verbs.

get on ~~go~~ go away go out go out
have have have pick up see

1 Are you going to _go_____ to the exhibition on Sunday?

2 Do you want to _____ for a meal or _____ a cookout on the beach?

3 It's your birthday soon. Are you going to _____ a party at home or are we going to _____ somewhere?

4 You and Em have never stayed at my house! We should _____ a sleepover. You can _____ the bus near the park on Saturday and my dad can _____ Em.

5 We're going to _____ this weekend. We're going to _____ my relatives in Idaho. It's my grandma's 75th birthday!

Performing arts

2 Complete the conversation with the verbs.

acting designed directing ~~performing~~ take

Will: Do you want to hang out this weekend?
Emily: I can't. I'm in a play.
Will: What? You mean, ¹ _performing_ on stage?
Emily: Yeah. I'm ² _____ in the school play.
Will: I forgot! I'm so sorry!
Emily: It's OK. You should come. Alfie's ³ _____ it and Sara ⁴ _____ the costumes. Come along and ⁵ _____ some pictures!

TV shows and movies

3 Complete the words.

Streaming What are you going to watch this weekend? Click and watch.

TV shows

1 r e a l i t y
  s h _ o w s

2 t _ _ k
  s _ _ ws

3 s _ _ _ _ _ s
  s _ _ ws

4 s _ _ _ p
  o _ _ _ as

Movies

5 a _ _ _ _ _ n
  m _ _ _ _ s

6 c _ _ _ _ _ ies

7 h _ _ _ _ r
  m _ _ _ _ s

8 s _ _ _ _ _ _ e
  f _ _ _ _ _ n
  m _ _ _ _ s

Past progressive with *when* and *while*

4 Complete the sentences with the past progressive or simple past form of the verbs.

1 Kayla _was performing_ (perform) on stage when someone's phone _rang_ (ring).

2 I'm sorry, but I _____ (not see) your texts while I _____ (hang out) with my friends.

3 We _____ (not see) our relatives while we _____ (stay) in Rio last week.

4 _____ (you / remember) to read my notes while you _____ (study)?

5 Jon _____ (get on) the train when he _____ (drop) his wallet.

Adverbs

5 Complete the sentences with the adverb form of the adjectives.

anxious ~~careful~~ confident quick

1 Antonia designed the costumes for the play _carefully_. She made them very _____, in just one weekend.

2 I was so scared before the play. I sat _____ waiting for it to start. But then I got on stage, and I acted really _____. My friends said I was great!

easy fast good noisy

3 The plane took off _____. It was going very _____ – over 250 km/h.

4 At the end of the concert, Adele performed my favorite song, *Hello*. She sang really _____ and I could hear the lyrics _____.

Present perfect (experiences)

6 Write true sentences. Use the correct affirmative or negative form of the present perfect.

1 do capoeira
  I've never done capoeira.

2 have a sleepover
  _____

3 travel on a plane
  _____

4 save money
  _____

5 perform on stage
  _____

6 watch a horror movie
  _____

7 ride a motorcycle
  _____

8 go to an amusement park
  _____

9 score a goal
  _____

10 do a bungee jump
  _____

👉 Your turn

7 In pairs, ask and answer questions about the sentences in exercise 6.

> Have you ever done a bungee jump?

> Yes, I have!

8 Tell the class about your partner.

> Rafael has done a bungee jump, but he hasn't …

Introducing ...

Video Watch the video.
Complete the sentences.

Hi! I'm Victoria, but most people call me Vicky. I love **1** <u>sports</u>. **2**_____ is my favorite, but I also enjoy **3**_____. This weekend I'm running a half marathon. That's 21 kilometers!

Hey! My name's Rob. I love technology – especially **4**_____ and **5**_____. I'm saving money for a new camera at the moment. I love **6**_____ and I take a lot of photos. In fact, stay there … Nice! Do you want to see?

Hello. I'm Amy. I'm quite **7**_____ and I enjoy studying. I also love **8**_____ – especially for clothes. What do you think of my T-shirt? It's **9**_____!

Hi there. I'm Tripp. I'm not as hard-working as Amy. I'm not lazy – just **10**_____. Like Vicky, I love sports, especially **11**_____ and **12**_____. I'm on the school basketball team.

In this unit ...

- describe your feelings and emotions
- describe body language
- share problems and offer advice
- choose appropriate definitions for words with more than one meaning
- understand a video about happiness in Mexico

 **Video** Watch the warm-up video.

Body and mind

1

> Any good pictures?

> There are some good ones of _____.

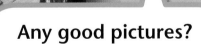

1 Why does Rob agree to delete the pictures of Vicky?

2 Do you take lots of pictures of your friends?

Feelings and emotions

1 🔊 02 ▷ **Read Vicky's message to a friend. What is Woodlands?**

 Vicky McKay
@_victoria

↩ Reply ♥ Like   **Following**

@jen_jones. Do you remember losing that game against Woodlands? A friend took this photo of me after the game. I was really annoyed. Their teacher was the referee!

2 Look at the pictures and read the comments. Choose the correct adjectives to complete the comments.

3 🔊 03 ▷ Listen, check, and repeat.

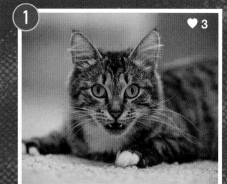

1 ♥ 3
I got up early today. Bertie is **shocked** / **relaxed**!

2 💬 12
True! It's important to be **positive** / **annoyed**!

3 ♥ 5
I know how you feel, Bertie! I'm **exhausted** / **confused**, too.

4 ♥ 2
Lucy gets **embarrassed** / **positive** when I take pictures of her! Long hair can be useful when your best friend has a new camera …

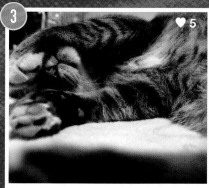

5 ♥ 18
My brother has an easy life! Gaming, messaging, and listening to music. I'm **jealous** / **frightened**.

6 ♥ 14
At the beach with a good book – Sophie is really **relaxed** / **stressed**!

7 ♥ 1
At the beach. I'm **confused** / **embarrassed**! Is it left or right for information?

8 ♥ 9
Two weeks before exams! Rob is getting a bit **stressed** / **annoyed**.

9 ♥ 8
Grrrr! After two weeks, my new white sneakers are gray! I'm **annoyed** / **exhausted**!

10 ♥ 5
Sleepover time! We ALWAYS watch a horror movie and we ALWAYS get **frightened** / **jealous**!

4 Match the words with their definitions.

1 embarrassed	_d_	6 relaxed	___
2 confused	___	7 exhausted	___
3 frightened	___	8 annoyed	___
4 positive	___	9 shocked	___
5 stressed	___	10 jealous	___

a when you can't understand something

b happy and enthusiastic

c a little angry

d ~~shy or worried about what other people think of you~~

e worried and tired

f unhappy or mad because you want something that someone else has

g very surprised, and maybe upset

h scared

i calm and not worried

j very tired

5 How do you feel in these situations? Use adjectives from exercise 4.

1 You spend the day at the beach. _relaxed, positive_

2 Your mom sings in front of your friends.

_____

3 You run ten kilometers.

_____

4 Your friend buys an expensive phone.

_____

5 Someone borrows your stuff, but doesn't ask you first. _____

6 You have lots of homework.

_____

7 Your best friend is rude to you for no reason.

_____

 Stop -ed adjectives describe emotions – how someone feels about something: *I'm bored.*
-ing adjectives describe the thing or person that causes the emotion: *This is a boring movie.*

6 Complete the words with -ed or -ing.

1 I don't understand this movie. It's really confus_ing_.

2 I like this music. It's really relax_____.

3 Did you hear the news about Tom? I was shock_____.

4 I forgot the teacher's name. It was really embarrass_____.

5 Don't be frighten_____. Bill is a friendly dog.

6 I'm going to bed early tonight. My weekend was exhaust_____!

☞ Your turn

7 Copy and complete the sentences for you. Then, in pairs, compare your sentences.

1 I feel relaxed when I **don't have any homework.**

2 I feel annoyed when I …

3 The most confusing subject at school is …

4 I get stressed when I …

5 When …, I sometimes feel jealous.

→ *METRO EXPRESS* P.109

Workbook P.W2   **Online Homework**

L **Listening**

Fears and phobias

1 Read the definition. Do you know the names of any phobias?

> **phobia** *noun* /ˈfoʊbiə/
> a very strong fear or dislike that you cannot explain: *She has a phobia about spiders.*

2 🔊 04 Listen and match the phobias with the definitions.

a clowns   b ~~dogs~~   c speaking in public   d going to school

1 cynophobia _b_   3 scolionophobia ___

2 coulrophobia ___   4 glossophobia ___

3 🔊 04 Listen again. Choose the correct answers.

1 We can get phobias …
  a from bad experiences.   c from our family.
  b when we are stressed.   ⓓ a, b, and c

2 The interviewer is frightened of …
  a spiders only.   c spiders and snakes.
  b dogs only.   d snakes and dogs.

3 Psychologists think some people are frightened of clowns because …
  a clowns are always smiling.
  b clowns are often in horror movies.
  c they had a bad experience at the circus.
  d people can't see clowns' real faces.

4 Dr. Thompson doesn't enjoy …
  a being on the radio.
  b speaking to groups of people.
  c being in unusual situations.
  d being in crowded places.

1 🔊 05 **Read the comments. Match the titles 1–3 with the stories A–C.**

1 It wasn't for me!   2 My dad, the teenager   3 I just wasn't ready

Emotional moments

We all experience strong emotions sometimes. Can you remember a time when you felt super stressed, totally shocked, or really embarrassed? Tell us your stories for a chance to win two movie tickets.

A Ruby ___

Singing was one of my favorite hobbies when I was younger. When I started high school, my parents suggested auditioning for the school choir. They paid for some singing lessons, and I practiced for weeks before I had my audition. It was on a Saturday, at 3 p.m. I arrived an hour early with my dad so that I had time to practice singing the music first. But another student was late for their audition, and I had to start immediately.

I never get nervous about performing, but suddenly I felt very stressed! I sang really badly. It was the worst fifteen minutes of my life. But the most surprising thing? I passed the audition and I'm in the choir!

B Marco ___

My twin brother, Alex, is great at playing sports. I'm more interested in reading and music. And this was true when we were young. But I can never forget our 10th birthday. We got lots of presents, but there was one huge present. Was it for both of us? Then Dad said, "Open it, Alex." I was so jealous!

My brother opened it quickly and inside was a bike. I hated riding bikes, but I was still annoyed. I wanted a big, exciting present, too.

Mom says I got lots of other presents, but I can't remember them. She says I was miserable all day!

C Keira ___

I remember my first party without any adults. It was a friend's 15th birthday and I was really excited. The party was cool, but by midnight I was feeling exhausted and ready to go.

Then some parents started arriving to pick up their kids. Suddenly I heard my dad's voice: "I LOVE this song!" he was shouting. I ran into the living room, but I was too late. My dad was already dancing WITH MY FRIENDS! I was so mad at my dad. I didn't speak to him for a week!

2 **Read the text again. Write the correct people.**

1 _Marco_ had a bad experience on his or her birthday.

2 _____'s dad didn't want to go home at the end of a party.

3 _____ was shocked about something after his or her experience.

4 _____ was embarrassed by someone.

5 _____'s parents paid for some lessons.

6 _____ has different interests from his or her brother.

3 **Answer the questions.**

1 Why did Ruby do her audition early?
   Because the other student was late.

2 How long was Ruby's audition? _____

3 Why didn't Marco's parents give him the same present as his brother? _____

4 What did Marco's parents give him?
   _____

5 What was special for Keira about the party?
   _____

6 How did Keira know her dad was at the party?
   _____

G Grammar

Use of gerund (-ing form)

1 🔊 06 **Read the text. Why didn't the boy's dad help him?**

Climbing was one of my favorite hobbies when I was young. Once, on vacation, I climbed a really tall tree, but I couldn't get down. I was really frightened of falling. My dad hates climbing and has a phobia about heights so my uncle had to climb up and help me.

2 Complete the chart.

We use gerunds:	
a as a subject	**1** <u>Climbing</u> was one of my favorite hobbies.
b after some verbs, e.g. *enjoy, finish, hate, like, love, practice, start, suggest*	My dad hates **2** _____.
c after prepositions	I was really frightened of **3** _____.

Stop climb → climb**ing**   get → get**ting**
drive → driv**ing**

3 Complete the sentences with the gerund of the verbs. Then match the sentences with the uses of the gerund in exercise 2.

~~be~~ feel listen lose perform swim

1 I'm sorry for <u>being</u> late.   <u>c</u>
2 _____ on stage can be embarrassing.   ___
3 Did you enjoy _____ in the ocean?   ___
4 Jo is annoyed about _____ the game.   ___
5 _____ to music is relaxing.   ___
6 I hate _____ stressed about tests.   ___

4 Complete the sentences with the gerund of the verbs for you. Then compare your answers.

1 <u>Writing</u> English is harder than <u>speaking</u> it. (speak, write)
2 _____ is more fun than _____. (chat online, talk on the phone)
3 _____ is more exciting than _____. (bungee jump, scuba dive)
4 _____ is more interesting than _____. (study for tests, see your relatives)

5 Complete the sentences with one word or phrase from A and one from B.

A
don't like ~~enjoy~~
finished 's suggesting
started

B
going playing
running
washing ~~watching~~

1 They <u>enjoy watching</u> horror movies.

2 She _____ _____ to the mall.

3 My mom _____ _____ tennis last year.

4 They _____ _____ the dishes.

5 They _____ _____ a few minutes ago.

👉 **Your turn**

6 In pairs, make questions. Then ask and answer.

1 how / you / feel before / take / a test
  <u>How do you feel before taking a test?</u>
2 how / you / feel after / finish / your homework
  _____
  _____
3 you / think / of / go / to college
  _____
4 what / you dream of / be / in the future
  _____
  _____

How do you feel before taking a test?

I always feel positive before taking a test.

→ *METRO EXPRESS* P.109

Body: actions

1 🔊 **07** Match the verbs with the pictures. Then listen, check, and repeat.

> bite   blush   breathe   cross
> nod   ~~raise~~   shake   smile

1 ___raise___ your eyebrows

2 _____ your nails

3 _____

4 _____

5 _____ your arms

6 _____

7 _____ your head

8 _____ your head

2 Complete the sentences with the correct form of the actions in exercise 1.

1 __Raising your eyebrows__ can mean you're surprised or shocked.

2 You _____ fast when you're frightened.

3 _____ means "yes" in many cultures.

4 _____ means you're feeling positive.

5 _____ can mean you're stressed.

6 _____ can mean you're embarrassed.

7 People often say "no" by _____.

8 _____ can mean you're annoyed.

👉 **Your turn**

3 In pairs, ask and answer the questions.

1 What makes you blush?   3 What makes you smile?

2 Do you bite your nails?   4 Can you raise one eyebrow?

→ *METRO EXPRESS* P.109

L Listening

Speaking in public

1 🔊 **08** Listen. What is the topic of the interview?

a Tips for speaking in public

b Tips for good body language

c Why we feel anxious about speaking in public

2 🔊 **08** Listen again. Choose *T* (True) or *F* (False).

1 Martina has glossophobia.   T ☐ F ☑

2 Martina thinks crossing your arms is positive body language.   T ☐ F ☐

3 Martina says difficult questions can make people blush.   T ☐ F ☐

4 Martina says that audiences should smile at presenters.   T ☐ F ☐

5 Martina feels practicing your talk is the most important tip.   T ☐ F ☐

3 🔊 **08** Complete Martina's tips for public speaking with one word. Then listen again and check.

1 Practice __talking__ in front of a mirror.

2 _____ at your body language carefully.

3 Be prepared to _____ any questions.

4 Learn to _____ slowly.

5 Everyone makes mistakes. Try to _____ relaxed and continue with your talk. It isn't necessary to _____ perfect!

Use of infinitives

1 🔊 09 **Read the conversation.
Why is Sal stressed?**

Ann: Hi, Mrs. Moss. I'm here to pick up Sal. We're going out.

Mrs. Moss: She's upstairs. But she's stressed about something …

Ann: What's wrong?

Mrs. Moss: I don't know. I asked her this morning, but she didn't want to talk to me.

Ann: OK. I think she's worried about her project. I can help her.

Mrs. Moss: Thanks, Ann. She's lucky to have a friend like you!

2 Complete the chart.

We use infinitives:	
to talk about purpose	I'm here ¹ to pick up Sal.
after some verbs, e.g. *decide, expect, learn, need, offer, plan, want*	She didn't want ²_____ to me.
after adjectives	She's lucky ³_____ a friend like you.

3 Complete the sentences with the infinitive of the verbs.

> ~~answer~~ buy celebrate log out say

1 I raised my hand **to answer** the question.
2 Click on this button _____ of the website.
3 My parents lent me $30 _____ a jacket.
4 We went out _____ Dad's birthday.
5 Turkish people nod their heads _____ "no".

4 Complete the sentences with the correct form of the verbs.

1 I **decided to stay** at home last night. Was the movie good? (decide, stay)
2 What time are you _____ to the party? (plan, go)
3 I was shocked. I _____ the test, but I passed! (expect, fail)
4 Do you _____ at the mall on Saturday? I don't have any plans. (want, meet)
5 We _____ last summer. I loved it! (learn, surf)

5 Look at the pictures. Write sentences in the simple present, using an infinitive.

1 Jack's number / easy / remember   2 They / excited / see her

3 That word / hard / say   4 I / lucky / have great parents

1 **Jack's number is easy to remember.**
2 _____
3 _____
4 _____

Gerund or infinitive?

6 Complete the questions with the gerund or infinitive of the verbs.

1 Do you practice **speaking** (speak) English outside of school?
2 Do you get stressed about _____ (be) late?
3 Outside of school, are you learning _____ (do) anything at the moment?
4 Do you enjoy _____ (make) new friends?
5 Is it important _____ (smile)? Why?
6 What things are fun _____ (do) in your city?
7 Do you offer _____ (help) your parents with chores or do they have to ask you?
8 Is _____ (hang out) with your friends more interesting than _____ (see) relatives?

 **Your turn**

7 In pairs, ask and answer the questions in exercise 6.

> Do you practice speaking English outside of school?

> Yes, I sometimes practice speaking to my brother in English.

→ *METRO EXPRESS* P.109

Sharing problems

1 🔊 10 **Listen and complete the conversation.**

Sophia: ¹ <u>What's</u> up, Jacob?

Jacob: I'm really ² _____.

Sophia: Oh, no. Why's that?

Jacob: I need ³ _____ for a test tomorrow,
I have a lot of homework, and I have
⁴ _____ some chores tonight.

Sophia: Try ⁵ _____ positive. Can you
⁶ _____ the chores tomorrow?
Ask your parents.

2 🔊 11 **Listen to two more conversations.
Complete the chart.**

Feeling	Reason	Advice
Jacob is stressed.	He has to study, do homework, and do chores tonight.	Ask your parents if you can do chores tomorrow.
Ava is ¹ <u>exhausted</u>.	She had ² _____ last night.	Maybe you should ³ _____ _____.
Ryan is ⁴ _____.	His brother borrowed his ⁵ _____ without asking.	You could ⁶ _____ _____.

Stop

Useful phrases

What's up? / What's wrong?

Why's that? / How come?

Try to … / Maybe you should … / You could …

3 **Use the chart in exercise 2 and act out the conversations.**

4 **In pairs, plan a new conversation. Copy and complete the chart in exercise 3 to plan your conversation. Use exercise 1 as a model.**

5 **In pairs, practice your conversation.**

6 **Act out your conversation for the class.**

1 🔊 12 **Read and listen. What is the best title?**

a Technology that reads your emotions

b Technology you can have a relationship with

c Technology that can help at home

2 **Read the tip.**

Tip **Good readers** can use dictionaries and context to find the appropriate meaning of unknown words.

Both definitions for these words are correct. Find the highlighted words in the article and choose the most appropriate definition.

> 1 **tough** /tʌf/
> a (adjective) very difficult
> b (adjective) very strong
> 2 **offer** /ˈɔfər/
> a (verb) to give or provide something
> b (verb) to ask someone if they want something
> 3 **expression** /ɪkˈsprɛʃn/
> a (noun) phrase
> b (noun) the look on someone's face

3 **Read the article. Choose _T_ (True) or _F_ (False).**

1 The Subconscious Menu chooses you a perfect pizza from 20 different pizzas. T ☐ F ☑

2 The Subconscious Menu is good at choosing people's perfect pizzas. T ☐ F ☐

3 Understanding your emotions is important for Pepper. T ☐ F ☐

4 Pepper is always happy. T ☐ F ☐

5 The Affectiva software can understand more emotions than Pepper. T ☐ F ☐

6 There are two main uses of the Affectiva software. T ☐ F ☐

4 **Complete the sentences with one or two words.**

1 The article says it's tough <u>to choose</u> a pizza.

2 There are 4,896 different combinations of the _____ at the pizza restaurant.

3 The pizza menu uses the camera on the tablet _____ your eyes.

4 The _____ of a Pepper is $1,800.

5 It took _____ to sell the first 1,000 robots.

6 Affectiva's software uses millions of examples of _____ from all over the world.

7 Affectiva can make _____ safer.

Choosing a pizza can be tough. There are just so many combinations of ingredients. The "Subconscious Menu" at this pizza restaurant tries to solve the problem. The menu is on a tablet and shows a customer 20 different pizza ingredients. In just 2.5 seconds it presents, from 4,896 combinations, your perfect pizza. The menu works by using the camera on the tablet. It follows your eyes and decides which ingredients you look at the longest. The "Subconscious Menu" claims to choose the correct pizza 98% of the time!

Like the pizza menu, Pepper the robot uses cameras to read your emotions. It can understand a range of expressions, from smiling to nodding your head, and react to what it sees. Pepper can offer to have a chat when you are stressed, or do a funny dance when you are feeling miserable! Pepper shows its own emotions, too: it's pleased to see you in the morning, and it feels confused when it doesn't understand people. The realistic robot even looks like it's breathing! And Pepper's helpful: it accesses the Internet to find information, like weather forecasts, and suggests taking an umbrella when it's rainy!

The robots are so popular that the company sold the first 1,000 (at $1,800 each) in just one minute!

Robots like Pepper can understand some human emotions. But imagine a computer that knows exactly how you are feeling, just by looking at your face.

Affectiva, a U.S. company, has developed software that analyzes facial expressions of emotion. The company has analyzed over 4.7 million faces from 75 different countries.

Affectiva believes there are thousands of uses for the software in our daily lives. For example, it wants to use the software in cars to know when drivers are tired, and in learning apps to know when students are bored or confused.

twenty-one

Happiness in Mexico

Vicky

Before you watch

1 What do you think is important for happiness? Number the words in order from 1 (most important) to 5 (least important).

a health _____

b money _____

c friends and family _____

d good government _____

e good weather _____

2 Look at the map. What do you know about these countries?

1 Iceland   5 Mexico
2 Denmark   6 Puerto Rico
3 The Netherlands   7 Costa Rica
4 Switzerland

Iceland   The Netherlands   Denmark

Switzerland

Puerto Rico

Mexico

Costa Rica

While you watch

3 ▶ Video Watch the preview video. Check (✓) the things that you see in the video.

1 older people and young people together ☑

2 teenagers using cell phones ☐

3 people dancing in the street ☐

4 expensive cars ☐

5 a family playing a game together ☐

6 cold weather ☐

7 a family eating together ☐

8 people playing sports outdoors ☐

9 a concert ☐

10 people relaxing outdoors ☐

4 ▶ Video Look at the ideas in exercise 1. Which of these things make Mexico a happy country? Watch the video and check.

_____

5 ▶ Video Watch the video again. Choose the correct answers.

1 The United Nations made the World __Happiness__ Report.

ⓐ Happiness   b Health   c Money

2 The world's happiest country in 2016 was

_____.

a The Netherlands   b Switzerland   c Denmark

3 Mexico is happier than some countries that have more

_____.

a doctors   b money   c good weather

4 According to the video, in Mexico,

_____ are very important.

a music   b food   c friends and family

5 People spend a lot of time _____.

a outdoors   b sleeping   c at work

6 Mexicans spend a lot of time outdoors

_____.

a to improve their health

b because of the weather

c while they are working

7 Spending time with friends and family

_____.

a can't make us happy

b is part of what makes us happy

c is more important than being happy

After you watch

6 Discuss the questions.

1 Do you think people in your country are happy? Why? / Why not?

2 What do you think a country needs in order to be happy?

3 Do you think the world is becoming a happier place? Why? / Why not?

7 Make a video or project about happiness in your home country.

• Say what families do when they spend time together.

• Explain how people relax and enjoy free time.

• Say how happy you think people are.

Online Homework   ON THE MOVE   Challenge

In this unit ...

- talk about rules and bullying
- use the zero conditional to talk about things that always happen, and to give instructions and advice
- ask for and give permission
- practice skim reading
- understand video interviews about rules

Video Watch the warm-up video.

2
Follow the rules

> Tripp, stop that! _____ is against the rules in the library!

1 How does Amy feel at the end of the video? Why?

2 Have you ever gotten into trouble for something you didn't do?

do and make

1 🔊 13 **Read the conversation. Who finished their project?**

Victoria: I finished my project last night. Did you finish yours?

Amy: Yes, I did mine in the library. Tripp was there, but he just made a lot of noise!

Tripp: Amy, did the librarian ask you or me to be quiet?

Amy: Tripp!

2 🔊 14 **Complete the conversations with the phrases. Listen and check.**

made this mess   make excuses   makes mistakes

2 **Coach:** Who ⁵_____? The sign says: "No dirty soccer boots"! Charlie?

Charlie: I know – I usually take off my boots, but I'm late for my next class. I didn't have time!

Coach: Come on – don't ⁶_____. You know the rules.

Charlie: I'm sorry.

Coach: Don't worry! Everyone ⁷_____ sometimes. Clean the floor quickly, and then you can go to class.

doing something wrong   made a complaint
make the rules   makes a lot of noise

1 **Doorman:** Hey! Stop!

Lola: Why? Am I ¹ _doing something wrong_?

Doorman: Yes. You can't skateboard here.

Lola: Oh, I had no idea. Why is that?

Doorman: It ²_____.

Lola: But …

Doorman: Listen, I don't ³_____. The residents make them. And a resident ⁴_____ about noisy skateboarders.

did a great job   doing my best   doing your chores

3 **Dad:** Hazel? Are you ⁸_____?

Hazel: Yes, take a look in the kitchen.

…

Dad: Wow! You ⁹_____ of cleaning the kitchen! It's super-clean.

Hazel: Thanks. I'm cleaning my room now. I'm ¹⁰_____, but this vacuum cleaner isn't working very well!

3 Choose the correct words.

1 Listen, I don't **make the rules** / **make a mess**. I just work here.

2 My dad is mad at my sister. She **did some chores** / **did something wrong** at school.

3 Stop **making excuses** / **making noises**. I need your homework tomorrow morning!

4 I want to get a good grade, so I'm going to **do my best** / **do anything wrong**.

5 Don't **make a mess** / **do a great job**. Grandma is coming soon.

6 Isla **made a complaint** / **made a mistake** because she didn't like her food.

👉 Your turn

4 Complete the sentences with members of your family and the correct form of *do* or *make*. Compare answers.

At home, …

1 _My brother never does_ anything wrong.

2 _____ _____ the rules.

3 _____ _____ the most mess.

4 _____ have / has to _____ chores.

→ *METRO EXPRESS* P.110

→ **Workbook** P.W3   **Online Homework**

L Listening

Home rules

1 🔊 15 Read the questions. Then listen to three people talking about rules. Which question are they answering?

a Who makes the rules at home?

b What are your parents like?

c Do you have a lot of rules at home?

d Which home rules don't you like?

e Do you have to do chores at home?

2 🔊 15 Which things do Isy, Matt, and Eva mention? Listen and write the correct letter. There is one extra thing.

Isy   Matt   Eva

1 Isy   _b,_____

2 Matt _____

3 Eva   _____

a cleaning

~~b coming home late~~

c horror movies

d devices

e music

f studying

3 🔊 15 Listen again. Choose *T* (True) or *F* (False).

1 Isy has to eat in the kitchen.   T ☑ F ☐

2 Isy's family wears shoes at home.   T ☐ F ☐

3 Matt can't use his phone in his bedroom.   T ☐ F ☐

4 Matt plays online games in the evenings.   T ☐ F ☐

5 Eva goes to bed at eleven o'clock on
  school nights.   T ☐ F ☐

6 Eva agrees with all the rules in her house. T ☐ F ☐

4 Discuss the questions.

1 What do you think of the rules that Isy, Matt, and Eva have at home? Why?

2 What rules do you have at home? Which do you like? Which don't you agree with?

1 🔊 16 **Read the texts. Does each writer feel positive 👍, negative 👎, or both positive and negative 🤚 about devices at school?**

DEVICES @ SCHOOL: Cool 👍 or not cool 👎?

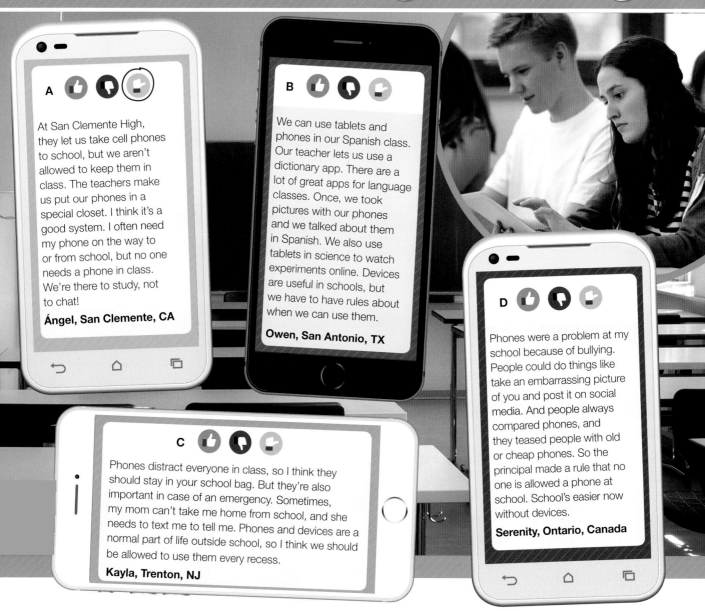

A 👍 👎 🤚

At San Clemente High, they let us take cell phones to school, but we aren't allowed to keep them in class. The teachers make us put our phones in a special closet. I think it's a good system. I often need my phone on the way to or from school, but no one needs a phone in class. We're there to study, not to chat!

Ángel, San Clemente, CA

B 👍 👎 🤚

We can use tablets and phones in our Spanish class. Our teacher lets us use a dictionary app. There are a lot of great apps for language classes. Once, we took pictures with our phones and we talked about them in Spanish. We also use tablets in science to watch experiments online. Devices are useful in schools, but we have to have rules about when we can use them.

Owen, San Antonio, TX

C 👍 👎 🤚

Phones distract everyone in class, so I think they should stay in your school bag. But they're also important in case of an emergency. Sometimes, my mom can't take me home from school, and she needs to text me to tell me. Phones and devices are a normal part of life outside school, so I think we should be allowed to use them every recess.

Kayla, Trenton, NJ

D 👍 👎 🤚

Phones were a problem at my school because of bullying. People could do things like take an embarrassing picture of you and post it on social media. And people always compared phones, and they teased people with old or cheap phones. So the principal made a rule that no one is allowed a phone at school. School's easier now without devices.

Serenity, Ontario, Canada

2 Match the sentences with the texts.

1 School is a place for studying, not for using phones.
   __A__

2 Students should be able to use phones between classes. _____

3 Devices can be useful during classes. _____

4 Students leave their phones in a safe place in school. _____

5 Phones cause bad behavior at school. _____

6 People need a phone if there's a problem or if plans change. _____

3 Complete the notes with information from the texts. Which do you agree and disagree with?

How phones can be useful in school

1 _dictionaries and other apps – I agree_

2 _____

3 _____

4 _____

5 _____

How phones can be a problem in school

6 _____

7 _____

4 What other ideas could you add? Discuss and compare in pairs.

be allowed to, let, and make

1 🔊 17 Read Mark's message. When can Mark use his phone? Check (✓) the times.

1 before school starts at 9.00 a.m. ☐
2 9.00–12.00 ☐
3 at lunchtime 12.00–1.00 ☐
4 1.00–3.30 ☐
5 after school, from 3.30 p.m. ☐

My school lets us use our cell phones at lunchtime, but we aren't allowed to use them during class. The teachers make us put our phones in our school bags. But I can use my phone before, and after, school.

Mark, Boston, Mass.

2 Complete the chart.

Permission: *be allowed to* and *let*
We**'re allowed to use** devices at lunchtime. We ¹ _aren't allowed to use_ them during class. **Are** you **allowed to hang out** here?
My school ² _____ **us use** our cell phones at lunchtime. She **lets us use** a dictionary app. My parents **don't let us shop** online. **Do** your parents **let you chat** online after 11 p.m.?
Obligation: *make*
The teachers ³ _____ **us put** our phones in our school bags. He **doesn't make us study** on the weekend.

3 Choose the correct alternatives.

1 Our school lets us wear sneakers.
  (a) We can wear sneakers.
  b We have to wear sneakers.
2 Our teachers make us study for tests every week.
  a We have to study for tests every week.
  b We don't have to study for tests every week.
3 We aren't allowed to talk loudly in the library.
  a We can't talk loudly in the library.
  b We can talk loudly in the library.
4 Our teachers don't let us eat in class.
  a We can eat in class.
  b We can't eat in class.
5 My school doesn't make us wear a uniform.
  a We don't have to wear a uniform.
  b We have to wear a uniform.
6 We aren't allowed to take pictures in school.
  a We don't have to take pictures in school.
  b We can't take pictures in school.

4 Complete the sentences. Use the affirmative (✓) or negative (✗) form of *be allowed to*, *let* (*me*), or *make* (*me*) and the verbs.

1 Emily passed her driver's test, so
  she _'s allowed to drive_ . (✓ / drive)
2 My sister says I can use her tablet. She always
  _____ it. (✓ / borrow)
3 We have to walk inside school. We
  _____ here. (✗ / run)
4 I don't have to clean the kitchen. My parents
  _____ it. (✗ / clean)
5 I can't ride a motorcycle, but my brother has a
  licence. He _____ one. (✓ / ride)

👉 **Your turn**

5 Write true sentences. Use *be allowed to*, *let*, or *make*.

1 my dad / me / do chores
  My dad doesn't make me / makes me do chores.
2 I / stay / in bed late on Sundays
  _____
  _____
3 my parents / me / stay out late on Saturday nights
  _____
  _____
4 my mom / me / clean / my room
  _____
  _____
5 I / go / for sleepovers on the weekend
  _____
  _____
6 my parents / me / watch TV in the morning before school
  _____
  _____

6 Write five more sentences about yourself. Compare in pairs.

→ *METRO EXPRESS* P.110

Bullying

1 ◀ᴗ 18 ▶ Complete the gaps on the poster with the verbs. Listen and check.

> ~~fight with~~ gossip about ignore
> play a joke on tease threaten

Give me your phone, or I'm going to hit you!

Look at those sneakers!

They look like my mom's sneakers!

Have you heard about Jake … ?

What is bullying?

Bullying can take many different forms, physical, or emotional. Bullies make their victims feel frightened. Bullies may …

¹ **fight with** people – kicking or hitting them.
² _____ to hurt someone.
³ _____ someone, calling them rude names or laughing at them.
⁴ _____ someone, talking about their private life, including saying things that aren't true.
⁵ _____ someone.
⁶ _____ someone: not including someone in a conversation or a group.

2 ◀ᴗ 19 ▶ Complete the conversations with the simple present or past form of the verbs in exercise 1. Listen and check.

1 "You look mad. What's up?"
"Cassa __played a joke__ on me. She sent a silly message to all my contacts!"

2 "Did you hear about Hailey's new boyfriend?"
"Jayden? Yeah! But I guess we shouldn't _____ them."

3 "Does your sister _____ you?"
"Yes. She never talks to me!"

4 "What's up?"
"Gina took an embarrassing picture of me and _____ to post it online."

5 "What did Joshua say to you?"
"He was laughing at me and he _____ me about my clothes."

6 "Why did you _____ Michelle?"
"She started hitting me for no reason. Luckily a teacher saw and she stopped."

→ *METRO EXPRESS* P.110

L Listening

Restorative justice

1 ◀ᴗ 20 ▶ You are going to hear two people talking about *restorative justice* and *dialogue circles*. Look at the picture. What do you think a *dialogue circle* is? Listen and check.

2 ◀ᴗ 20 ▶ Listen again and choose the correct words.

1 Detention means students have to stay (late after class)/ home for a while.

2 Olivia Fenton's school uses **restorative justice / traditional punishments**.

3 Olivia **teased / fought with** someone.

4 In the dialogue circle, Olivia mainly **talked / listened**.

5 In the dialogue circle, Olivia felt **annoyed / embarrassed**.

6 The dialogue circle **changed / didn't change** how Olivia felt about her behavior.

3 Discuss the questions.

1 Why are dialogue circles effective? What reasons does Olivia mention?

2 What do you think of dialogue circles?

3 What other ways are there to stop people doing something wrong?

 G Grammar

Zero conditional

1 🔊 21 > **Read the sentences. Which do you agree with?**

1 If students follow the rules, they learn more!
2 Don't make noise if you're in the library.
3 Students don't get good grades if they're always late for school.
4 If you see bullying, tell a teacher.

2 Complete the chart.

We use the zero conditional to talk about things that always happen.	
if	simple present
If students ¹ _follow_ the rules,	they ² _____ more.
simple present	***if***
Students ³ _____ good grades	if they ⁴ _____ always late for school.

3 Match the sentence halves.

1 If you hit people, ...   a if he has a test.
2 If my teacher asks a   b if people are late.
   hard question, ...   c if you don't do
3 You get into trouble ...   your homework
4 Jon never gets stressed   d if she feels nervous.
5 Sonia bites her nails   e I never answer.
6 I don't get annoyed   f they get upset.

Stop The *if* clause can come first or second in conditional sentences. The meaning is the same. Notice where we use a comma.

*The principal writes to students' parents **if** they do something wrong.*

***If** students do something wrong, the principal writes to their parents.*

Conditional imperative

4 Look at exercise 1 again and complete the chart.

We use the conditional imperative to give instructions and advice.	
if	imperative
If you ¹ _see_ bullying,	² _____ a teacher.
imperative	***if***
³ _____ noise	if you ⁴ _____ in the library.

5 Write conditional imperative sentences. Use *if* and add a comma if necessary.

1 you see bullying / tell a teacher
   If you see bullying, tell a teacher.
2 don't take a taxi / you can't afford it
   _____
3 your sister is asleep / be quiet
   _____
4 use hot water / you wash the dishes
   _____
5 you make a video / please send me a copy
   _____
   _____
6 don't click on links / you aren't sure they're safe
   _____
   _____

6 Complete the zero conditional and conditional imperative sentences.

1 My dad _gets_ confused if he _watches_ movies in English. (get, watch)
2 If Max _____ in the coffee shop, _____ his party. It's a surprise. (be, not mention)
3 _____ this word if you _____ the meaning. (look up, not know)
4 If you _____ once a week, it _____ you healthy. (jog, keep)
5 _____ to an exhibition if it _____ sunny. Do something outdoors. (not go, be)
6 You _____ to the next level in this game if you _____ over 1 million points. (move, score)
7 _____ with your friends if you _____ a lot of homework. Do the homework first. (not hang out, have)
8 The teacher _____ extra marks if you _____ neatly. (give, write)

→ *METRO EXPRESS* P.110

Asking for and giving permission

1 **22** **Listen and read. Who is allowed to go out?**

a Ann   b Ben   c Chloe   d David

Ann: Is it OK if I go to the movie theater tomorrow?

Dad: Yes, of course.

Ben: Do you mind if I meet some friends downtown this afternoon?

Mom: Sorry, I'm afraid that your uncle is visiting soon.

Chloe: Do you mind if I go to the mall later?

Mom: No, not at all.

David: Is it OK if I go to Tom's house?

Dad: Sorry, but you need to study this evening.

Stop

Asking for and giving permission

Is it OK if I … ?   Do you mind if I … ?

✓ Yes, of course.   ✓ No, not at all.

✗ Sorry, but …   ✗ Sorry, I'm afraid that …

---

2 **Match the activities with reasons not to do them. (There may be more than one match.)**

1 go to the skatepark   _____

2 meet my friends at the mall   _____

3 go hiking   _____

4 go to the beach   _____

5 play soccer in the park   _____

6 hang out with friends   _____

7 go to the movies   _____

a The weather forecast isn't good.

b It's too dangerous.

c It's too expensive.

d You need to do homework.

e You need to do your chores.

3 **Write three new conversations. Use the conversations in exercise 1 as a model.**
Use the ideas in exercise 2, or your own ideas.
Practice your conversations.

> Do you mind if I go to the skatepark?

> Sorry, but you need to do your chores.

1 **Read the tip.**

Tip **Good readers** can skim a text very quickly, without reading every word, to get the general idea.

Read the text quickly and without stopping. Choose the best title for the text.

a Cyberbullying and how to stop it

b Together we can stop bullying

c Bystanders are bullies

2 **Find the verbs and nouns in the text.**
Match them with the definitions.

1 cyberbullying _c_   4 mind ___

2 control ___   5 community ___

3 acceptable ___   6 report ___

a to give information about something you've seen

b something that's OK or that you're allowed to do

c ~~hurting people using messages on social media~~

d the group of people in a certain area

e to be annoyed or worried about something

f to have the power to make someone do what you want

3 **23** **Read the text and choose the correct answers.**

1 Bullying happens

  a in public places and at school.

  b when you're at home.

  ⓒ in public places, at home, and at school.

2 Bystanders … bullying.

  a see   b start   c stop

3 Bystanders

  a are too lazy to tell teachers about bullying.

  b sometimes feel afraid of bullies.

  c think bullying is embarrassing.

4 You can be an upstander by

  a inviting bullies to join you.

  b being friendly to people who are alone.

  c deleting negative messages online.

5 The writer thinks that

  a it is impossible to stop bullying.

  b bystanders believe bullying is acceptable.

  c it is possible for people to help stop bullying.

4 **Discuss the questions.**

1 How can cyberbullies reach their victims?

2 What do bullies think if bystanders do nothing?

3 Why shouldn't you laugh at bullies?

4 Why should you invite a victim of bullying to join your group of friends?

BULLYING is hard to control and it affects millions of teenagers every day. In the past, it mostly happened at school or in public places, but nowadays the Internet makes it possible for bullies to reach their victims at home. We call it cyberbullying – when a bully teases or threatens someone online. Experts believe that almost all children and teenagers will experience bullying at some point in their lives.

SO WHAT CAN WE DO TO STOP BULLYING?

Most people know that if someone bullies you, you can tell a teacher or a parent. But what should you do if you see bullying happening to someone else? If you see bullies threatening someone or teasing someone, should you do something? Many people try to ignore bullying. They become *bystanders*: they stand by and see bullying happen, but don't do anything to stop it. Sometimes bystanders are frightened of the bullies, or they're embarrassed about telling their parents or a teacher. Or they just feel confused about what to do, so they don't do anything.

But if you don't do anything, bullies think that their behavior is acceptable. They think that people don't mind, and more bullying happens. That's why we need to be *upstanders*. Upstanders say "no" to bullies because bullying is not acceptable!

Bullying is hard to stop – but together, we can stop it by being upstanders, not bystanders.

HOW CAN YOU BE AN UPSTANDER?

- If you see people teasing someone or playing a joke on them, don't laugh. If you laugh, bullies think you like what they're doing. Invite the person they're bullying to join you.

- Try to make new friends. If you see someone who is alone, or who people are ignoring, invite them to have lunch with you or hang out after school.

- If you see negative messages or gossip online, don't send it to other people. Spreading negative messages about someone online is cyberbullying. You should report it to the website, if possible, or to a teacher or adult.

- If people are fighting, don't stand too near – you need to stay safe. And don't watch – bullies love an audience. Tell an adult.

Every school and every community has more kind people than bullies. If we work together, we can help to stop bullying!

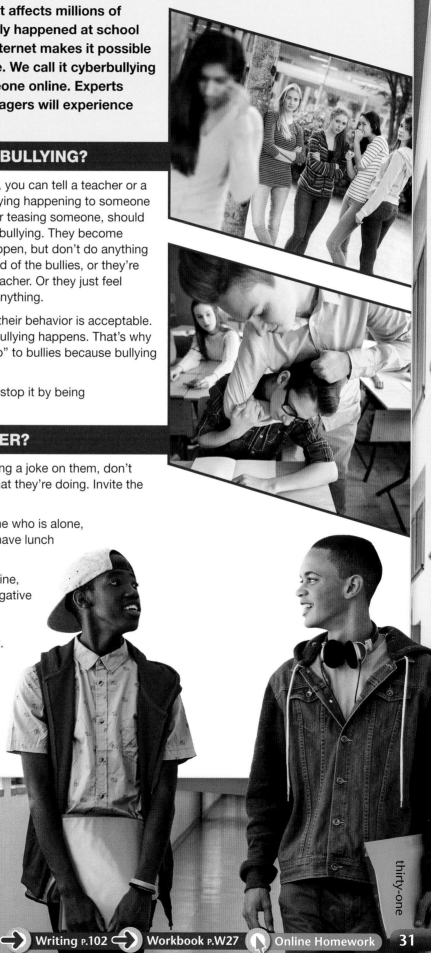

thirty-one

 **Watch**

Rules at home and at school

Tripp

Before you watch

1 Match the pictures with the words. Which things do some parents make kids do at home? Which things do some parents let kids do?

do laundry   do the vacuuming   go on the computer   play drums   watch TV   water the plants

2 Do you do any of the activities in exercise 1? Or would you like to? Why? / Why not?

While you watch

3 ▶Video Watch the video. Number the topics in the order they speak about them.

a Rules about washing the dishes, taking out the trash, and vacuuming _____

b Rules about homework, going out with friends, and living with family _____

c Rules about bullying, being on time, and being quiet in class _____

4 ▶Video Watch the video again. Choose *T* (True) or *F* (False).

1 Ollie's family has a rule about homework.   T ☑ F ☐
2 Piper isn't allowed to go on sleepovers.   T ☐ F ☐
3 Jack's parents are very strict.   T ☐ F ☐
4 Naomi isn't always allowed to play her drums.   T ☐ F ☐
5 Ollie sometimes washes the dishes.   T ☐ F ☐
6 Piper thinks her chores are unfair.   T ☐ F ☐
7 Jack has to wash the towels.   T ☐ F ☐
8 Naomi's mom doesn't let her water the plants.   T ☐ F ☐
9 Students at Ollie's school are usually late.   T ☐ F ☐
10 The students help make the rules at Piper's school.   T ☐ F ☐
11 Jack thinks his school is too strict.   T ☐ F ☐
12 Naomi's school has strict rules about phones.   T ☐ F ☐

5 ▶Video Watch the video again. Think about the rules they talk about. Answer the questions.

1 Who do you think has the strictest rules at home? Why?
2 Who do you think has the strictest rules at school? Why?
3 Which rules do you think are fair? Why?
4 Were there any rules mentioned that you think are unfair? Why?

Jack   Naomi   Ollie   Piper

After you watch

6 Ask and answer the questions with a friend.

1 Which chores at home do you think teenagers should have to do?
2 Are there any chores you think teenagers should never have to do?
3 Which rules do you think every school should have?
4 Are there any rules you think schools shouldn't have?

7 Interview your friends using the questions in exercise 6. Make a video or project about their answers.

Online Homework   ON THE MOVE   Challenge

Review

V Vocabulary

1 Match the sentences 1–10 with a–j.

1 I'm sure you're going to do well on the exam.
2 I had to give a speech at school.
3 I didn't understand the homework.
4 I got up at six this morning.
5 I love sunbathing and reading a book.
6 I forgot to watch the final of the soccer last night.
7 I'm taking pictures of everyone in the class for a project.
8 It was my first bungee jump.
9 Someone broke into my neighbor's apartment yesterday.
10 Christina and Lucy often have sleepovers without me.

a It's so relaxing.
b It was really confusing.
c I got really stressed before it.
d I'm exhausted!
e Be more positive!
f But I don't get jealous.
g He was really shocked.
h I'm so annoyed.
i Please don't be embarrassed.
j It was really frightening.

2 Complete the verbs.

1 b _lush_
2 s_____
3 c_____ your arms
4 b_____ your nails
5 s_____ your head
6 r_____ your eyebrows

3 Complete the sentences with the correct form of *make* or *do* and the words.

> a complaint   ~~a great job~~   a lot of noise
> anything wrong   excuses   my best   some chores

1 You _did a great job_ of helping your brother with his project yesterday. Thank you.
2 You're _____ in here. Please be quiet.
3 I have to _____ for my parents so I can't hang out tonight.
4 I _____ to clean my bedroom, but it isn't perfect.
5 This food is terrible. I'm going to _____.
6 Why are you annoyed with me? I didn't _____!
7 You're always late! Don't _____.

4 Look at the pictures and complete the sentences with the correct form of the verbs.

> fight   gossip   ignore   play   ~~tease~~   threaten

1 Julia is _teasing_ Marcos because he's too frightened to watch the movie.
2 Daniel is _____ his sister.
3 Marcos and Jose are _____.
4 Jenna's mom is _____ to take away her phone.
5 They're _____.
6 Livia is _____ a joke on Gaby.

G Grammar

1 Complete the conversation with the gerund or infinitive of the verbs.

1 **A** What's wrong with your brother?
   B He's really upset about __losing__ (lose) the match.

2 **A** Your sister's homework is really hard.
   B I offered _____ (help) her, but she ignored me.

3 **A** I finished the homework, but I think some of my answers are wrong.
   B Don't worry about it. _____ (make) mistakes is normal.

4 **A** Have you heard about Clare?
   B Don't tell me! It isn't kind _____ (gossip) about people.

5 **A** Why are you doing all the chores?
   B _____ (earn) some money.

6 **A** What are you doing this weekend?
   B Seb suggested _____ (go) to the mall on Saturday morning. Do you want _____ (come)?

2 Rewrite the sentences with *be allowed to*, *let*, or *make*.

1 We can't wear jeans at school. (be allowed to)
  We __aren't allowed to wear jeans at school.__

2 Do your parents allow you to have parties at home? (let)
  Do _____
  _____

3 The teacher said I had to stay after school. (make)
  The teacher _____

4 Can you use cell phones at school? (be allowed to)
  Are _____
  _____

5 My parents say I have to clean my room every week. (make)
  My parents _____
  _____

6 Our coach says we can't go out the night before a big game. (not let)
  Our coach _____
  _____

3 Complete the zero conditional and imperative sentences with the correct form of the verbs.

> do / pay   feel / breathe   ~~get / tease~~
> not let / get back   not take / be   not worry / make

1 I _get_ annoyed if my sister _teases_ me.

2 If I _____ the bus at seven, I_____ late for school.

3 _____ if you _____ a mistake.

4 If you _____ anxious, _____ deeply.

5 My parents _____ me go out for a week if I _____ late.

6 If I _____ chores, my mom _____ me.

Consolidation

Read the conversation. Choose the correct words.

Amy: What's wrong? You look [1] __confused__.

Paul: I am. I expected [2]_____ a really good grade on this test.

Amy: I know how you feel. It's [3]_____ hard for something and then get a bad grade. You [4]_____ your best.

Paul: But I practiced [5]_____ these questions every night last week. I thought the test was easy! Is Mr. Clifton [6]_____ a joke on me?

Amy: If you think your grade is wrong, [7]_____ him. He sometimes [8]_____ mistakes.

Paul: I'm going to do that. Mr. Clifton …

1 **a** relaxed   **(b)** confused   **c** exhausted
2 **a** getting   **b** get   **c** to get
3 **a** annoyed studying   **b** annoying to study
   c annoyed to study
4 **a** did   **b** made   **c** worked
5 **a** doing   **b** do   **c** to do
6 **a** making   **b** doing   **c** playing
7 **a** telling   **b** tell   **c** you tell
8 **a** makes   **b** does   **c** lets

In this unit ...

- talk about man-made and natural disasters
- make predictions about the future
- made predictions based on present evidence
- ask for and give opinions
- understand a video about a smart city

Big issues

Video Watch the warm-up video.

_____ are the biggest causes of air pollution in the U.S.

1 How many answers did you get right?

2 Is air pollution a problem in your city?

Main St.

STOP

Man-made and natural problems

1 🔊 24 Read the text. At the end of your class today, how much bigger will the world's population be?

2 🔊 25 Complete the facts with the words. Listen, check, and repeat.

> climate change   disease   drought   flood
> ~~heat wave~~   overpopulation   pollution   wildfire

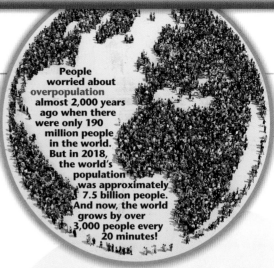

People worried about overpopulation almost 2,000 years ago when there were only 190 million people in the world. But in 2018, the world's population was approximately 7.5 billion people. And now, the world grows by over 3,000 people every 20 minutes!

DID YOU KNOW?

In 2100, experts believe there will be 11 billion people in the world. Some people think that ² _____ will be a serious problem.

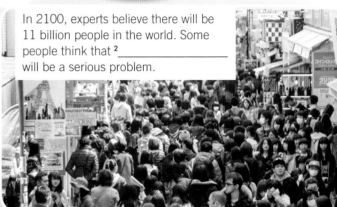

WARMEST WELCOME FROM AUSTRALIAS HOTTEST TOWN

The longest ¹ **heat wave** was from October 31, 1923 to April 7, 1924 in Marble Bar, Australia. The temperature in the town was higher than 37.8°C (or 100°F) for 160 days.

Mosquitoes are the most dangerous animals in the world because they carry the ³ _____ malaria. About 3.2 billion people in the world are at risk of malaria.

The longest ⁴ _____ on record was in Australia, from 1995 until 2012. The government paid $4.5 billion to farmers who didn't have any water.

In cities, cars cause up to 90% of air ⁵ _____.

A ⁶ _____ can travel up to 20 km/h. That's faster than the average cyclist.

In a ⁷ _____, water only needs to be 1 m deep and it can carry away cars.

3 Complete the sentences with words from exercise 2.

1 After a <u>flood</u>, it can take a long time for the water to disappear.

2 If it doesn't rain for a long time, we sometimes get a _____.

3 A _____ can start from lightning.

4 In a _____ you should always carry some water to drink.

5 _____ describes the way the Earth's weather is changing.

6 _____ happens when there are too many people for resources like food and water.

7 There are several types of _____, for example, air, land, sea, light, and noise.

8 The Black Death was a _____ in Europe in the 14th century. It killed 60% of the population of Europe.

Stop
too much / too many means a large amount of something – more than you want.
Count nouns: *too many people*
Non-count nouns: *too much pollution*

As a result of ⁸_____, there is now 14% less ice in the Arctic than there was 50 years ago.

Your turn

4 Answer the questions about your city or country.

1 Are there too many tourists?
2 Is there too much pollution?
3 Do any areas have wildfires?
4 Do any areas have floods?
5 Are there heat waves?

→ *METRO EXPRESS* P.111

Workbook P.W4   **Online Homework**

L **Listening**

Wildfires at Yellowstone Park

1 🔊 26 **Listen. What is the main topic?**

a The effects of climate change on wildfires in Yellowstone Park
b The history of wildfire in Yellowstone Park
c The story of the 1988 Yellowstone Wildfires

2 🔊 26 **Listen again. Choose *T* (True) or *F* (False).**

		T	F
1	Wildfires can be good for large forests.	☑	☐
2	Humans started the first wildfire in 1988.	☐	☐
3	The fire moved quickly because of the weather.	☐	☐
4	On some days, the fire traveled at 16 km/h.	☐	☐
5	The weather stopped the wildfires.	☐	☐
6	Lightning caused most of the wildfires.	☐	☐

3 Read the tip.

Tip **Good readers** take notes when they listen to longer texts.

🔊 26 **Listen again for these dates and numbers. Take notes about what happened or what they mean.**

1 June 23 – <u>wildfire started in park</u>

2 July 21 – _____

3 September 11 – _____
_____

4 3,000 km² – _____

5 $120 million – _____

4 🔊 26 **Use your notes to complete the summary. Then listen again and check.**

On June 23, ¹<u>a wildfire started in Yellowstone Park</u>. At first, the park workers allowed it to burn. But on July 21, the park ²_____. The firefighters couldn't control the fires. Suddenly on September 11 ³_____ heavily and the fires stopped. ⁴_____ 3,000 km² of the park and ⁵_____ $120 million.

1 🔊 27 Read the article. Which problem do you think is the most serious? Why?

Our Greatest Threats

In the future, our planet will face many different challenges. But will the greatest threats to our survival come from space, from the Earth, or even from ourselves?

Space

On February 15, 2013, an asteroid entered the Earth's atmosphere over Russia. It was 20 m long, and weighed more than the Eiffel Tower. When it exploded, 30 km above the ground, it was traveling at about 65,000 km/h. Many glass windows broke in the explosion and about 1,500 people were injured. The largest piece of the asteroid weighed 654 kg and landed in a lake.

Many scientists think that another large asteroid will hit the Earth one day. It will probably land in the ocean and it will cause a tsunami – a huge wave. When tsunamis travel to land, they cause floods.

💬 78

The Earth

From March to May, 2010, a volcano erupted in Iceland, and there was a huge cloud of ash in the sky over Europe. Twenty countries didn't allow planes to take off for over a week. No one was injured, but millions of people couldn't get home, and the disaster cost $7.3 billion.

But that was just a normal volcano. Supervolcanoes are over 1,000 times bigger than normal volcanoes. There is one under Yellowstone Park in the U.S. It is about the same size as Mount Everest. One day, it will erupt. A huge cloud of ash will block the sun and some countries will become too cold for humans.

💬 55

Humans

At the moment, 750 million people in the world don't have access to clean water. Three billion people earn less than $2.50 every day.

By 2050, experts think that there will be over 9.6 billion people on the planet. Will there be enough natural resources for everybody? All of these people need food, water, and somewhere to live. Cities will become more crowded; traffic and pollution will get worse. More people use more energy and this causes climate change, too. Is overpopulation our greatest threat?

💬 42

2 Read the article again. Choose the correct answer.

1 The asteroid …
   a was longer than the Eiffel tower.
   b hit Russia 30 km from a city.
   c weighed 654 kg.
   d broke windows in buildings.

2 The volcano in Iceland …
   a was a supervolcano.　　　c hurt lots of people.
   b caused problems for travelers.　d erupted for a week.

3 The article says …
   a access to clean water will be our biggest problem in the future.
   b the current population of the world is 750 million people.
   c overpopulation causes environmental problems.
   d at the moment, there are enough natural resources for everyone.

3 Read again. Complete the sentences with one word.

1 The asteroid in Russia was __heavier__ than the Eiffel Tower.

2 One day, a large asteroid will cause a _____.

3 The _____ of the eruption in Iceland was $7.3 billion.

4 The Yellowstone Park _____ is as big as Mount Everest.

5 The _____ of the world will be 9.6 billion in 2050.

6 Environmental problems will get _____ in the future.

will / won't: future predictions

1 🔊 28 **Read the question and answer. Why don't we need to worry about the sun dying?**

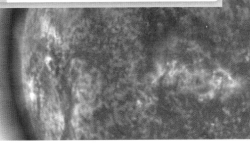

Q Will the sun die one day?

A Yes, scientists think that it will. The sun burns hydrogen gas to make heat and light. But one day, there won't be any hydrogen. The sun will get bigger and hotter. It'll become very hot on Earth, and there won't be any water in the oceans. But don't worry. Experts say this will start in about 5 billion years.

2 **Complete the chart.**

We use *will* / *won't* to make predictions about the future based on opinion.	
Affirmative	**Negative**
The sun ¹ _will_ get bigger and hotter.	There ² _____ be any hydrogen.
Questions	**Short answers**
³ _____ the sun _____ one day?	Yes, it ⁴ _____. / No, it won't.
When **will** another asteroid **hit** the Earth?	

Stop We can contract *will* with subject pronouns.
It'll (= It will) become very hot.
You'll (= You will) be late.

3 **Look at the pictures. Complete the sentences with 'll or won't and the verbs.**

1 I _won't score_ any goals today. (score)

2 I_____ in a big house like that one day. (live)

3 You _____ this movie. (like)

4 She_____ a software developer one day. (be)

5 Do your homework now, please. You _____ time tomorrow. (have)

4 **Make questions about the future with the words.**

In 25 years …
1 people / drive / cars / will / ?
   Will people drive cars?
2 will / a luxury food / chocolate / be / ?
   _____

In 50 years …
3 masks / everyone / will / because of pollution / wear / ?
   _____
   _____

4 all their classes online / have / will / students / ?
   _____
   _____

In 100 years …
5 live / people / on a different planet / will / ?
   _____

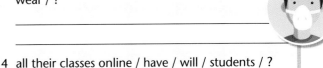
WELCOME TO MARS

6 will / exist / diseases / ?
   _____

Stop After *I think* / *I don't think*, use *will*, not *won't*.
I think it will rain.   *I don't think it will rain.*

👉 **Your turn**

5 **What do you think? In pairs, use *I think* / *I don't think* to answer the questions in exercise 4.**

I don't think people will drive cars. Travel will be relaxing.

→ *METRO EXPRESS* P.111

V Vocabulary

Environmental problems and solutions

1 Match the problems with the solutions.

PROBLEMS

1

We are **RUNNING OUT** of the world's **NATURAL** RESOURCES.

2

We **THROW AWAY** too many **THINGS.**

3

Animals are **BECOMING EXTINCT.**

SOLUTIONS

a

We need to **PROTECT** the places where they live.

b

We need to **SAVE** resources like WATER and ELECTRICITY.

c

We need to **REDUCE** the number of things we buy. **REUSE** plastic bottles by washing them. And if you put something in the trash, remember to **RECYCLE** it!

2 🔊 29 Match the green words in exercise 1 with the meanings 1–8. Then listen, check, and repeat.

1 _become extinct_ : when a plant or animal doesn't exist anymore

2 _____: finish or use all of something

3 _____: keep something safe

4 _____: to use less of something and not waste it

5 _____: make something less or smaller

6 _____: put something in the trash

7 _____: use something again

8 _____: make trash into something that can be used again

👉 Your turn

3 Discuss the questions.

1 How can you save natural resources in your daily life?

2 What things do you reuse and recycle at home?

3 Which animals are in danger of becoming extinct in your country?

→ *METRO EXPRESS* P.111

L Listening

Cleaning the world's oceans

1 Look at the items. Do you know how long they take to decompose? Match the items with the times.

3–4 weeks   50–100 years   450–1,000 years   ~~never~~

a _never_

b _____

c _____

d _____

2 🔊 30 Listen. What is Boyan Slat's company trying to do?

a collect plastic in the ocean

b stop plastic going into the ocean

c recycle plastic we only use once

d make diving safe

3 🔊 30 Listen again. Choose the correct words.

1 About 8 million (tons)/ **kilograms** of plastic goes into the ocean every year.

2 Every year, about **100,000 / 1 million** sea birds die because of eating plastic.

3 Boyan is from **the Netherlands / Greece**.

4 He started his company **before / after** leaving college.

5 It's going to take his company **a year / ten years** to remove 70 million kg of plastic from the ocean.

6 We use **15% / 50%** of the world's plastic only once.

4 🔊 30 Answer the questions. Then listen again and check.

1 What is microplastic?

   Microplastic is very small pieces of plastic.

2 Why was Boyan shocked on vacation in Greece?

   _____

   _____

3 Why did he leave college early?

   _____

   _____

4 What is the company going to do with the plastic?

   _____

5 Why do some scientists think Boyan's idea won't be successful?

   _____

   _____

G Grammar

be going to: future predictions

1 🔊 31 **Read the conversation. Who is Mrs. Hall?**

Jack: Look at that blue sky! It's going to be a hot day today, especially for this time of year.

Cassie: Yeah, I think it's because of climate change.

Jack: Are you worried about it?

Cassie: I'm *really* worried. You should come to the after school Environment Club. It's interesting … and frightening.

Jack: OK. Tell me about it later. Right now, we're late for math. Mrs. Hall isn't going to be happy!

2 **Complete the chart.**

We use *going to* to make predictions based on present evidence.	Look at that blue sky! It ¹ _'s going to be_ a hot day today. Right now, we're late for math. Mrs. Hall ² _____ happy!

Stop Remember we also use *going to* to talk about plans and intentions.

I'm going to meet some friends at the mall later.

3 **Look at the pictures. Complete the predictions with the correct form of *be going to*.**

1 The volcano _is going to_ erupt.

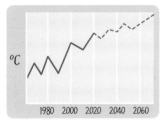

2 The temperature on Earth _____ increase.

3 They _____ become extinct.

4 The traffic _____ get worse.

4 **Read the situations. Then complete the sentences with the affirmative or negative of *be going to* and the verbs.**

~~be~~ be be finish get lose

1 It's 8:20 and Sue is still in bed. School starts at 8:30 a.m.
Sue _is going to be_ late.

2 Marvin only spent ten minutes on his homework.
He _____ a good grade.

3 It's winter, but the weather forecast predicts hot and sunny weather for the next five days.
There _____ a heat wave.

4 Italy is winning 3–0 against Mexico. There's only a minute of the game left.
Mexico _____.

5 Josh made a mess in the kitchen. His parents are coming home in five minutes.
They _____ happy.

6 Today is Sunday and I'm seeing my relatives this afternoon. I have a lot of homework to do before Monday.
I _____ everything.

5 **Choose the correct words. Use *be going to* for predictions based on present evidence, and *will* for predictions based on opinions.**

1 My sister **will** / **is going to** have a baby next month.

2 One day, I think governments **will** / **are going to** ban plastic bags.

3 Look! The bus **will** / **is going to** leave. Run!

4 Some scientists think that in the future humans **will** / **are going to** live for hundreds of years.

5 The printer **will** / **'s going to** run out of paper soon. Can you get some more?

6 Do you think you **'ll** / **'re going to** be famous one day?

→ *METRO EXPRESS* P.111

Asking for and giving opinions

1 **32** **Complete the conversation. Then listen and check.**

| ~~do~~ it'll will will be |

A What **1** _do_____ you think life **2** _____ be like in 20 years?

B I think **3** _____ be awesome. For example, technology will be amazing. Do you agree?

A I'm not sure. I agree about technology, but personally, I believe climate change **4** _____ a huge problem.

2 **In pairs, practice the conversation in exercise 1.**

> **Stop**
>
> **Useful language**
> *What do think life will be like in … years?*
> *Personally, I think / believe …*
> *I think it'll be awesome / cool / difficult / very different.*
> *How about you?*
> *I agree. / I disagree.*
> *I'm not sure.*

3 **Read the predictions. Check (✓) the predictions you think will be true in 20 years.**

1 Your phone will recognize your emotions. ☐

2 Robots at home will be common. ☐

3 Lions will be extinct. ☐

4 We will run out of oil. ☐

4 **In pairs, write a conversation about future predictions. Use the conversation in exercise 1 as a model. Use the ideas in exercise 3, or your own ideas.**

> What do you think life will be like in 20 years?

> I think it'll be cool. I think your phone will recognize your emotions.

> I disagree …

5 **Act out your conversations. Does the class agree or disagree with your opinions?**

1 **Look at the comments about the article on page 38. Match the name of the writer with the section he / she is commenting on.**

1 Patricia	a space
2 Matt	b the Earth
3 Chloe	c humans

2 **Read the tip.**

> **Tip**
> **Good readers** can find and understand people's opinions in their writing.

33 **Read the comments. Underline each person's opinions in their comments. Then choose the correct answers.**

1 Patricia thinks …
   a volcanoes are a bigger threat than supervolcanoes.
   b we need to study supervolcanoes carefully.

2 Matt thinks richer countries should …
   a share their resources with poorer countries.
   b reduce their consumption of resources.

3 Chloe thinks …
   a living in space is a good solution for the future.
   b the chance of an asteroid disaster is very small.

3 **Read the comments again. Answer the questions.**

1 Where and when did the last supervolcano erupt?
   It erupted in New Zealand 27,000 years ago.

2 What is the "red zone"?
   _____
   _____
   _____

3 What are some examples of natural resources we use?
   _____

4 Why do you think richer countries use more natural resources?
   _____
   _____

5 What are scientists doing about asteroids?
   _____
   _____

6 How much does it cost to put a 75 kg person into space?
   _____

4 **In pairs, discuss the questions.**

1 Do you agree with Patricia, Matt, and Chloe?

2 Can you think of any other solutions to the problems?

Our Greatest Threats

HOME | VIDEOS | LINKS | COMMENTS Search

Comments (217)

Patricia
Naples, Italy

Interesting article, but there are only seven supervolcanoes in the world and the last one erupted in New Zealand – 27,000 years ago. There are 1,500 smaller volcanoes like the one in Iceland!

I think studying volcanoes is more important than worrying about supervolcanoes. We need to know when volcanoes are going to erupt – so we have time to escape.

About 600,000 people (including me!) live in the "red zone" near Mount Vesuvius, a volcano in Italy. If the volcano erupts, we are at risk. The city has an evacuation plan, and it will take 72 hours for everyone to escape the area. I don't think that will be quick enough!

💬 55

Matt
Washington, D.C.

Overpopulation doesn't need to be a problem. If we change our lifestyles, I think there is space on our planet for everyone. Everything we do in our daily lives uses natural resources: water, energy, materials, and land. At the moment, people in richer countries use about 90 kg of natural resources every day! In poorer countries, it's only 10 kg. People in richer countries (that includes me) need to throw away less food, reuse things like plastic bags and bottles, and recycle more trash. In short, we have to reduce our use of resources. It's simple!

💬 42

Chloe
Sydney, Australia

The asteroid in Russia was large, but it's not unusual for material to enter our atmosphere from space – in fact about 100,000 kg of material enters our atmosphere every day! Scientists watch the largest asteroids in space carefully, but they think there is a one in 10,000 chance that one will hit the Earth in the next 100 years. That's tiny!

Some experts talk about building places to live in space or on other planets like Mars or Titan (Saturn's largest moon). I'm not sure. It costs around $5,000 to put 1 kg into space at the moment, so it's going to be very expensive to move from the Earth.

💬 78

Watch

Amy

Before you watch

1 Look at the pictures. Describe the cities with the words.

clean   crowded   green   noisy   open   polluted   quiet

Seoul, South Korea

Songdo, South Korea

_____

_____

2 Answer the questions.

1 Does your city or town have parks or green spaces? Where?

2 Which parts of your city or town are crowded? When are they the most crowded?

3 Which parts of your town or city have a lot of businesses? What types of business are there?

4 Does your town or city have a lot of traffic?

5 How do most commuters get to work in your town or city?

While you watch

3 ▶ Video Watch the video and choose the correct words.

1 Seoul is a **smart** / **huge** city.

2 Songdo is a **new** / **polluted** city.

3 Songdo has a lot of **green space** / **traffic**.

4 Computer technology helps Songdo to **protect animals** / **recycle waste**.

5 Smart cities may **help** / **cause** problems such as overpopulation and climate change.

4 ▶ Video Watch again. Complete the sentences.

1 Nearly _26_____ million people live in Seoul.

2 Songdo is about _____ kilometers from Seoul.

3 Songdo is called a _____ city because it is environmentally friendly.

4 In the middle of Songdo, there's a large _____.

5 Songdo has _____ apartments.

6 The city uses _____ to make energy.

7 There is space in Songdo for new _____.

8 Families love Songdo because of the _____.

After you watch

5 Answer the questions.

1 What are the similarities and differences between your home town and Seoul?

2 What are the similarities and differences between your home town and Songdo?

3 Would you like to live in a city like Songdo? Why? / Why not?

6 Imagine you are a city planner. Design a city that you would love to live in. Make a map, poster, or drawing of it. Include:

• places for people to live

• entertainment

• recreation and outdoor space

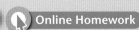 Online Homework    Challenge

In this unit …

- talk about truth and lies
- listen to and read texts about hoaxes and myths
- talk about possible or probable future events
- express disbelief
- practice scanning for information when reading
- understand video interviews about truth and lies

4

Tell the truth

▶ Video Watch the warm-up video.

OK! Listen, do you have plans for Saturday? I'm _____. Can you come?

Oh. Saturday? I'm sorry, I can't on Saturday…

1 Why can't Rob tell Vicky the truth?

2 Is it ever OK to lie?

Truth and lies

1 🔊 34 ▷ Read the conversation. What is a *white lie*?

Tripp: Happy birthday, Vicky! Did you know about the party?

Vicky: No, I had no idea. I thought my friends were busy …

Rob: I feel really guilty about lying to you, Vicky.

Vicky: It's OK, Rob. It was only a white lie. You promised Amy not to tell me about the party. I should trust my friends more.

2 🔊 35 ▷ Complete the quiz with the verbs. Listen and check.

> admit   believe   lie   make up
> pretend   promise   ~~tell the truth~~   trust

3 Do the quiz.

4 Add up your points and look at the key. Compare your results in pairs. Do you agree?

> **KEY**
> **5–6:** You try to be honest, but you don't mind being "creative" with the truth. Be careful!
> **7–8:** It's hard to be honest all the time, especially if it hurts someone's feelings. A white lie isn't a real lie!
> **9–10:** You're super-honest! Your friends are very lucky. Can you trust them 100%, too?

 **Your turn**

5 Discuss the questions.

1 Do you always tell the truth? Or do you make up stories sometimes?

2 Is it ever OK to lie? What about telling white lies?

3 Do you always admit to doing something wrong?

4 Who do you trust the most? Why?

➔ *METRO EXPRESS* P.112

TRUTH AND LIES QUIZ

1 Your sister has a terrible new hairstyle. She asks what you think. What do you say?

a "I liked your old hairstyle better." – It's best to ¹ <u>tell the truth</u>. **(2 points)**

b "You look awesome!" – Why not ² _____ to like it? That way you won't hurt her feelings. **(1 point)**

2 You get home late because you were hanging out with friends. Your parents were worried. What do you say?

a "There weren't any buses so I had to walk." – Sometimes it's easier to ³ _____ a reason for being late. **(1 point)**

b "I didn't realize the time. I ⁴ _____ not to be late again." – It's best to be honest about these things. **(2 points)**

3 A friend is upset. He isn't a great soccer player and he didn't get onto the team. What do you say?

a "Forget about the team, you're very good at lots of other things." – Nobody's good at everything! **(2 points)**

b "You're great! I can't understand why you didn't make the team." – There's no need to hurt people's feelings. It's OK to ⁵ _____ if it helps someone feel better. **(1 point)**

4 You forget a friend's birthday party – then you see messages about it on social media. What do you say?

a "I forgot about your party. I'm really sorry. Was it good?" – It's better to ⁶_____ to making a mistake than to be dishonest. **(2 points)**

b "Sorry I couldn't go to your party. I had to see my relatives." – That's not true, but you don't want your friend to know you forgot his or her birthday! **(1 point)**

5 Your parents let you have a party while they go away for a night. You spill soda and it leaves a dark stain on the sofa. What do you say?

a "I think there was already a stain there." – It's better not to admit to everything you do wrong. This way you can avoid an argument, and you can have a party another time. **(1 point)**

b "It was an accident. Can I pay for a cleaner?" – At least your parents know they can ⁷_____ you. They'll ⁸_____ you if something goes wrong again. **(2 points)**

L Listening

The Apollo moon landings

1 🔊 36 > **Read the quotation. Who do you think said this and what do you think it means? Listen and check.**

> That's one small step for a man, one giant leap for mankind.

a Yuri Gagarin, the first man in space
b Neil Armstrong, the first man on the moon
c Buzz Aldrin, the second man on the moon

2 🔊 37 > **Listen and label the pictures 1–3 in the order Alex and Beth mention them.**

a ____   b ____   c ____

3 🔊 37 > **Listen again. Who says these lines?**

1 How do we know he was on the moon?
  _Beth_____

2 Do you really think they made up the whole story?
  _____

3 Maybe the U.S. pretended they landed on the moon.
  _____

4 That's easy to explain. _____

5 It looks like they took the picture in a studio, with bright lights. _____

4 Read the tip.

> **Tip** **Good listeners** can infer a speaker's opinion without the speaker saying it exactly.

🔊 37 > **What do you think is the speakers' opinion? Listen and check. How did you infer this?**

	Alex	Beth
Yes, they landed on the moon.		
Maybe they landed on the moon.		
No, they didn't land on the moon.		

1 Read the title of each paragraph. Only one is true and the rest are myths. Can you guess which is true?

2 Read quickly and check. Complete the gaps 1–5 with *true* or *myth*.

3 🔊 38 Match the missing lines 1–5 with a–e in each paragraph. Read, listen, and check.

1 Astronauts have even seen the Pyramids in Egypt.
2 It doesn't matter what the color is.
3 Subjects like biology and languages were hard for him.
4 They were using a new invention called "radar".
5 These are your elbows, shoulders, knees, etc. where two bones fit together and move.

4 Complete the sentences with one word in each gap.

1 Carrots are good for your _eyes_ because of the _vitamins_ in them.
2 Some large man-made objects like _____, _____, and the _____ are visible from space.
3 Bulls can't see in _____.
4 The weather can affect your _____.
5 At school, Einstein was good at _____ and _____.

TRUTH *OR* MYTH?

Only one of these common beliefs is true – the rest are myths! Can you guess which isn't a myth?

"Carrots help you to see in the dark."

Seventy years ago, British pilots were able to "see" enemy planes at night. They said that this was because their pilots ate lots of carrots. In fact, the real reason was a secret. **a** 4

Verdict: ¹ _myth_! The vitamins in carrots are good for your eyes, but you won't be able to see in the dark if you eat carrots.

"You can see the Great Wall of China from space."

It's possible to see cities and big roads from the International Space Station's orbit 200 km above the Earth. **b** _____

Verdict: ² _____! The Great Wall of China isn't visible from space because it is the same color as the sand and rocks on the ground around it.

"Bulls will attack if they see the color red."

Matadors use red cloaks when they fight bulls and most people think that bulls hate the color red.

Verdict: ³ _____! Bulls (and cows) see in black and white, not in color! Bulls will run if they see movement. **c** _____

"If your knees ache, a storm might be coming."

Atmospheric pressure affects your body's joints. **d** _____

Verdict: ⁴ _____! If a storm is near, the pressure in the atmosphere will increase, and some people can feel this pressure in their joints.

"Einstein failed his math exams at school."

Einstein was a math genius. This story suggests that exams don't tell you everything about a person's abilities.

Verdict: ⁵ _____! Albert Einstein wasn't a grade A student. **e** _____ However, he never failed math. In fact, his teachers said he was brilliant at math and physics.

G Grammar

First conditional

1 🔊 39 Read about the superstitions about cats. Complete the sentence.

People in _____ think that black cats bring good luck.

In Russia, people believe you'll have good luck if you see a gray cat. In the U.K., people think you'll have good luck if you see a black cat. But in the U.S., if a black cat walks in front of you, people say you *won't* have good luck.

2 Complete the chart.

We use the first conditional to talk about possible or probable future events.	
if + simple present	*will* / *won't*
If a black cat ¹ _walks_ in front of you,	you ² _____ good luck.
will / *won't*	*if* + simple present
You³ _____ good luck	*if* you ⁴ _____ a gray cat.

3 Choose the correct words.

1 What will they get if they **'ll win** / **win** the game?
2 My brother **won't mind** / **don't mind** if you borrow his skateboard.
3 We **go** / **'ll go** for a walk if the weather gets better.
4 Where **you hang out** / **will you hang out** if it's rainy later?
5 If Leah **got** / **gets** onto the team, she'll be really pleased.
6 If you **don't know** / **won't know** what the weather forecast is, I'll look online.
7 Will you help me if I **get** / **will get** lost?
8 If you **will see** / **see** Logan, will you say "hi" from me?

4 Complete the first conditional sentences.

Superstitions in the U.S.

1 If you _break_ a mirror, you _'ll have_ seven years of bad luck. (break, have)

2 If you _____ your fingers, it _____ you from bad luck. (cross, protect)

3 Don't buy shoes for your boyfriend or girlfriend. They _____ you if you _____ them a pair of shoes! (leave, buy)

4 You _____ bad luck if you _____ under a ladder. (have, walk)

5 If your left hand _____ itchy, you _____ money. (be, lose)

6 But you _____ money if your right hand _____ itchy. (get, be)

7 And you _____ any money if you _____ your wallet on the floor. (never have, leave)

👉 **Your turn**

5 Read the superstitions in exercise 4 again.

1 Which are the same in your country?
2 Which do you believe?
3 Can you add any other superstitions to the list?

→ *METRO EXPRESS* P.112

 Workbook P.W16 | Online Homework

Vocabulary

Nouns ending with -ion

1 ◀)) 40 ▶ **Match the verbs and nouns. Complete the chart. Listen and repeat.**

act explain connect describe decide
imagine prepare communicate discuss
invite collect invent

discussion invention action connection
collection description decision invitation
imagination preparation communication
explanation

Verb	Noun
act	action
explain	explanation

Stop Notice that some of the nouns end in -ion and some end in -ation.

2 Look at the chart and underline nouns ending in -ion in one color, and nouns ending in -ation in another color.

3 Complete the sentences with the correct form of the verbs and nouns from the chart.

1 I didn't understand the homework, so I called Amy and she __explained__ it.

2 I didn't do much _____ for the test.

3 Sam has a _____ of over 1,000 soccer stickers!

4 Virtual reality headsets are the coolest _____ ever!

5 Jo's a vegetarian, but I don't know why she _____ not to eat meat.

6 Did you _____ Emma to your party?

7 Lee's very good at talking to people. He has great _____ skills!

8 I _____ the thief: he was tall, with dark hair and glasses.

→ *METRO EXPRESS* P.112

L Listening

The five-second rule

1 ◀)) 41 ▶ **Listen to the conversation. Can you infer the speakers' opinions about the five-second rule?**

Who believes in the five-second rule?
a Jacob   b Emma   c Emma's mom

2 ◀)) 41 ▶ **Listen and complete the sentences with *J* (Jacob) or *E* (Emma).**

1 __E__ was eating a donut.

2 _____ dropped the donut.

3 _____ didn't want to eat the donut.

4 _____ gave an explanation of the five-second rule.

5 _____ didn't believe the five-second rule.

6 _____ was waiting for his or her mom.

3 ◀)) 42 ▶ **Complete the paragraphs. Use each word once in each paragraph. Listen and check.**

eat ~~food~~ ground seconds

If you drop **1** __food__ on the ground, quickly blow on it or wipe it on your clothes. It's OK to **2**_____ it if it's on the **3**_____ for less than five **4**_____.

It doesn't matter if you leave **5**_____ on the ground for one second or 30 **6**_____. If you drop food and there's bacteria on the **7**_____, the bacteria will contaminate it. So don't **8**_____ it, or you might find yourself in the emergency room!

Your turn

4 Do you believe in the five-second rule?

G Grammar

Modals: *might, must,* and *can't*

1 🔊 43 **Read the conversation. When will Mia celebrate her 20ᵗʰ birthday?**

a 2076 **b** 2080 **c** 2084

Mia: Guess how old I am. I have to warn you – you might not guess right!

Jon: Hmm. You might be 17 or 18. Am I right?

Mia: No! It's a trick question. I celebrated my fourth birthday in 2016.

Jon: What? That can't be true! You must be much older than that!

Mia: Let me explain: I was born on February 29, 2000.

Jon: Oh, a leap year, with 29 days in February. Leap years only happen every four years, right?

Mia: Yes. So my tenth birthday will be in 2040! I might not have more than 20 birthdays in my whole life!

2 Complete the chart. Which sentences are present possibility and which are future possibility?

> We use *might / might not* to talk about present and future possibility.
>
> You ¹ _might not_ guess right!
> You ² _____ be 17 or 18.
> I **might** have a party on my next birthday.
> I ³ _____ have more than 20 birthdays.

3 Complete the conversations.

> might be   ~~might buy~~   might not arrive
> might not do   might not have   might see

1

Lisa: Look at that bag! It's lovely.

Kate: Yeah, and it isn't too expensive.

Lisa: Wow, I _might buy_ it! Oh, no. Wait a minute. I _____ enough money.

2

Ben: The train _____ on time today. It's often late on Saturdays.

3

Kris: Do you have plans this weekend?

Stan: Not really. We _____ relatives, or we _____ anything. Sometimes it's good to stay home and do nothing.

4

Leo: Did you hear the door?

Silas: Yeah. It _____ Sonia. She wanted to visit today.

 **Your turn**

4 In pairs, take turns to make sentences about the future using *might* (*not*) and the words.

> college   jobs   next weekend   tonight   vacations

> I might not go out tonight. I might stay in and watch soccer.

5 Read the conversation in exercise 1 again and complete the chart.

> We use *must* to talk about present certainty.
> We use *can't* to talk about present impossibility.
>
> That ¹ _____ be true! (*It's impossible.*)
> You ² _____ be much older than that!
> (*I am sure / certain about this.*)

6 Choose the correct answers.

1 My watch says 12:45, but it's dark outside.
  It (must be) / can't be nighttime.
  It **must be / can't be** daytime.

2 Simon won the 100 m race.
  He **must feel / can't feel** proud!

3 Leo's mom is on a 25-km bike ride.
  She **must enjoy / can't enjoy** biking.

4 There's snow on Isla's coat and scarf.
  It **must be / can't be** hot outside.

7 Look at the picture and write sentences. Use *might, must,* and *can't.*

1 these girls / be at home
  These girls might be at home.

2 they / be in a movie theater
  _____

3 they / be at the beach
  _____

4 they / be watching a comedy
  _____

5 they / feel / cold
  _____

6 they / like / popcorn
  _____

→ *METRO EXPRESS* P.112

Expressing disbelief

1 ◄)) 44) **Read the web page. Then listen and check (✓) the stories you hear.**

That can't be true!

1 ☐ **Insects in lipstick**
Some lipsticks contain small beetles! The cochineal beetle produces a red dye, and cosmetics companies use this to give some lipsticks a bright red color!

2 ☐ **Folded paper**
It's impossible to fold a piece of paper in half more than seven times. Try it!

3 ☐ **Headless cockroaches**
Cockroaches live for a year, and they can live for a week without their head! They only die because they can't drink water.

4 ☐ **The Mona Lisa's eyebrows**
The Mona Lisa doesn't have eyebrows. Take a look! This might be because it was fashionable to remove eyebrows in Florence, Italy, 500 years ago.

Stop

Useful phrases
Hey, listen to this.
You won't believe this, but …
Really? I find that hard to believe.
You're joking!
That can't be true.

2 ◄)) 45) **Listen and complete the conversations.**

be true   's true   ~~won't believe~~

A You ¹ _won't believe_ this, but it's impossible to fold a piece of paper in half more than seven times.

B You're joking! That can't ² _____.

A It ³ _____! Try it!

be true   listen to   to believe

A Hey, ⁴ _____ this. They make some lipsticks with beetles!

B Really? I find that hard ⁵ _____.

A Look, it says here that …

B Wow! I guess it might ⁶ _____.

3 **Practice your own conversations. Use exercise 2 as a model. Use the information about cockroaches, the Mona Lisa, or your own ideas.**

Online Homework

R) Reading)

1 **Read the tip.**

Tip **Good readers** can scan a text quickly to find specific information such as dates and proper nouns.

◄)) 46) **Read the article. How many countries and nationalities does it mention?** Underline **them while you read.**

2 **Scan the text and find the answers. (The answers are all dates or proper nouns.)**

1 What was Google's smell service called?
   Google Nose BETA

2 What do they call April Fools' Day in France?
   _____

3 Which company did an April Fools' Day joke about animals? _____

4 Who made the documentary about spaghetti trees? When? _____

3 **Choose the correct answers.**

1 Google Nose BETA …
   a produced smells.
   b delivered roses.
   ⓒ was a joke.

2 With Google Nose, the writer …
   a breathed quickly.
   b didn't smell anything.
   c smelled roses through the screen.

3 Around the world, April 1 …
   a has a few names.
   b is called April Fools' Day.
   c is also called April Fish.

4 The idea for Google Street Roo included …
   a cameras on animals.
   b spaghetti in trees.
   c cans of tomato sauce.

5 The BBC …
   a made a video of British farmers.
   b grew spaghetti trees in Switzerland.
   c played a joke on thousands of people.

Your turn

4 **Discuss the questions.**

1 Which April Fools' Day joke in the text do you think was the funniest?

2 Why might media companies play April Fools' jokes?

3 Have you ever heard a funny April Fools' joke? What was it?

4 Have you ever played an April Fools' joke? What was it?

APRIL FOOLS' DAY

A few years ago, I received an e-mail invitation:

Have you ever smelled flowers on your computer? No? Google it! With Google Nose BETA you can enjoy millions of smells from around the world. What do wild roses smell like? Google knows – try Google Nose!

I smiled and shook my head: "That can't be true." But when I read a description of its database of 15 million smells, I quickly changed my mind: "This invention might be real. Google is the world's largest media company." I clicked on the link to the Google Nose page. I put my nose near the screen and I breathed in slowly. There was no smell at all. I was confused. Then I made the connection and I started to laugh. The date was April 1.

The day has different names around the world – Americans call it April Fools' Day, in France it's *Poisson d'Avril* (April Fish), and in Brazil, April 1 is *Dia da Mentira* (Day of Lies). The equivalent in Spanish-speaking countries, *Día de los Inocentes* (Day of the Innocents), is on December 28. People play jokes on friends and family, and media companies often play jokes, too. Google plays jokes every April Fools' Day. Did you hear about the version of Google Street View called Google Street Roo? That was a plan to take pictures of the Australian continent with 3-D cameras on wild kangaroos. People believed it, but it was just another April Fools' joke.

Google wasn't the first and they won't be the last company to play April Fools' jokes. Perhaps the best was a BBC documentary on British TV in 1957. It was about farmers in Switzerland and their spaghetti trees. In the video, the farmers were taking spaghetti from trees. Afterwards, thousands of people asked the BBC how they could grow their own spaghetti trees. The BBC said: "Put a piece of spaghetti in a can of tomato sauce and hope for the best."

Writing P.104 Workbook P.W29 Online Homework **53**

Truth and lies

Rob

Before you watch

1 Look at the pictures. Answer the questions.

1 Who do you think the skateboarder in picture 1 is sending a text to? Why?

2 Who do you think gave the girl in picture 2 her gift? Why is she saying she loves it?

3 Have you ever said something like this? Why?

1 I'm studying for my English test.

2 It's perfect. I love it.

While you watch

2 Video Read the list of topics. Then watch the video and check (✓) the topics that it discusses.

1 Lying to a friend about a new haircut ☐	4 Lying to a teacher about homework ☐
2 Lying to your parents ☐	5 Believing an April Fools' Day joke ☐
3 Lying in a store ☐	

3 Watch the video. Choose the correct person.

	Ollie	Piper	Jack	Naomi
thinks you should never be dishonest				
might lie about a friend's appearance	✓			
will lie to be polite				
talks about lying at a store				

	Ollie	Piper	Jack	Naomi
sometimes lies to friends?				
didn't talk to his / her parents about a bad grade				
lied about his / her age				
lied as a small child				

	Ollie	Piper	Jack	Naomi
believed a joke about money				
believed a joke about school				
believed a joke about a prize				
believed a joke about food				

After you watch

4 Interview your friends with the questions from the video.

1 Is it ever OK to be dishonest?

2 Have you ever lied?

3 Have you ever believed an April Fools' joke, or a story that someone has made up?

5 Make a video or project about truth and lies. You can include the answers to the questions in exercise 4, or think about the following questions.

- When is it wrong to lie?
- Is it ever OK to lie? When?
- What problems can lying cause?

Online Homework  Challenge

Review

V Vocabulary

1 Label the pictures of man-made and natural problems.

> ~~climate change~~ disease drought flood
> heat wave overpopulation pollution wildfire

1 _climate change_

2 _____

3 _____

4 _____

5 _____

6 _____

7 _____

8 _____

2 Match the sentence halves.

1 Don't throw away
2 We should protect
3 The world is going to run out
4 Remember to keep and reuse
5 We're going to reduce
6 Take shorter showers and
7 It should be easier to recycle
   I think the human race will become

a your plastic bags.
b of oil and gas in 100 years.
c our natural environment.
d that book. You can sell it online.
e glass and metal.
f extinct one day.
g our carbon emissions by 20%.
h save water!

3 Complete the conversations about truth and lies.

A I don't ¹ b _elieve_____ you. Did you
  ² m_____ this ridiculous story?

B No, it's true, I ³ p_____!

A Don't ⁴ l_____ to me. ⁵ T_____ me the truth!

C We know Jonnie stole our money, but he won't
  ⁶ a_____ it.

D Did he ⁷ p_____ it was his money?

C Yes. I can't ⁸ t_____ him anymore.

4 Complete the sentences with the *-ion* noun form of the verbs.

1 Did you do much _preparation_ (prepare) for the test?

2 Here's a _____ (describe) of what you need.

3 Our class had a _____ (discuss) about truth and lies.

4 What's your _____ (explain) for being late?

5 Did you receive a party _____ (invite)?

6 I have a good _____ (imagine).

7 Who's going to make the final _____ (decide)?

8 Good _____ (communicate) is important in any relationship.

G Grammar

1 Complete the predictions with *will* / *'ll* or *won't*.

I love studying at high school so
I ¹ _'ll go_____ (go) to college.
I think I ² _____ (choose)
science or math because I'm
good at those subjects at school.
I ³ _____ (study)
literature. I'm not a big fan
of novels.

Serena

Alfie

I have a good feeling
about today's game. I think
I ⁴ _____ (score) a goal.
The other team is very good, so
we probably ⁵ _____ (win),
but I'm looking forward to the
game. It ⁶ _____ (be)
good fun.

2 **Complete the predictions with the correct form of** *be going to.*

Abi: What's the weather like? **¹** Is_____ it
going to be (be) warm and sunny again?

Fran: No, it **²**_____. There are dark clouds in
the sky. It **³**_____ (rain).

Zac: Can I have some juice, please?

Mom: Sure. The bottle's nearly empty so we
⁴_____ (need) some more.
Can you stop by the store after school?

Kris: You look exhausted. **⁵**_____ you
_____ (feel) OK to play soccer later?

Anita: Yes, I **⁶**_____. I look tired, but I feel good.
I **⁷**_____ fine (be).

Livia: Watch out! You **⁸**_____ (fall)!

Jude: No, I **⁹**_____. I know there's a hole in the
sidewalk so I **¹⁰**_____ (walk)
into it!

3 **Complete the first conditional sentences with the**
correct form of the pairs of verbs.

> do / not be   get / miss   not get / not study
> not mind / arrive   ~~rain / leave~~   see / chase
> stay / take   tell / believe   text / finish

1 It _'ll rain_____ if we _leave_____ our umbrellas at
home, and it _____ dry if we _____
them. I know it!

2 We _____ good grades if we
_____.

3 How _____ you _____ to school if
you _____ the bus?

4 If the dog _____ the cat, it _____ it.

5 Dad _____ if we _____ a little
late.

6 _____ you _____ me if the movie
_____ after 11:30?

7 If they _____ the truth, everyone
_____ them.

8 What _____ you _____ if it
_____ sunny this weekend?

4 **Complete the sentences about present and future**
possibility with *can't, might, might not,* **or** *must.*

1 It's a nice day, so I _might_____ ride my bike.

2 I heard Oscar lost your phone. You _____ be
mad at him!

3 We're tired, so we _____ go out this evening.

4 This is the news. It _____ be the music channel.

5 I called them at the apartment, but there was no
answer. They _____ be home today. Or maybe
they didn't want to talk.

6 I'm not sure what's in your sandwich. It _____
be ham, but I can't remember what Mom said.

Consolidation

Read the conversation. Choose the correct words.

Grant: Did you see that documentary about climate
change? They say it **¹** _'s going to be__ really cold
this winter. If it **²**_____ a lot in the fall,
it'll be a cold winter.

Cody: But it **³**_____ cold! Last year it rained all
fall, but the winter was warm and dry.

Grant: Well, the scientists in the documentary said there's
a **⁴**_____ between wet falls and cold
winters. I don't understand the science, but I
⁵_____ the scientists. Don't you?

Cody: Yeah, I guess so. The effects of climate change are
getting worse every year, with extreme weather like
⁶_____ and floods. I think the scientists
⁷_____ be right. Some animals will
⁸_____, but I don't think life on Earth
⁹_____.

1	**a** won't be	**b** 'll be	**ⓒ** 's going to be
2	**a** will rain	**b** rain	**c** rains
3	**a** might not be	**b** must be	**c** can't be
4	**a** connects	**b** connection	**c** connecting
5	**a** pretend	**b** believe	**c** promise
6	**a** heat waves	**b** pollution	**c** overpopulation
7	**a** must	**b** can't	**c** mustn't
8	**a** become extinct	**b** run out	**c** throw away
9	**a** won't end	**b** will end	**c** is going to end

In this unit …

- talk about stages of a relationship
- talk about past habits
- talk about recent events
- identify the main events in a story
- understand a video about a relationship

Video Watch the warm-up video.

Getting along

Give me your phone.
I can call Tripp and …

This is so _____.

1 What mistake did Vicky make?

2 What are all the ways you communicate with your friends?

V Vocabulary

Relationship verbs

1 🔊 47 **Read the conversation. Which part of Amy's message isn't true?**

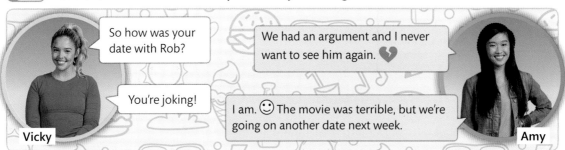

Vicky: So how was your date with Rob?

Amy: We had an argument and I never want to see him again. 💔

Vicky: You're joking!

Amy: I am. ☺ The movie was terrible, but we're going on another date next week.

2 🔊 48 **Match the pictures with the expressions. Then listen, check, and repeat.**

ask someone out   be attracted to someone   break up (with someone)   ~~fall in love (with someone)~~   get along (with someone)   go on a date   have an argument (with someone)   make up (with someone)   miss someone

a   fall in love (with someone)

b   _____

c   _____

d   _____

e   _____

f   _____

g   _____

h   _____

i   _____

_____

3 (49) Complete the story about Dan and Lucy. Use the simple past of the verbs in exercise 2. Then listen and check.

Dan and Lucy met at a party and they
¹ got along really well. Dan
²_____ Lucy because she was really funny.
At the end of the party, he took her phone number and
³_____ her _____. Lucy said "yes" so they
⁴_____ to the movies. They both had a
great time and soon they **⁵**_____.
Lucy was often late, and one day, they
⁶_____ about it. They were both really
mad, and after the argument they **⁷**_____.
But Dan **⁸**_____ Lucy and so he sent
her a message. She felt the same way and they
⁹_____.

4 Put the pictures of Dan and Lucy in exercise 2 in the correct order. In pairs, practice telling the story.

a _____   d _____   g __1__
b _____   e _____   h _____
c _____   f _____   i _____

> **Stop**
> We use *each other* to show that each person in a group of two or more does something to the others.
> *We get along with **each other** really well.*
> *They often wear **each other**'s clothes.*

5 Complete the sentences with the correct form of the verbs from exercise 2.

1 Tyler and Libby have a good relationship with each other. They _get along_ with each other.
2 Owen ended his relationship with Zoe last week. They _____.
3 Ana and Jack had an argument, but they are friends again now. Ana sent Jack a present and said sorry, and they _____ with each other.
4 Lily invited James to go on a date with her. Lily _____ James _____.
5 Ryan started to love Ashley as soon as they met. He _____ with her very quickly.
6 Ava feels sad about Ethan because they aren't together now. She _____ him.
7 Alexis wanted to go to a Chinese restaurant and Evan wanted to eat pizza, and they couldn't agree. They _____ about where to eat.
8 Clare _____ to Gavin. She thinks he's very good-looking and funny.
9 Ben asked Jo to go to the movies with him. They are _____ this Friday.

L **Listening**

Couples

1 (50) Listen to the conversations about couples. Match the conversations 1–3 with the sentences a–f. There are three extra sentences.

a They're just good friends. _____
b They get along, but she isn't attracted to him. _____
c They made up recently. _____
d They broke up recently. _____
e They have a lot of arguments. _____
f They're going on a date. _____

2 (50) Listen again. Choose the correct answers.

1 Why are the speakers surprised?
 a Ethan and Abbie have different personalities.
 b Ethan and Abbie aren't interested in the same things.
 c Abbie isn't attracted to Ethan.
2 Why did Simon and Sofia break up?
 a He wanted to get married.
 b Simon's parents didn't get along with Sofia.
 c The speakers don't know exactly.
3 Which statement is true about Pete and Jenny?
 a They first met when they were small children.
 b They broke up after a few dates.
 c She asked him out but he said no.

3 (50) Complete the sentences with the words. Then listen and check.

> ~~different~~   get   like
> relationship   spend   together

1 a They're so _different_ from each other.
 b That's going to be an interesting _____.
2 a Now they're _____ again.
 b I think they'll _____ married soon.
3 a They _____ a lot of time with each other.
 b They're more _____ brother and sister, really.

Romeo Montague

Mercutio

Juliet Capulet

Tybalt Capulet

Prince of Verona

1 🔊 51 Look at the title of the story. What do you know about this story? Read, listen, and check.

Romeo and Juliet

I've just met an awesome girl.

Who?

Juliet ... Juliet Capulet.

Capulet?!

1 Romeo and his friend Mercutio go to a party. Romeo meets Juliet at the party and they immediately fall in love. But there is a problem: Romeo is a Montague and Juliet is a Capulet. And the two families don't get along …

Perhaps our families will make up now.

2 Romeo and Juliet decide to get married secretly.

You've just killed my best friend!

3 After the wedding, Romeo meets Juliet's cousin, Tybalt. He tries to be friends, but Tybalt isn't listening. Tybalt kills Mercutio. Romeo gets really mad and kills Tybalt.

Leave! If you ever come back, you will die.

4 Romeo isn't allowed to stay in the city.

Romeo — I'm not really dead. Wait for me! J xxx

5 Juliet's father doesn't know that Juliet has already gotten married. He chooses a husband for her, Paris. Juliet wants to escape, so she pretends to be dead. First, she sends a message to Romeo and then she takes a special sleeping potion.

If I can't be with you, I don't want to live!

6 Romeo visits Juliet secretly. He hasn't received the message from Juliet yet and he is really upset when he finds her.

7 Soon after, Juliet wakes up. She quickly realizes Romeo's mistake. She also can't live without her new husband …

Our argument caused this tragedy.

We are so sorry.

8 When both families learn the truth, they are very upset. They decide to make up.

2 Read the story again. Put the events in the correct order.

a Romeo has to leave the city. _____
b Romeo dies. _____
c Romeo and Juliet get married. __1__
d Juliet dies. _____
e Juliet sends Romeo a message. _____
f Mercutio dies. _____
g The Montagues make up with the Capulets. _____
h Romeo kills Juliet's cousin. _____
i Juliet takes a sleeping potion. _____

3 Write questions for the answers.

1 Why is Romeo and Juliet's relationship a problem ?
Because their families don't get along.

2 Why _____?
Because Tybalt killed his friend Mercutio.

3 Why _____?
Because he killed Tybalt.

4 Why _____
_____?
Because she didn't want to marry Paris.

5 Why _____?
Because they didn't want another tragedy like Romeo and Juliet.

Present perfect: *just*, *already*, and *yet*

1 🔊 52 **Read the conversation. Is the sentence true, false, or do we not know?** _____

Toby's going on a date with Sarah on Saturday.

A Have you heard Toby's news yet?

B No, I haven't. What's happened?

A He's already found another girlfriend.

B No way! He's just broken up with Sarah!

A I know!

B So who is she?

A He hasn't told me yet.
Look at his message: I can't meet you on Saturday. I'm going on a date!

B Maybe he and Sarah made up.

A I hope so. They're a cute couple.

2 **Complete the chart.**

Affirmative	Negative
He's ¹ _just_ broken up with Sarah.	He hasn't told me ³ _____.
He's ² _____ found another girlfriend.	
Questions	**Short answers**
Have you heard Toby's news ⁴ _____?	Yes, I have. / No, I ⁵ _____.

3 **Complete the sentences with the present perfect and *just*.**

a He _'s just asked out_ (ask out) Macy and she said "yes"!

b He _____ (break up) with Jen.

c They _____ (have) an argument about soccer.

d We _____ (make up). We're together again.

e I _____ (go) on a date with Tom. It was fun!

4 **Match the answers in exercise 3 with the questions 1–5.**

1 Why are you smiling? _____

2 Are you still mad at your boyfriend? _____

3 Why are Seb and Matt ignoring each other? _____

4 Alex looks cheerful. What's happened? _a_____

5 What's wrong with Mark? _____

5 **Write sentences and questions with the present perfect and the words.**

1 you / make / any mistakes? (yet)
   Have you made any mistakes yet?

2 I / do / all the chores (already)
   _____

3 we / not / have / one argument. (yet)
   _____

4 I / make / a big decision. (just)
   _____

5 They / see / the movie. (already)
   _____

6 he / tell / you the truth? (yet)
   _____

6 **Carly is going on a date with Josh. Look at the picture. Write the things she has already done and the things she hasn't done yet.**

charge her phone   ~~choose her clothes~~
dry her hair   send Josh a message   take a shower

1 _Carly hasn't chosen her clothes yet._

2 _____

3 _____

4 _____

5 _____

7 🔊 53 **Listen to five people. What do you think has just happened? Use the verbs.**

fail   find   finish   forget
hurt   pass   ~~remember~~   score

1 He's just remembered something important.

→ *METRO EXPRESS* P.113

V Vocabulary

Expressing emotions

1 🔊 54 > **Match the verbs with the pictures and the definitions. Then listen, check, and repeat.**

cry   hug   laugh   shout   stare   sulk

1 _cry_ : make tears from your eyes because you are unhappy or something hurts

2 _____ : be quiet or unhappy because you are mad with someone about something

3 _____ : smile and make a noise with your mouth because something is funny

4 _____ : put your arms around someone, usually because you love him or her

5 _____ : speak very loudly

6 _____ : look at someone or something for a long time

2 Choose the best verbs.

1 Do you **shout at** / **hug** your friends when you see them in the morning?

2 Do you ever **cry** / **sulk** when you watch sad movies?

3 Is it rude to **stare** / **cry** at people in your country?

4 Do any of your friends **laugh** / **sulk** after arguments?

5 Have you ever **shouted** / **stared** at a good friend when you were mad at them?

6 What TV shows make you **hug** / **laugh**?

3 In pairs, ask and answer the questions in exercise 2.

> Do you hug your friends when you see them in the morning?

> Yes, we always hug.

→ *METRO EXPRESS* P.113

L Listening

Siblings: brothers and sisters

1 🔊 55 > **Ryan, Grace, and Lucas are talking about relationships. Listen and decide which question they are answering.**

a What are the most common reasons you have arguments with your siblings?

b Do your siblings get along with each other?

c Is your relationship with your sibling different now from it was in the past?

2 🔊 55 > **Listen again. Choose *T* (True) or *F* (False).**

1 Ryan gets along with his brother's friends.   T ☑ F ☐

2 Ryan gets upset when his brother teases him.   T ☐ F ☐

3 Ryan's relationship with his brother was better in the past.   T ☐ F ☐

4 Grace gets along better with her cousin than her sister.   T ☐ F ☐

5 Grace never has arguments with her cousin.   T ☐ F ☐

6 Lucas's sisters get along better with each other than with him.   T ☐ F ☐

7 Lucas's relationship with his sisters is better now than it was in the past.   T ☐ F ☐

8 Lucas was helpful to his sisters when they were younger.   T ☐ F ☐

3 🔊 56 > **Complete the sentences. Then listen again and check. What do you think the phrases mean?**

close   ~~close in age~~   fall out
like a sister   little brother   only child

1 **Ryan:** We're pretty _close in age_ – 16 and 17. I'm always his _____, of course, and he sometimes teases me.

2 **Grace:** I'm an _____, so I don't have any brothers or sisters. My cousin is _____ to me.

3 **Lucas:** They have a really _____ relationship. My sisters used to shout and _____ with each other all the time.

4 In pairs, discuss the questions.

1 What are the advantages of having a sibling?

2 What are the advantages of being an only child?

used to

1 🔊 **57** **Read the conversation. Which statements are true?**

1 Frank is Ella's mom's older brother.
2 Frank got upset when Ella's mom teased him.
3 Frank and Ella's mom get along now.

a 1 and 2   **b** 2 and 3   **c** 1, 2, and 3

Ella: Mom. Did you use to get along with your brother when you were young?
Mom: Uncle Frank? No, we didn't use to be friends at all. Frank was my little brother, and I used to think he was really annoying!
Ella: Did you use to tease him?
Mom: Yes, I did. A lot! It was so easy to make him cry!
Ella: Oh, poor Uncle Frank!
Mom: I know. But we're close now, of course.

2 **Complete the chart.**

Affirmative	Negative
I ¹ used to ___ think he was so annoying.	We ² _____ be friends at all.
Question?	Short answers
Did you ³_____ get along with your brothers?	Yes, I ⁴_____. / No, I didn't.
What toys did you use to play with?	

Stop We use *used to* + infinitive to talk about things that:
1 happened regularly in the past, but don't happen now.
2 were true in the past, but aren't true now.

3 **Complete the sentences with the phrases.**

used to believe   used to hug
used to shout   ~~used to think~~

1 People _used to think_ that the Earth was flat.

2 My brother and I _____ at each other all the time!

3 When I was young, I _____ a teddy bear at night.

4 Until 400 years ago, some people _____ that lambs grew on trees!

4 **Complete the sentences with *used to* or *didn't use to* and the verbs.**

cry   eat   enjoy   have arguments   ~~laugh~~   worry

1 I _used to laugh_ at all my brother's jokes, but now they're just annoying.
2 I _____ about exams, but now I get really stressed about them.
3 My parents and I _____ all the time, but now we get along really well.
4 I _____ when my sister teased me. Now I don't get upset about it.
5 Tom _____ meat because he was a vegetarian.

5 **Make questions with *used to*.**

When you were younger …
1 what / you / hate eating?
  What did you use to hate eating?
2 you / go to a different school?
  Did you use to go to a different school?
3 what / you / to be frightened of?
  _____
4 what / you / watch on TV?
  _____
5 you / sleep with a favorite toy?
  _____

👉 **Your turn**

6 **In pairs, ask and answer the questions in exercise 5.**

What did you use to hate eating?

I used to hate eating vegetables.

➔ *METRO EXPRESS* P.113

sixty-three

Talking about recent events

1 🔊 58 **Read and listen. Then complete the summary of the conversation.**

Zoe: Have you heard about Lauren and Rob?

Alison: No, what's happened? Tell me!

Zoe: They've just split up.

Alison: Are you kidding? I'm shocked! They got along really well.

Zoe: I know. I can't believe it.

Lauren and Rob ¹ _have just split up_ . Zoe and Alison are ² _____ because Lauren and Rob ³ _____ .

2 **In pairs, practice the conversation in exercise 1.**

3 🔊 59 **Listen to another conversation and complete the summary.**

Stella ¹ _has just asked out_ Luis, but he said no. Maria ² _____ because he ³ _____ with his last girlfriend.

Stop **Useful phrases**
Have you heard about … ?
What's happened?
They've just …
Are you kidding?
I'm shocked! / I'm not surprised.

4 **In pairs, write two conversations about these situations. Use the conversation in exercise 1 as a model.**

1 Two friends have just made up. You're surprised because they had a really big argument recently.

2 Two friends have just been on a date. You aren't surprised because they share a lot of interests.

Have you heard about … ?

No, what's happened? Tell me!

5 **In pairs, practice your conversations.**

1 🔊 60 **Read the story. Match the sentences a–e with the gaps 1–5. Then listen and check.**

a They had a meeting with all the workers in the company and explained the situation.

b Rudi, two years older, was loud and confident.

c The people of Herzogenaurach became either Puma or Adidas fans.

d But the two wives didn't get along.

e Their business became successful very quickly.

2 **Read the tip.**

 Tip **Good readers** can identify the main events in a story.

Read the story. Match the beginnings and ends of the sentences to make the main events in the story of Adidas and Puma.

1 In 1920,	a the brothers stopped getting along.
2 In 1924,	b Jesse Owens made the company famous.
3 In 1936,	c Adi formed Adidas.
4 In the early 1940s,	d Rudi Dassler started working with his brother.
5 In 1948,	e Adi Dassler started designing sports shoes.
6 In 1949,	f Rudi left Dassler Brothers.

3 **Complete the sentences with one word.**

1 Rudi was good at _selling_ shoes because he was confident.

2 The athlete Jesse Jones _____ the brothers' shoes at the 1936 Olympic Games.

3 Friedl and Katherina didn't have a good _____ .

4 We don't know the _____ why the brothers fell out.

5 The workers had to make a _____ about which brother they wanted to work for.

6 Adi invented his company's name from the first three _____ of his first and second names.

7 The companies _____ up by having a soccer match.

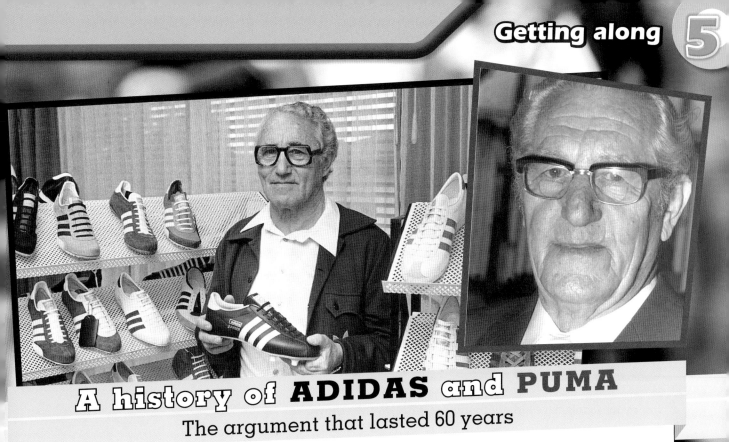

A history of ADIDAS and PUMA
The argument that lasted 60 years

As young brothers, Adi and Rudi Dassler used to get along well. They both loved sports, but they had very different personalities. Adi was quiet and hard-working. **1** _b_____

In 1920, Adi started making sports shoes at home, in the small town of Herzogenaurach, Germany. Adi was a brilliant designer, but he needed help to sell his shoes. So four years later, his brother, a talented salesman, joined the company. They called it Dassler Brothers Shoes. **2**_____ It made sneakers for Olympic athletes – including the American athlete Jesse Owens. In 1936, Owens won four Olympic gold medals while he was wearing Dassler Brothers sneakers. Suddenly their shoes were world famous.

At that time, both brothers used to live in the same house with Rudi's wife, Friedl, and their young children. In 1937, Adi fell in love with and married Katherina Martz. Now there were two families living together. **3**_____

Then in the early 1940s, the brothers fell out. No one knows exactly why, but in 1948 they decided not to work together anymore. **4**_____ The workers had to decide: did they want to work for Adi or Rudi?

The same year, Rudi started his own company, just 500 meters from the house they used to share. He called it Ruda (from Rudi and Dassler), but soon he changed the name to Puma. A year later, Adi started Adidas (from Adi and Dassler).

The brothers never spoke to each other again and their argument divided their town. **5**_____ The town even had two different soccer teams – one wore Puma shoes and the other wore Adidas! But in 2009, the companies decided to make up. They played a game of soccer together – 61 years after the brothers fell out!

W Watch

Milton and Phyllis

Vicky

Before you watch

1 Look at the pictures. Answer the questions.

1 Which person appears in all four of the pictures?
2 What order were the pictures taken in? How can you tell?
3 What do you think the relationship is between the man and the woman?
4 What important event does picture a show?

2 Does your family have old photographs? What do they show?

While you watch

3 ▶Video Watch the preview. Choose the best word to complete the descriptions of the photographs.

1 Great ⟨Grandma⟩ (Phyllis) / **Grandpa** (Milton) as a child
2 **Phyllis** / **Milton** graduating
3 Phyllis and Milton **dating** / **getting married**
4 Milton **on vacation** / **in the army**
5 Milton with his **kids** / **new car**
6 **Phyllis** / **Milton** with the grandchildren
7 Phyllis **graduating** / **with her granddaughter**

4 ▶Video Watch the video. Choose *T* (True) or *F* (False).

1 Milton and Phyllis didn't have brothers
or sisters.   T ☐ F ☑
2 They met at a dance.   T ☐ F ☐
3 They dated after Milton joined the army.   T ☐ F ☐
4 Milton wrote letters to Phyllis.   T ☐ F ☐
5 Milton and Phyllis had three kids.   T ☐ F ☐
6 Milton and Phyllis are very happy together.   T ☐ F ☐

5 ▶Video Watch the video again. Complete the sentences with one word.

1 Phyllis was __born__ in 1925.
2 Milton had _____ sisters.
3 Milton graduated from high school in _____.
4 Phyllis was _____ when she met Milton.
5 When they first met, they went for a _____.
6 Milton says on their first date, they saw a _____.
7 After they were married, Milton had to go to _____ to fight.
8 Their first child was born in _____.
9 Phyllis was _____ when she started college.
10 Phyllis and Milton have _____ great-grandchildren.

After you watch

6 Make a video or project about your family. If possible, include information about your parents, grandparents, or great grandparents.

• What are / were their names?
• Where did they meet?
• How many kids / grandkids / great-grandkids do they have?
• Any other information, including photographs, that you would like to include.

 Online Homework   Challenge

In this unit ...

- talk about what things look, smell, taste, and feel like
- talk about experiences, using the simple past and present perfect
- practice predicting before reading
- understand a video about synesthesia

Video ▶ Watch the warm-up video.

I'm doing an _____ for my _____ class.

The senses

1 What flavors does Vicky taste in the red, yellow, and orange jellos?

2 What does Tripp's experiment show?

Sense verbs and adjectives

1 🔊 61 〉 **Read the conversation. How does Vicky feel? Choose two adjectives.**

a confused **b** embarrassed **c** stressed **d** surprised

Tripp: Try this.
Vicky: Mmm! I love chocolate. Woah!
Tripp: What's up?
Vicky: It's hot! My tongue is burning!
Tripp: It's chili chocolate. I thought you liked spicy food.
Vicky: I do. But I didn't expect *chocolate* to be *spicy*!

2 🔊 62 〉 **Label the pictures. Listen and check.**

colorful   disgusting   fresh   hard   rough   ~~salty~~   shiny   smooth   soft   sour   spicy   sweet

TASTES ...

These pretzels taste ¹ <u>salty</u>.

This curry tastes ²_____.

This candy tastes ³_____.

Lemons and limes taste ⁴_____.

LOOKS ...

These balloons look ⁹_____.

These bugs look ¹⁰_____.

FEELS ...

This wood feels ⁵_____.

This blanket feels ⁶_____.

This sandpaper feels ⁷_____.

These pebbles feel ⁸_____.

SMELLS ...

These flowers smell ¹¹_____.

This trash smells ¹²_____.

3 🔊 63 **Choose the correct words. Listen and check.**

durian

jackfruit   rambutans

Some fruits, like the durian, jackfruit, and rambutan, have a **¹ hard** / **sweet** skin on the outside, and **²soft** / **salty** fruit on the inside. In Vietnam, they call rambutans *chom chom*, meaning "messy hair", because of their unusual skin! On the inside, there is **³ shiny** / **rough**, white fruit.

mango sticky rice

luk chup

These **⁴ fresh** / **spicy** flowers at the market in Kunming, China, were very **⁵ colorful** / **smooth**. They **⁶ felt** / **smelled** amazing!

Mango sticky rice was my favorite Thai dessert. It **⁷ tasted** / **looked** delicious, but it was very **⁸ disgusting** / **sweet**.

4 🔊 64 **Complete the phrases with the verbs. Listen and repeat.**

~~feels~~ looks smells tastes

1 It _feels_ smooth. / It _feels_ like glass.

2 It _____ sweet. / It _____ like coffee.

3 It _____ disgusting. / It _____ like old shoes!

4 It _____ shiny. / It _____ like some kind of metal.

5 **Play a guessing game with the pictures in exercise 2, and with other things.**

They taste salty.

Pretzels!

No. What else tastes salty?

Fries?

→ *METRO EXPRESS* P.114

Workbook P.W7   Online Homework

L **Listening**

An Asian food market

1 **Read the tip.**

Tip **Good listeners** think about the topic of a listening exercise and predict key words they might hear.

Find the *durian* and *luk chup* in the pictures. You are going to listen to conversations about them. Choose four phrases you might hear.

1 It smells disgusting.   ☑

2 It feels soft.   ☐

3 It tastes salty.   ☐

4 They're very sweet.   ☐

5 It tastes spicy.   ☐

6 They're smooth and shiny.   ☐

2 🔊 65 **Listen to the conversations and check.**

3 🔊 65 **Answer the questions. Listen again and check**

1 What difference between durians and jackfruits do they mention?
Jackfruits have rough skin. Durians have big,
hard spikes.

2 Where does the durian come from?
_____

3 How do the speakers describe the durian's flavor?
_____
_____

4 Where does *luk chup* come from?
_____

5 What are three ingredients in *luk chup*?
_____

👉 **Your turn**

4 **Discuss the questions.**

1 Have you ever eaten any unusual fruits?
2 What fruits are typical in your country? What do they taste like?

The brain: our sixth sense

Humans have five senses: sight, hearing, smell, taste, and touch. We get 80% of our sensory information through our eyes. This makes sight our most important sense. The second most important is hearing. Although smell, taste, and touch are vital for many animals, humans don't rely on these senses for survival. If we lose our hearing or our sense of smell, we can use our sight to understand the world around us. But it's harder to replace our sight with the other senses.

Erik Weihenmayer became blind when he was 13, but that has never stopped him doing the things he loves. He first tried rock climbing when he was 16, and since then he's climbed hundreds of mountains. In 2001, he became the first (and only) blind person to climb Mount Everest!

Erik Weihenmayer

Now, Weihenmayer climbs with the help of a BrainPort. The BrainPort sends pictures from a camera, via a micro-processor, to a pad on his tongue. Electrodes on this pad form shapes. The tongue feels the shapes, and sends information to the brain. The brain then transforms the information into simple pictures. The idea of the technology is that we "see" with our brains, not just with our eyes. The company that makes BrainPort is still developing the technology, but it already allows Weihenmayer to do things that used to be impossible – he can "see" a ball and play ball games with his daughter, and he can climb without help from others.

Craig Lundberg lost his sight when he was 24, and like Weihenmayer, Lundberg has continued to live an active life. Since losing his sight, he has run a marathon, completed a 550-km bike ride, and climbed Mount Kilimanjaro! Lundberg was one of the first people to try the BrainPort, and he was excited about how the device might improve life for blind people. He was able to identify objects, read words, and walk without help when using the BrainPort.

Blind people can't replace their sight with other senses, but their other senses, especially hearing and touch, help them to understand what's around them. The BrainPort can add to this, by helping blind people to "see" their environment and objects around them.

1	micro-processor unit
2	_____
3	_____
4	_____

Craig Lundberg wearing a BrainPort

1 🔊 66 **What do the men in the pictures have in common? Read and check.**

2 Label the parts of the BrainPort in the picture.

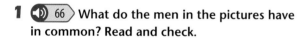

camera   electrodes
~~micro-processor unit~~   pad

3 Answer the questions.

1 Which is the most important sense, and why?
 Sight, because we get 80% of our information from it.

2 To survive, which two senses do humans need the most?
_____

3 What record does Erik Weihenmayer hold?
_____

4 What can Weihenmayer do now he has a BrainPort?
_____

5 What adventure sports has Craig Lundberg done since he went blind?
_____

6 What could Craig Lundberg do when he used the BrainPort?
_____

 **Your turn**

4 In pairs, discuss the questions.

1 Order the senses from most important to least important. Explain your reasons.

2 Which senses are important for animals, and why?

3 In the future, how do you think technology will help us with other physical problems?

G Grammar

Present perfect: *for* and *since*

1 🔊 67 **Read the conversation. Why is the pool closed?**

a Because it smells disgusting.
b Because it feels horrible.
c Because it looks awful.

Gavin: What's that smell?
Riley: The pool. Disgusting, isn't it? It looks bad, too.
Gavin: Yeah. How long has it smelled like that?
Riley: It's been like this since Friday.
Gavin: Really?
Jose: Yes, the pool's been closed for five days.
Riley: I heard they haven't cleaned it since last month!

2 Complete the chart.

Affirmative	It's **been** like this ¹ _since___ Friday. The pool's **been** closed ² _____ five days.
Negative	They **haven't cleaned** it ³ _____ last month.
Questions	⁴ _____ **has** it **smelled** like that?

Stop
We can use the present perfect to talk about an action or state that started in the past and that continues now.
We use the present perfect and *for* to talk about periods of time. We use *since* to specify a point in time.
*I've been here **for** 20 minutes. I've been here **since** 10:30.*
We use *How long … ?* to ask about the duration of the action or state.

3 Match the sentence halves.

1 We haven't lost a game since
2 Have you been here since
3 Rudy has been at college for
4 How long have
5 I've known you since
6 Has Alice lived in L.A. for
7 How long has

a you studied English?
b six o'clock?
c I joined the team.
d two years.
e Lara played soccer?
f ten years?
g we were five.

4 Complete the sentences with *for* or *since*.

1 We have lived in New York _for_____ ten years.
2 I've had this tablet _____ my last birthday.
3 This store hasn't been open _____ long.
4 We've been in this school _____ we were 12.
5 Has she been here _____ 3:30?
6 Have you liked soccer _____ a long time?
7 I haven't felt well _____ I had breakfast.
8 They've had the same teacher _____ a few months.

5 Write questions with *How long* and the present perfect. Write answers with *for* or *since*.

1 you / live here?
I / live / here / I was three
  How long have you lived here?
  I've lived here since I was three.

2 you / study English?
I / study / it / eight years
  _____
  _____

3 we / be / in this class?
we / be / in this class / 9:30
  _____
  _____

4 you / know / your best friend?
we / know / each other / ten years
  _____
  _____
  _____

👉 **Your turn**

6 Ask and answer the questions in exercise 5 for you.

How long have you lived here?

I've lived here for fifteen years. How about you?

→ *METRO EXPRESS* P.114

Workbook P.W20   Online Homework   **71**

Sleep

1 🔊 68 Look at the quiz and complete the gaps. Listen and check.

2 Do the quiz. Choose *T* (True) or *F* (False).

3 Add up your points. Look at the key and compare in pairs. Do you agree?

→ *METRO EXPRESS* P.114

Are you a SLEEPY-HEAD or a NIGHT OWL?

| feel sleepy   lie in bed   ~~yawn~~ |

1 I __yawn__ as soon as someone else yawns.
T ☐ (2) F ☐ (1)

2 I always _____ after school.
T ☐ (2) F ☐ (1)

3 I hate getting up. I _____ for hours on weekends.
T ☐ (2) F ☐ (1)

| fall asleep   lie awake   wake up |

4 I _____ as soon as my head touches the pillow.
T ☐ (2) F ☐ (1)

5 I sometimes _____ at night.
T ☐ (1) F ☐ (2)

6 I _____ early on the weekend.
T ☐ (1) F ☐ (2)

| have a nightmare   have dreams   snore |

7 I _____ a lot. I'm a heavy sleeper.
T ☐ (2) F ☐ (1)

8 I _____ about sleeping!
T ☐ (2) F ☐ (1)

9 After I _____ ,
I just turn over and go back to sleep.
T ☐ (2) F ☐ (1)

KEY
9–12: You're happier awake than asleep. That's OK, but remember you need sleep to stay healthy.
13–16: You like a good night's sleep, but you can get out of bed when you need to.
16–18: You're a real sleepy-head! Nothing will get you out of bed.

L **Listening**

Teenagers and sleep

1 🔊 69 Listen to the podcast and choose the main idea.

a Teenagers should go to bed earlier than 11 p.m.

b High schools should start later than 7:30 a.m.

c High school students should stop sulking.

d Parents should change their body clocks.

2 🔊 69 Read the questions. Listen again and answer.

1 What is the body clock?

2 If high schools start after 9 a.m., what effects does it have on students' … ?   **a** sleep   **b** behaviour   **c** grades

3 🔊 70 Complete the summary of the podcast. Listen and check.

| 6   7   7:30   ~~9~~   9   9½   10   11   13 |

Most people feel sleepy at around ¹__9__ p.m. until they are ²_____. After this age, people feel sleepy at around ³_____ p.m. Teenagers need up to ⁴_____ hours' sleep. If high school starts at ⁵_____ a.m., you need to get up at ⁶_____ a.m. Your body needs more than ⁷_____ hours' sleep. Some high schools have changed classes to start at ⁸_____ or ⁹_____ a.m.

👉 **Your turn**

4 Discuss the advantages and disadvantages of high schools starting after 9 a.m.

G Grammar

Simple past or present perfect?

1 🔊 71 **Read the conversation. Who can you see in the picture?**

Liv: Have you ever fallen asleep anywhere unusual?

Lou: No, I've never done that, but my brother has fallen asleep in some strange places!

Liv: Ha ha! Where?

Lou: Last week, we went to the movie theater, and he fell asleep during the movie. And he snored!

2 Complete the chart.

Present perfect
¹ Have_____ you ever _fallen_____ asleep anywhere unusual?
I **²**_____ that.
Simple past
Last week, we **³**_____ to the movie theater. He **⁴**_____ asleep. And he **⁵**_____!

Stop
We use the present perfect to talk about past experiences in our life. We don't say the time when they happened.
*My brother **has fallen asleep** in lots of strange places!*
We don't use the **present perfect** with past time phrases.
*My brother **has fallen asleep** at the movies last week.* ✗
We use the simple past to say when past events happened.
*My brother **fell asleep** at the movies last week.* ✓
We also use the **simple past** to add more information.
*I've eaten chili chocolate. It **was** delicious!*

3 Choose the correct words.

1 We **'ve visited** / visited Florida lots of times.
The last time we **have gone** / **went** was two years ago.

2 I **saw** / **'ve seen** that movie before.
I **saw** / **'ve seen** it last month.

3 I **'ve had** / **had** a nightmare last night.
Did you ever have / **Have you ever had** one?

4 **Julia:** **Have you got** / **Did you get** a lift yesterday?
Riley: No. I **walked** / **'ve walked**.

5 **Kevin:** **Did you ever go** / **Have you ever gone** to an amusement park?
Elliot: No. There **was** / **has been** a school trip to one last year, but I **haven't gone** / **didn't go**.

4 Complete the conversations with the pairs of verbs. Use the present perfect and the simple past.

drive / ride   earn / pay   give / speak   ~~have / stay~~

1 " _Have you_ ever _had_ a sleepover at Amy's?"
"Yes. I _stayed_____ at her house last Friday."

2 "_____ ever _____ any money?"
"Sure. My parents _____ me $10 for cleaning the car last weekend."

3 "_____ ever _____ a presentation to more than 100 people?"
"Yes. I _____ about the environment to the whole school last year."

4 "_____ ever _____ a car?"
"No, but I _____ a motorcycle last summer."

5 Write true sentences. Use the present perfect to talk about your experience. If there is more information, write a sentence in the simple past.

1 swim in the ocean
 I've swum in the ocean. I swam in the ocean last
 summer. / I haven't swum in the ocean.

2 have an argument with a friend
 _____
 _____

3 sleep in a tent
 _____
 _____

4 forget something important for school
 _____
 _____

5 sell something to a friend
 _____
 _____

👉 **Your turn**

6 Ask and answer the questions in exercise 5.

Have you ever swum in the ocean?

Yes, I have. I swam in the ocean in Florida last July.

→ *METRO EXPRESS* P.114

Talking about experiences

1 🔊 72 **Listen and complete the conversations.**

liked it ~~missed my stop~~ saw it on Saturday
woke up at the bus station

Austin: Have you ever fallen
asleep on the bus?

Xavier: Yes, I have!

Austin: What happened?

Xavier: I ¹_missed my stop_
and I ²_____!

Phil: Have you seen the new Pixar movie yet?

Alex: No, I haven't. Have you seen it?

Phil: Yes, I ³_____, and I
really ⁴_____.

2 **Look at exercise 1 and:**

1 underline verbs in the present perfect tense.
2 circle verbs in the simple past.

3 🔊 73 **Listen to two conversations and complete
the chart.**

Have you ever … ?	When? / What?
¹_won a competition_	¹_when I was 11_
²_____	²_____
	_____
Details	
¹_art competition, won $10_	
²_____	

🛑 **Stop** **Useful phrases**
Have you ever … ? / Have you … yet?
Yes, I have. / No, I haven't.
Really? When? / What happened? /
What was it like?

4 **Use the chart in exercise 3 and act out the
conversations.**

5 **In pairs, plan two more conversations.
Copy and complete the chart in exercise 3.
Use exercise 1 as a model. Use the activities
below or your own ideas.**

do a martial art   eat an insect   go surfing
perform on stage   try parkour   visit Los Angeles

6 **Act out your conversations in small groups.**

1 **Read the tip.**

Tip **Good readers** can predict what a
text is going to say. This helps you
understand ideas while you are reading.

You are going to read an article about the
importance of sleep. Think about the questions
and make notes before you read the article.

1 What problems can we have if we don't get
enough sleep?
2 How can we make sure we sleep well?

2 🔊 74 **Read the article quickly. Which of your ideas
does it mention?**

3 **Look at the pictures and explain how each one
relates to the text.**

4 **Choose the correct answers.**

1 Thái Ngoc's story about never sleeping …
   a must be true.
   b might be true.
   ⓒ can't be true.
2 A British man has stayed awake …
   a for over a week.
   b forever.
   c for two weeks.
3 Not sleeping is bad for your …
   a eyes.   b ears.   c mouth.
4 Your … can make you angry.
   a hormones
   b pimples
   c immune system
5 When we're tired, we feel …
   a colder.   b hungrier.   c weaker.
6 It's good to take a nap …
   a at the same time every night.
   b after lunch.
   c in the evening.

👉 **Your turn**

5 **Discuss the questions.**

1 Do you sleep enough (7+ hours)?
2 Have you ever stayed up all night? How did
you feel?
3 Can you think of any more advice about
sleeping well?

Sleep well!

Imagine never sleeping

How long do you sleep every night? Think of all the things you could do instead of wasting every night sleeping! Thái Ngoc, a Vietnamese farmer, says he hasn't slept since 1973. He works on the farm while his family sleep at night. However, doctors say Ngoc hasn't really been awake for over 40 years. No one can stay awake for that long. The world record-holder for staying awake is Tony Right from the U.K. He stayed awake for 264 hours – that's eleven days! He found it very hard.

The idea of never sleeping might sound great, but we have to sleep to stay healthy. Getting a good night's sleep isn't a waste of time – it's vital for our health.

What happens if you don't get enough sleep?

Most people need more than seven hours' sleep a night, and teenagers might need more than that – around nine hours. Research shows that if you sleep for four to five hours, you get more illnesses (like coughs and colds) than if you sleep for at least seven hours. This is because tiredness makes your immune system weaker. If you don't sleep enough, you can also get headaches, and your sight can get worse. Being too tired changes your hormones, too. This change in hormones can affect your skin and give you pimples, and it can also make you eat too much. Scientists found that tired people prefer fast food over healthy food, and they eat around 549 more calories per day than people who sleep well. All of this can affect your mood, and many teenagers who don't get enough sleep feel more angry and miserable than people who do.

How to sleep better

Do you sleep at least seven hours per night? Start a sleep diary and check. If you don't sleep enough, try going to sleep at the same time every week night. Avoid drinking coffee and sodas with caffeine in the evening because the caffeine keeps you awake. And don't use tablets or smartphones just before going to bed because the light from the screens stops you feeling sleepy. If you feel really tired during the day (and you're at home), try taking a nap. A short sleep of about 20 minutes can help your body. For teenagers, the best time to nap is from 2–3 p.m.

seventy-five

W Watch

Tripp

Before you watch

1 Look at the picture. Answer the questions below.

The brain

touch

taste

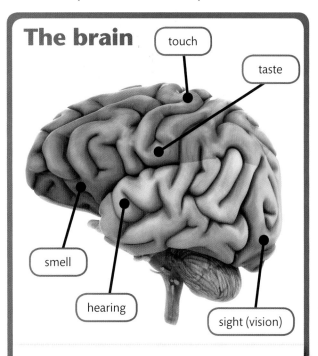

smell

hearing

sight (vision)

The sensory cortex is in the outer part of the brain. It deals with the five senses.

Which sense do you use when you experience ...

1 the orange color of a sunset?
  sight

2 the sweetness of a piece of fruit?
  _____

3 the roughness of a stone?
  _____

4 the sound of someone's voice?
  _____

5 the sweet smell of a flower?
  _____

2 Can you think of things that you experience with more than one sense?

> When I watch TV, I hear it and I see it.

> When it rains, I can feel it, see it, and smell it.

While you watch

3 ▶ Video Watch the video. Number the ideas in the order they appear.

a Synesthesia – people "seeing" sound or "tasting" color _____

b Using all of the senses in the perception of food _____

c Multisensory perception – senses working together _____

d Using the research to design product packaging _____

e Meet Charles Spence, a scientist who studies the senses ___1___

4 ▶ Video Read the text below. Watch the video again and choose the correct words.

Professor Charles Spence

Making sense of the senses

Professor Charles Spence is a specialist in [1] **the brain / the senses.** He does research on synesthesia: a condition where people's [2] **memories / senses** are pushed together in their heads. Scientists have known about it for more than [3] **20 / 200** years, but recently have learned a lot more using new technology. About [4] **four / forty** percent of people have synesthesia. It's [5] **very different from / a type of** multisensory perception. Synesthesia is rare, but [6] **most / few** people use multisensory perception regularly. When you eat, you taste the food, but feeling, smelling, and hearing food is [7] **not important / important, too.** Professor Spencer does research on food and food [8] **prices / packaging** to understand more about how people experience it with their senses.

After you watch

5 Think about a food or drink you enjoy. Make notes about ...

• how it feels.
• what it tastes like.
• how it smells.
• what it looks like.
• what it sounds like.

6 Make a video or project about the multisensory experience of the food you described in exercise 5.

 Online Homework  Challenge

Review

V Vocabulary

1 Match the sentence halves.

1 Liam and Grace get along well
2 Antonio fell in love
3 Lucas and Chloe broke up
4 Myra made up
5 Flo had an argument
6 Kit asked out

a Ariadne three times before she said "yes".
b with Adam when he sent her some flowers.
c because they both love playing sports.
d with Rachel the first time he saw her.
e and now she has a new boyfriend.
f with Ruben when he forgot her birthday.

2 Complete the sentences with the correct form of the verbs.

cry hug ~~laugh~~ shout stare sulk

1 They're __laughing__ .
2 Someone has just _____ Jack's name.
3 The boys are _____ at each other.
4 Leah was _____, but now she's stopped.
5 They're going to _____.
6 He's _____ because he isn't allowed to watch TV.

3 Write sentences with the verbs and the adjectives. More than one answer is sometimes possible.

cold   colorful   feel   fresh   look
shiny   smell   smooth   soft   sweet

1 This soda tastes sweet.
  It feels cold.

2 _____
  _____

3 _____
  _____

4 _____
  _____

5 _____
  _____

6 _____
  _____

4 Complete the sentences with the correct form of the verbs.

fall   feel   have   lie   ~~wake up~~   yawn

1 Did you __wake up__ during that storm last night? It was so loud and frightening!
2 I have a lot of dreams, but I've never _____ a nightmare.
3 That TV show was so boring. I _____ asleep while I was watching it.
4 It's so hot in here. It's making me _____ sleepy.
5 Don't _____ in bed all day! The weather is beautiful today.
6 Please don't _____ while I'm talking to you. It's very rude!

Review

G Grammar

Present perfect: *just, already,* and *yet*

1 Write sentences.

1 Dan / just / admit / he was lying.
   Dan's just admitted he was lying.

2 Rosie / already / break up / with Sam.
   _____

3 I / just / do / my chores.
   _____

4 Jo / ask out / Mark yet?
   _____

5 we / already / see / that movie.
   _____

6 Jack / not / get back / yet.
   _____

2 Complete the sentences with the correct form of *used to* and the verbs.

1 My sneakers _used to be_____ (be) really comfortable, but I think my feet are bigger now.

2 Sue _____ (invite) me to her parties, but now she doesn't.

3 I _____ (not do) chores, but now I often cook dinner and clean my room.

4 I _____ (have) nightmares when I was younger, but I don't have any now.

5 A _____ (sulk) when you were younger?

   B Yes, I did. I _____ (go) to my room and ignore everyone.

6 My parents _____ (not let) me go out in the evenings. But now I'm allowed to stay out until ten.

3 Complete the sentences with the present perfect form of the verbs. Add a time phrase.

1 I _'ve known_____ (know) my English teacher for _two years_____.

2 I_____ (have) these shoes since _____.

3 I _____ (not eat) anything for _____.

4 I_____ (live) in this city since _____.

5 I _____ (not watch) a horror movie for _____.

4 Complete the sentences with the simple past or present perfect.

1 a _Have you ever gone_ (you / ever / go) on a date?

   b _Did Sam go_____ (Sam / go) on a date with Lucy last night?

2 a _____ (Milo and I / have) a big argument yesterday.

   b _____ (I / never / fall out) with Harry.

3 a _____ (Dinosaurs / become) extinct 65 million years ago.

   b _____ (Dinosaurs / be) extinct for 65 million years.

4 a _____ (I / visit) Mexico twice in my life.

   b Last year, _____ (my dad / go) to the U.S. three times.

Consolidation

Choose the correct answers to complete the conversation.

Ali: **1** _Did you go_ on a date last weekend?

Jack: Yes, Lauren and I **2**_____ to the movies.

Ali: How was it?

Jack: Not great. First, I bought the wrong popcorn. Lauren hates **3**_____ popcorn.

Ali: I hate all popcorn. I think it **4**_____ disgusting.

Jack: Then, the man next to us fell **5**_____ and started snoring. Everyone was **6**_____ us because they thought we were with him.

Ali: Then, at the end of the movie, Lauren started **7**_____. The story was sad.

Jack: So, are you going to go out again?

Ali: I don't know. I sent Lauren a text on Sunday, but she **8**_____.

1 **a** Have you gone	**b** You went	**c** Did you go
2 **a** went	**b** 've gone	**c** 're going
3 **a** shiny	**b** salty	**c** soft
4 **a** feels	**b** sounds	**c** tastes
5 **a** asleep	**b** sleepy	**c** sleep
6 **a** staring at	**b** hugging	**c** sulking with
7 **a** shouting	**b** laughing	**c** crying
8 **a** has just replied	**b** hasn't replied yet	**c** has already replied

In this unit …

- talk about positive actions
- talk about imaginary situations and their results
- give advice
- talk about people and places you might help
- identify the meaning of unknown words when reading
- understand a video about an environmental organization

7

Do the right thing

Video ▶ Watch the warm-up video.

> Sorry! Forgot to tell you.
> Did you find the _____
> I put in your pocket?

1 What did Rob do with the money?

2 Imagine you find some money in the street. What would you do?

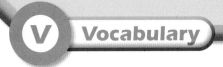

V Vocabulary

Positive actions

1 🔊 75 **Read Vicky's comment. How many half marathons has she run?**

Some of you might remember that I ran my first half marathon last year. My time was two hours and seven minutes. Yesterday, I ran another one to raise money for a children's charity. One hour and 59 minutes. And I raised over $200! Thank you, everyone!

2 🔊 76 **Complete the suggestions with the words. Then listen and check.**

donate   ~~give (somebody) a hand~~   look after   pick up litter   raise money   start a campaign   volunteer

Do Something Good Today

You only have 30 minutes? That's fine!

① **Give** your brother or sister **a hand** with their homework. And try not to fall out!

② _____ old books or clothes to a charity and make some space in your room at the same time.

Do you have a few hours? Awesome!

③ _____ a friend's dog for a few hours. Go to a park and have some fun!

④ _____ on the beach or on your street. And remember to recycle!

You want a bigger project? What about these?

⑤ _____ to help at a charity for half a day every week. Look online to find one suitable for your age, interests, and skills.

⑥ _____ for a charity. You could sell tickets to a fashion show at school, or have a cake sale.

⑦ Does your school need a better recycling system? Is there too much traffic outside your school?

_____ to tell people about the situation. You can make a difference!

3 Complete the sentences with the advice from exercise 2.

PLEASE HELP
OUTSIDE SCHOOL
Monday
3PM

1 "One of our teachers is organizing a group of students to _pick up litter_ near the school." "Really? Are you going to _____ to help?"

2 Can you _____ your little sister while I go to the store? I'll be back in ten minutes.

3 "The meals at our school are really unhealthy." "I agree. We should _____ to make them better."

4 I have an idea to _____ for our school trip. I'm going to sell all my old computer games.

5 Can you _____ me a _____ with these books? Dad's going to _____ them to a charity.

 Your turn

4 In pairs, discuss the questions.

1 Do you give your parents a hand with chores at home?
2 Do you always put litter in a trash can?
3 Have you ever looked after a friend's pet while they were away on vacation?
4 Have you ever donated money to charity?
5 Is there anything you would like to start a campaign for at your school?
6 Have you ever volunteered to help at a charity?

> Do you give your parents a hand with chores at home?

> Yes, I help with cooking and I clean my room.

→ *METRO EXPRESS* P.115

L **Listening**

Positive news stories

1 🔊 77 Listen to the podcast. Which statements are true?

1 Two people are presenting the podcast.
2 Natalie found the stories in the podcast.
3 The presenters talk about two news stories.
a 1 and 2   b 2 and 3   c 1 and 3

2 🔊 77 Read the questions carefully and underline key words. Then listen and choose the correct answer.

1 Before the idea about donating pizza …
  (a) homeless people paid $1 for a slice of pizza.
  b pizza was half-price for homeless people.
  c homeless people didn't eat at the restaurant.

2 What has happened at the restaurant since the idea started?
  a A café in Italy has started doing the same thing.
  b People have started donating pizza online.
  c The owner gave away 8,500 slices of pizza in the first year.

3 How can you earn points in the bank's campaign?
  a By helping your brother or sister with exams.
  b By picking up litter on the streets.
  c By visiting your doctor.

4 Which statement is true?
  a Natalie thinks extra classes are a good prize.
  b Andy is going to phone the bank.
  c Natalie would like to join the bank.

3 Read the tip.

> **Tip**   **Good listeners** can use context to infer ideas when listening.

🔊 77 Listen to the podcast again and complete the sentences.

1 Soon the restaurant's wall was covered in

_____.

2 An employee at the bank said "the phones have not _____."

Which idea(s) can you infer about sentences 1 and 2?

Story 1
a The restaurant owner probably donated a lot of money.
b Customers liked the idea of donating a slice of pizza.

Story 2
a Lots of people are complaining about the campaign.
b Lots of people want to join the bank and the campaign.

Workbook P.W8   Online Homework

1 🔊 78 ▷ **Read the text quickly. Complete the headings with the words.**

> parent   local politician   teacher

2 Read the comments. Write the correct names.

1 _____ gets along with his parents.

2 _____ doesn't want people to feel bad at school.

3 _____ and _____ want to do something with a connection to the environment.

4 _____ thinks his parents are too strict.

5 _____ has an unusual idea about education.

3 Read the text again. Answer the questions.

1 Who does Kylie want to help?
  <u>local schools and homeless people</u>

2 What problems does Chris see with James's idea?
  _____

3 What does Tyler think parents need to understand?
  _____

4 What can you infer from Nate's emoji?
  _____
  _____

5 What do teachers do at Claire's school?
  _____
  _____

6 Where did Helen get her idea?
  _____

4 In pairs, discuss the questions.

1 What do you think of James's idea?
2 What do you think Tyler's parents say to him about sleeping? Do you agree with him?
3 Do you agree with Nate?
4 What do you think of Helen's idea?

> I like James's idea. I hate litter, too.

---

askmetro

Our question this week:

How would you do these jobs better?

YOU'RE A ¹ _____.

KYLIE

I would start a campaign to donate books to local schools and clothes to homeless people. Everyone has too much stuff and we need to reuse it all.

JAMES

I hate litter on the streets. It looks terrible. I would start a campaign to pick it up and recycle it (if possible). Everyone would have to do it for 30 minutes every month! Our city would look so much better.

▶
CHRIS

But how would you know? People wouldn't do it!

▶
JAMES

Perhaps people could take a selfie when they're picking up litter, and post it online!

YOU'RE A ² _____.

TYLER

My family life is great and we're really close. But what would I do differently?

I would try to understand that being a teenager can be hard! We have a lot of things to do and we sometimes need to go to bed late. And in the mornings, we sometimes need to get up late because we're tired.

NATE

Sometimes Mom and Dad treat me like I'm 12! They need to trust me more and not make so many rules. I would give teenagers more freedom.

And I wouldn't make them go to museums on the weekend! 😝

YOU'RE A ³ _____.

CLAIRE

I wouldn't give people their tests back in front of the class. This always happens at my school. It makes people with bad grades feel really miserable.

HELEN

I would swap the classes and homework situation. So at home, students would research and learn about things. Then in class, they'd have more time for activities and discussion.

Some schools have already experimented with this idea. I read about it online.

would for imaginary situations

1 🔊 79 Look at the poster. Then listen and read. Which person should join the Student Council?

YOUR CHOICE

YOUR VOICE

What would YOU do to make our school a better place? Join Student Council today!

Alice: Are you going to join the Student Council?
Calvin: I'm not sure. I wouldn't have any good ideas.
Alice: That isn't true!
Calvin: So what would you change?
Alice: I'd ask for more recycling bins, a longer morning break – fifteen minutes is too short – and also …
Calvin: It sounds like you'd do a great job! Join!

2 Complete the chart with *'d, would,* and *wouldn't.*

Affirmative and negative	
Long form	**Short form**
I **¹** would _____ ask for more recycling bins.	I'd ask for more recycling bins. You **²**_____ do a great job!
I would not have any good ideas.	I **³**_____ have any good ideas.
Questions and short answers	
Would you join the student council?	Yes, I **would**. / No, I **wouldn't**.
What **⁴**_____ you change?	

3 Complete the sentences. Use *'d, would,* or *wouldn't* and the verbs.

1 I'm telling you the truth! I __wouldn't lie__ (lie) to you.

2 "_____ you _____ (know) how to look after a young baby?" "No, I _____!"

3 We should have "paper only" bins at school. Everyone _____ (recycle) more things.

4 "What _____ your ideal day _____ (be) like?"
"The weather _____ (be) nice – hot and sunny. And I _____ (do) anything!"

4 What would you do in these situations? Complete the sentences with *would / wouldn't* and the verbs.

donate   give them a hand   ~~look after~~   pick up

1 I _would / wouldn't_ _look after them._

2 I _____ _____

3 I _____ _____ all of the litter.

4 I _____ _____.

5 Order the words to make questions.

1 would / Where / on your perfect vacation / go / you / ?
Where would you go on your perfect vacation?

2 would / with a lot of money / you / What / do / ?
_____

3 you / What / do / and your friends / on your perfect weekend / would / ?
_____
_____

4 sing / at your dream party / would / Who / ?
_____

5 about your school / change / you / would / What / ?
_____
_____

6 In pairs, ask and answer the questions in exercise 5. Try to ask another question.

Where would you go on your perfect vacation?

I'd go to Australia.

What would you do there?

I'd go surfing!

→ *METRO EXPRESS* P.115

Helping: people and places

1 (80) Match the people you might help with the definitions. Then listen, check, and repeat.

1 senior citizen
2 teammate
3 neighbor
4 classmate
5 stranger

a someone who studies with you
b someone who plays sports with you
c someone you don't know
d someone who is over 65 years old
e someone who lives very near you

2 In pairs, discuss the questions.

1 Do you still know your classmates from elementary school?
2 Who is a senior citizen in your family?
3 Would you help a stranger in the street?
4 Which of your neighbors do you see the most often?
5 Have you ever had an argument with a teammate in a game?

3 (81) Match the words with the places you might volunteer to help at. Then listen, check, and repeat.

animal shelter   environmental organization
~~food bank~~   homeless shelter   thrift store

1 __food bank__   2 _____

3 _____   4 _____

5 _____

4 Complete the sentences with the places.

1 At Christmas, I made breakfast at a __homeless shelter__ for 50 people!
2 I bought this T-shirt at the _____. It was only $2.
3 Aww. She's cute! Did you get her from the _____?
4 The World Wildlife Fund is the world's largest _____.
5 My grandfather collects donations from our neighbors for the _____.

→ *METRO EXPRESS* P.115

L Listening

What would you do?

1 (82) Read the questions. Then listen and match the questions with the speakers.

1 Bex   2 Tom   3 Lu

a What would you do with a year off school? ____
b Who would you take on a trip around the world? ____
c What charity would you volunteer at? ____

2 (82) Listen. Which person, Bex, Tom, or Lu, mentions:

1 a parent? __Bex__ and _____
2 a sport? _____ and _____
3 a job? _____ and _____

3 (82) Listen again. Choose T (True) or F (False).

1 Bex is going to study on vacation.   T ☑ F ☐
2 Bex thinks volunteering at an animal shelter would be easy.   T ☐ F ☐
3 Tom would get a job first.   T ☐ F ☐
4 Tom would like to travel alone.   T ☐ F ☐
5 Lu would choose a teammate from volleyball.   T ☐ F ☐
6 Lu hasn't volunteered at the food bank yet.   T ☐ F ☐

4 Complete the sentences for you. Then compare your sentences with a partner.

1 With a year off from school, I would _____.
2 I would take _____ on a trip around the world.
3 I would volunteer at _____.

G Grammar

G Grammar

Giving and replying to advice

1 ◀)) 84 〉 **Complete the conversation. Then listen and check.**

| ~~ask~~ might that's tried were what's |

A Can I **¹** _ask_____ your advice about something?

B Yeah. **²**_____ up?

A I got really annoyed with my best friend yesterday, and now she doesn't want to talk to me.

B If I **³**_____ you, I'd apologize to her.

A I've **⁴**_____ that. But she's still mad at me.

B OK. It **⁵**_____ be a good idea to wait a few days and then write her a message. My advice would be to explain why you got annoyed.

A **⁶**_____ a good idea. Thanks.

2 **In pairs, practice the conversation in exercise 1.**

3 ◀)) 85 〉 **Listen to two conversations. What advice does each person give? Complete the sentences.**

1 You _____ spending some time with her without your boyfriend.

2 My advice _____ have a smaller lunch.

Stop | **Useful phrases**
Giving advice | **Replying to advice**
If I were you, I'd … | *I've tried that, but …*
It might be a good idea to … | *That's a good idea.*
You could try (calling …) | *I might try that.*
My advice would be to … | *I think I'll try that.*

4 **In pairs, write a conversation about two of these problems. Use the conversation in exercise 1 as a model.**

1 You lost something important.

2 You're feeling really stressed about an exam.

3 Some of your friends tease you about your clothes.

4 You don't have time to do your homework every night.

5 **In pairs, practice your conversation. Then act out your conversation for the class.**

1 ◀)) 86 〉 **Read and answer the four moral dilemmas. In pairs, compare your answers.**

2 ◀)) 87 〉 **Now read the real life stories A–D. Match the moral dilemmas 1–4 with the stories A–D.**

3 **Complete the stories with the words.**

| stole test thrift store ~~wallet~~ wallet |

4 **For stories A–D, which statement is true? Choose the correct answers.**

1 Story A:
   a Tristin e-mailed the actor about the wallet.
   b Chris gave Tristin $10,000 for finding his wallet.
   c Chris Hemsworth lost his wallet in the U.S.

2 Story B:
   a The thieves lived near each other.
   b Senior citizens steal $16.5 billion of things every year.
   c There were two thieves in the group.

3 Story C:
   a The friends bought the sofa from a 91-year-old woman.
   b At first, they wanted to spend the money.
   c They found the woman's address on one of the envelopes.

4 Story D:
   a 95% of students in the U.S. have copied from another person's homework.
   b The girl's mother had to pay $10,000.
   c Both the girl and her mother might get a punishment.

5 **Read the tip. Find the words in stories A–D and match them with their meanings.**

Tip | **Good readers** can identify the meaning of unknown words.

1 reward
2 refund
3 savings
4 fine

a money you must pay for committing a crime

b money that is given back to you because you are unhappy with something you bought

c something you get, e.g. money, because you have done something good

d money you haven't spent and you are keeping for a future event

 Online Homework

Moral Dilemmas

1 _____ If you found a celebrity's wallet, would you ...

a sell it online?

b try and find the celebrity?

2 _____ If a classmate (accidentally) showed you their answers during a test, would you ...

a quickly look at their answers?

b look in a different direction?

3 _____ If you saw an elderly person steal some food from a store, would you ...

a tell the store owner quietly?

b ignore it and leave the store?

4 _____ If you bought a jacket from a thrift store and found some money in a pocket, would you ...

a give the money back to the store?

b keep the money?

Real-Life Stories

A When Tristin Budzyn-Barker found a ¹ _wallet_____ in Los Angeles, he quickly recognized the photo ID inside. It was Chris Hemsworth, the Australian movie actor. Tristin found the name of Chris's manager and e-mailed him. When Chris heard, he invited Tristin on a TV show. As a reward, Chris gave Tristin all the money in the ² _____ for being so honest. And the TV show gave Tristin $10,000!

B Shoplifting costs U.S. stores $16.5 billion every year. And people of all ages shoplift.

Police recently caught a group of senior citizens. They were all neighbors and working together. One person in the group ³ _____ items from stores, and another person took them back to the store to get a refund.

C When three roommates bought a $20 couch from a ⁴ _____ in New York, it felt a bit uncomfortable. Soon they found the reason. Inside the couch, there were some envelopes. Each envelope had money in it – $41,000 in all! At first, they started thinking about what they might buy with the money. But then, they noticed a name on one of the envelopes. After some research, they found the owner of the sofa – a very pleased 91-year-old woman. The $41,000 was her life savings.

D In a survey, 64% of U.S. high-school students admitted to cheating on a ⁵ _____. And 95% have copied another person's homework. Some students even involve their parents. In France, police arrested a 52-year-old woman after she pretended to be her daughter in an important exam!

The mother might have to pay a fine of $10,000, and authorities might ban the girl from taking other exams for five years.

➡ Writing P.107   ➡ Workbook P.W32   Online Homework

W Watch

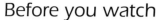

Bureo

Amy

Before you watch

1 Look at the pictures. Answer the question.

You are going to watch a video about a company that tries to make a difference to the environment. The video includes fishing, skateboarding, and plastic. What do you think the company does?

fishing

skateboarding

plastic

While you watch

2 ▶Video Watch the video and check your answer.

3 ▶Video Watch again. What do you see?

1 Chile's (coastline) / high mountains

2 **yellow** / **red** fishing boats

3 **sea animals** / **restaurant owners**

4 old **fishing nets** / **car tires**

5 machines for recycling **metal** / **plastic**

6 **skateboarders** / **politicians**

4 ▶Video Watch again. Choose *T* (True) or *F* (False). Correct the false sentences.

1 Chile has more than 6,000 km of coastline.   T☐ F☑
  Chile has more than 4,000 km of coastline.

2 Fishing nets are made of plastic.   T☐ F☐

3 *Bureo* means wheels.   T☐ F☐

4 The fishermen didn't want to give their nets to Bureo.   T☐ F☐

5 The factory melts the old nets.   T☐ F☐

6 Bureo raised $64,000 by selling skateboards.   T☐ F☐

7 Bureo skateboards are shaped like boats.   T☐ F☐

8 Ben, David, and Kevin ask the fishermen to give them free fish.   T☐ F☐

After you watch

5 Work in small groups. Think of three or four things that people throw away in your town or city. They can be big things, like furniture or old cars, or small things, like plastic bags.

6 Now imagine what you could make if you recycled some of the waste. Make a video or project about your recycling plan.

Online Homework    ON THE MOVE   Challenge

In this unit ...

- talk about being creative
- use relative clauses to define information
- talk about art you like and dislike
- prepare for reading by underlining key words in questions
- understand a video about street art

▶ **Video** Watch the warm-up video.

8

Creativity

> You have to think of as many uses as possible for a _____ in _____!

1 How many of Tripp's ideas can you remember?

2 How many alternative uses of a paper clip can you think of in three minutes?

Creativity: adjectives

1 🔊 88 ▷ **Look at the picture and read the description. Then listen and check.**

Can you see two animals at the same time in this clever picture? What are they?

2 🔊 89 ▷ **Complete the descriptions. Listen and check.**

old-fashioned ~~original~~ recycled strange tiny   ancient clever delicate enormous

a

This is an ¹ _original___ idea from West Africa.
It is a car made from ² _____ cans.

b

This ³ _____ sculpture by Dalton Ghetti
is made from a pencil! Ghetti only works
one or two hours every day, so it takes him
months to make a sculpture like this.

c

This ⁴ _____ object is an example of "steam
punk." It looks like a pair of ⁵ _____
glasses, but actually it was made recently.

d

Banksy is a street artist who paints pictures with a
⁶ _____ "message." This painting is about art,
artists, and their audience – the people who look at
art. It's ⁷ _____ – it's about five meters tall!

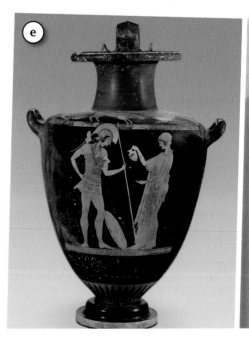

e

This vase comes from Greece.
It's ⁸ _____ – about 2,500 years old.
It is very ⁹ _____, so the archeologists
had to be very careful when they found it.

3 Match the adjectives from exercise 2 with the descriptions.

1 thousands of years old _ancient_

2 made with skill and intelligence _____

3 easily broken or damaged _____

4 very big _____

5 not modern _____

6 new and interesting _____

7 when a material is used again _____

8 unusual, surprising _____

9 very small _____

4 Describe the objects and pieces of art using words from exercise 2.

1 _This phone is old-fashioned._

2 _____
_____

3 _____
_____

4 _____
_____

Your turn

5 Discuss the questions.

1 What kind of art do you like?

2 Do you like making things? What creative activities do you do?

→ *METRO EXPRESS* P.116

L **Listening**

On the radio

1 (◄)) 90 ▷ Listen to three short recordings from the radio. Which pictures on page 90 are mentioned?

2 Read the tip.

Tip **Good listeners** try to understand the context of a listening text.

(◄)) 90 ▷ What is the context of each recording? Listen again and match the recordings a–c with the contexts 1–5. There are two extra contexts.

1 local news and events _____

2 an advertisement _____

3 a quiz _____

4 an interview _____

5 a play _____

3 (◄)) 90 ▷ Listen and choose the correct answers.

1 The Ancient Greece exhibition starts …
a Monday August 26.
b Monday August 28.
c Monday August 8.

2 The exhibition includes pottery and …
a flowers.
b street art.
c art.

3 The Ancient Greece website at lafayette.net sells …
a ancient objects.
b tickets.
c special pottery.

4 Banksy is …
a British.   b American.   c Greek.

5 The art critic says that Banksy's flower painting is …
a clever.
b original.
c famous.

6 The New Street Market starts at …
a ten o'clock on Saturday.
b ten o'clock on Monday.
c three o'clock on Saturday.

7 The New Street Market sells …
a burgers.
b recycled clothes.
c toy cars.

Your turn

4 Discuss which of the things in the recordings you would like to see.

Workbook P.W9   **Online Homework**

1 Look at the pictures and discuss what the title might mean.

But is it ART?

"Art" used to mean a painting, a drawing, or a sculpture in a gallery or on the walls of a wealthy home. These days, art has escaped from galleries, and people are creating non-traditional "art" in unusual places. The question is: "Is it really art?"

This guy who is lying on the sidewalk hasn't had an accident. He's painting. Ben Wilson does tiny paintings on gum that people have dropped. Why does he do it? When people drop old gum in the street, it gets dirty, and people find it disgusting. Ben likes to take the trash of our consumerist society and make it into something delicate and beautiful. It's creative – *but is it "art"?*

This sofa looks comfortable, but you shouldn't sit on it. It's made from chocolate! Prudence Staite is a British "food artist" who makes edible sculptures. She said: "I couldn't decide whether to become a chef or an artist. I wanted to be both. I wanted people to be able to touch art, smell art, enjoy art, bite art, and really get involved with art."

Chocolate is Prudence's favorite material to use, but she also uses butter, pasta, and vegetables. It's original and it's tasty – *but is it "art"?*

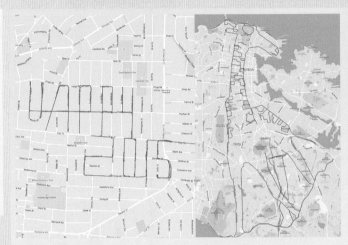

Stephen Lund draws enormous pictures online with his bike! How? He was using a GPS device to record his rides where he lives in Victoria, Canada. After each ride, he used to look at his route on the map. One day, Stephen realized that if he rode along certain streets, he could create words or a picture on the map. So he planned a route that would form the phrase "HAPPY 2015!" He recorded the ride using strava.com and posted the map of the ride on the site. His "GPS doodle" was an instant online success. Every week, he posts new GPS doodles on the site, mainly shapes of animals or people. Why not follow him on Strava or Instagram? It's fun and it's clever – *but is it "art"?*

2 🔊 91 ⟩ Read and complete the sentences with the names of the artists.

1 __Ben Wilson__ makes art as a reaction to modern society.

2 You can eat _____'s art.

3 _____'s art came from doing a sport.

4 _____'s art is digital, not physical.

5 _____ makes art using recycled materials.

6 _____ has made art that looks like furniture.

3 Answer the questions.

1 Where did people use to exhibit art?
   __In galleries and wealthy homes.__

2 Why does Ben Wilson work lying down?

3 What does Ben Wilson's art look like?

4 Which senses can we use to enjoy Prudence Staite's art?

5 How does Stephen Lund make GPS doodles?

6 Where can you see Stephen Lund's art?

☞ **Your turn**

4 Are gum paintings, edible sculptures, and GPS doodles really "art"? Explain your answer.

G Grammar

Relative clauses

1 🔊 92 ▷ **Read about** *Little People.* **What is it?**

a an artist   b an artwork   c an art project

LITTLE PEOPLE 🚶

Slinkachu is an artist who paints tiny figures of people doing "normal" things, like calling a taxi or going shopping. He puts the figures in places where people can see them, and he takes photographs that almost make the scenes look real. *Little People* is a series of photographs that explores the loneliness of living in a big city.

2 **Complete the chart.**

who
Slinkachu is an artist. He paints tiny figures of people.
Slinkachu is an artist **¹ who** paints tiny figures of people.

that
Little People is a series of photographs. It explores the loneliness of living in a big city.
Little People is a series of photographs **²_____** explores the loneliness of living in a big city.

where
He puts the figures in places. People can see them there.
He puts the figures in places **³_____** people can see them.

3 **Choose the correct words.**

1 Picasso was a Spanish artist (who) / **where** lived in France.

2 A studio is a place **that** / **where** an artist works.

3 A drawing is a picture **that** / **who** is made with a pencil.

4 A sculptor is a person **who** / **where** makes sculptures.

5 This is the museum **where** / **that** I saw the exhibition.

6 I liked the painting **who** / **that** looked like an enormous bird.

7 My uncle was the photographer **who** / **where** took these photos.

8 This is the kind of exhibition **who** / **that** I love.

4 **Complete the text with** *who, that,* **or** *where.*

Edgar Müller is a German street artist **¹ who** is famous for his street art. He paints amazing images of things **²_____** seem real. Actually, they're clever 3-D illusions **³_____** *look* real from certain angles. He usually draws in streets **⁴_____** there is lots of space. This picture shows people **⁵_____** are walking along the edge of a street in Geldern, Germany.

Use Your Eyes by Edgar Müller

5 **Complete the sentences with a relative clause.**

1 The gallery has a store. We always buy gifts there.
The gallery has a store **where we always buy gifts**.

2 Alex is my friend. He draws portraits.
Alex is my friend _____.

3 Cubism is an old-fashioned style of art.
My dad loves it.
Cubism is an old-fashioned style of art
_____.

4 This is a great art shop. I get my paper here.
This is a great art shop
_____.

5 This is the art campaign. I was telling you about it.
This is the art campaign
_____.

6 **Make sentences with relative clauses.**

1 artist is a person / paints
An artist is a person who paints.

2 library is a place / you can borrow books
_____
_____

3 bicycle is something / you can ride
_____

4 an author is someone / write
_____

5 a book is something / you read
_____

 **Your turn**

7 **Make two more sentences with relative clauses.**

→ *METRO EXPRESS* P.116

V Vocabulary

Creativity: verbs

1 **93** Complete the sentences. Listen and check.

what do you want to do when you're older?

build   compose   create   ~~design~~

1 I want to _design_ and make my own furniture.

2 My brother works in construction. I'm going to help my brother to _____ houses.

3 I love programming. One day, I'm going to _____ a new game for the iPad.

4 I can play the piano and read music. I want to _____ music for movies when I'm older.

discover   invent   paint   set up

5 I'd like to _____ a new form of transportation.

6 I've always wanted to have my own company. I plan to _____ an ice cream company with my friends.

7 I'd like to do something amazing one day, like _____ a cure for cancer.

8 I'm going to _____ fingernails to earn money before I go to college. I can make about $5 a customer.

Your turn

2 Talk about what you want to do when you're older.

> I want to set up my own website one day.

→ *METRO EXPRESS* P.116

L Listening

Creative people

1 Do the quiz. Compare your answers in pairs.

2 **94** Listen and check.

Who ... ?????????????????????

1 Who designed the Sydney Opera House?
Oscar Niemeyer / Jørn Utzon

2 Who built the first helicopter?
Igor Sikorsky / Leonardo da Vinci

3 Who discovered radioactivity?
Marie Curie / Albert Einstein

4 Who invented the World Wide Web (WWW)?
Tim Berners-Lee / Steve Jobs

5 Who painted *The Kiss*?
Frida Kahlo / Gustav Klimt

6 Who set up Google?
Larry Page and Sergey Brin / Mark Zuckerberg

7 Who composed music after he went deaf?
Mozart / Beethoven

8 Who created *The Lord of the Rings* series?
J.R.R. Tolkien / George R.R. Martin

3 **94** Listen again and choose *T* (True) or *F* (False).

1 Niemeyer designed buildings in Brasília.   T ☑ F ☐

2 Sikorsky designed the first parachute.   T ☐ F ☐

3 Einstein won two Nobel Prizes.   T ☐ F ☐

4 Berners-Lee made a lot of money from the web.   T ☐ F ☐

5 Gustav Klimt was a Mexican artist.   T ☐ F ☐

6 Google is older than Facebook.   T ☐ F ☐

Subject and object questions

1 🔊 **95** **Read the conversation.**
Complete the sentence.

Tamagotchis are from _____.

Milo: Wow! A Tamagotchi. I used to love my Tamagotchi.
Luke: I know.
Milo: Who told you?
Luke: You told me!
Milo: Really? When did I tell you?
Luke: You told me a few years ago.
Kim: What's a Tamagotchi?
Milo: It's a digital pet. They're Japanese. They're really cool.
Kim: How do they work?
Milo: You have to look after your Tamagotchi – you give it food, keep it warm, and do things to make it happy.

2 **Complete the chart.**

Subject questions	Object questions
¹ **Who** told you? You told me.	² _____ I tell you? You told me **a few years ago.**
Who invented them? **A company called Bandai** invented them.	³ _____ they work? You have to look after your **Tamagotchi** …

3 🔊 **96** **Match the questions and answers.**
Listen and repeat.

> He called me.   He gave me **a key ring.**
> Marcia helped me.   ~~Mason gave it to me.~~
> Noah called me.   She helped me.

1 Who gave you this key ring?
  Mason gave it to me.

2 What did Mason give you?
  _____

3 Who helped you?
  _____

4 Who did Marcia help?
  _____

5 Who called you?
  _____

6 Who did Noah call?
  _____

4 **Do the quiz. What can you remember? Write the questions and answers. Then ask and answer in pairs.**

MEMORY TEST

1 discovered / Who / relativity / ?
  Who discovered relativity?
  Albert Einstein discovered relativity.

2 Marie Curie / did / What / discover / ?
  _____
  _____

3 set up / did / What / Page and Brin / ?
  _____
  _____

4 Facebook / set up / Who / ?
  _____
  _____

5 painted / Who / the Mona Lisa / ?
  _____
  _____

6 invent / did / Leonardo da Vinci / What / ?
  _____
  _____

7 What / Slinkachu / does / make / ?
  _____
  _____

8 3-D illusions in the street / Who / paints / ?
  _____
  _____
  _____

👉 **Your turn**

5 **Write five more quiz questions about things you learned in** *Metro.* **Use subject or object questions. Then in groups, ask and answer them.**

> Who said: "That's one small step for a man, one giant leap for mankind."?

> Neil Armstrong said that.

> What does "glossophobia" mean?

> It means a fear of speaking in public.

→ *METRO EXPRESS* P.116

S Speaking

Talking about likes and dislikes

1 🔊 **97** Look at the pictures on page 90. Listen to the conversation and answer the questions.

1 Which picture are they talking about?

2 Which three adjectives do they use to describe it?

a ancient   d original

b delicate   e unusual

c old-fashioned

2 🔊 **98** Listen and complete the conversation. In pairs, practice the conversation.

> for   kind   much   thing   ~~think~~   to

Amy: What do you ¹ <u>think</u> of the Banksy picture?

Ben: I don't like it that ² _____. Street art isn't really my ³ _____. It's too messy ⁴ _____ me. It reminds me of a child's drawing. Do you like it?

Amy: Yeah, I really like this ⁵ _____ of thing. It looks cool ⁶ _____ me. It's an interesting idea.

Stop **Useful phrases**

What do you think of … ?

I really like this kind of thing. / I love it!

It isn't really my thing.

It's too … for me. / It looks … to me.

It reminds me of …

Do you like it?

3 In pairs, look at other pictures in Unit 8 and have conversations. Talk about which pictures you like and dislike, and explain why. Use the adjectives on page 90 or some of the adjectives below.

> beautiful   boring   colorful   different
> exciting   messy   modern   simple   unusual

> What do you think of this?

> I really like this sort of thing. It's modern. It looks like something out of a movie. Do you like it?

> No, it's not really my thing. It reminds me of …

R Reading

1 🔊 **99** Read the article quickly. Which is your favorite invention? Why?

2 Read the tip.

Tip **Good readers** look at questions before they read. As you read, underline key words that might be useful for answering the questions. This makes it easier to go back and find possible answers.

<u>Underline</u> the key words in exercise 3.

3 Read the article and answer the questions.

1 Why did Ann Makosinski invent a flashlight?

<u>Because she wanted to help her friend.</u>

2 In what way are Ann's two inventions similar?

_____

3 How does Guillaume Rolland's alarm clock wake you up?

_____

4 How could Guillaume afford to make his alarm clock?

_____

5 What can help teenagers to be more creative?

_____

_____

4 Read the article again and choose the correct answers.

1 Ann got the idea for her flashlight …

 a from her friend.

 ⓑ because she knew about thermoelectric power.

 c from looking at people's hands.

2 Ann's travel cup …

 a can heat coffee.

 b charges cell phones.

 c gets power from people's hands.

3 Before Guillaume invented the SensorWake clock, waking up in the morning was …

 a annoying.   b easy.   c relaxing.

4 The SensorWake clock can …

 a smell things.

 b make croissants or coffee.

 c make different smells.

5 As a child, Ann …

 a didn't use to watch TV.

 b used to play games on her cell phone.

 c wasted time watching TV.

5 Discuss the questions.

1 Why did not having gadgets help Ann to be creative?

2 Which invention would be the most helpful around the world? Why?

TEEN CREATORS

Some evidence shows that teenage brains are the most creative! But it's hard to be creative when you are a busy student. Today, we meet two young people who invented incredible things while they were still at high school.

Ann Makosinski was chatting one day with her friend from the Philippines. Her friend was worried because she wanted to study in the evenings, but there was no power at home. Ann decided to help. She remembered someone telling her that people are like "walking 100 W light bulbs" because of thermoelectric power (the energy and heat in their bodies). This gave her the idea of a flashlight that works on thermoelectric power. Her clever design uses the heat of a person's hand on the flashlight to produce electricity. Ann was 16 when she won an award for her invention, and since then she has also invented a travel cup phone charger. It uses the heat from the coffee to power a cell phone.

French student Guillaume Rolland couldn't wake up for school one day, and his noisy alarm clock made him feel stressed! He wanted to wake up feeling relaxed, so he decided to invent a new alarm clock. Instead of waking you up with loud noises, his SensorWake clock wakes you up with a smell!

He developed the idea in his parents' garage in Nantes, France, and raised money online, using a crowdfunding website called Kickstarter. Now he's set up his own company that builds and sells the clocks. You put a smell capsule into SensorWake, and it releases your favorite scent when it's time to wake up: chocolate, peppermint, coffee, croissants, or even grass!

So, how can teenagers be more creative? It's surprising, but sometimes feeling bored can increase your creativity! When Ann was younger, her parents didn't use to give her toys or let her watch TV, and as a teenager, she wasn't allowed to have a cell phone. "My parents didn't want me distracted and playing games on it because that would be wasting time," Ann said. "Not being given everything encourages you to create. That was one of the first steps for me learning to invent things."

Ann Makosinski

Guillaume Rolland

W Watch

Graffiti Life

Rob

Before you watch

1 **Match the pictures a–c with the descriptions 1–3.**

1 street art – an enormous painting on a building or wall _____

2 a street artist at work _____

3 graffiti – words and tiny pictures painted on a wall or a public place, by a lot of different people _____

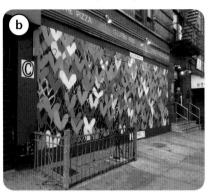

2 **Answer the questions.**

1 Does your area have any graffiti or street art?

2 Is it art or vandalism?

3 Do you like any of it? Why? / Why not?

While you watch

3 **Video Watch the preview. What do you see?**

1 a policeman photographing graffiti ☑

2 a policeman arresting a street artist ☐

3 tourists photographing street art ☐

4 street art in a museum ☐

5 people learning how to paint ☐

6 people planning and making an enormous painting ☐

4 **Video Watch the video. Choose the best words to complete each sentence.**

1 Street art is **popular** / **a big problem** in cities.

2 Graffiti Life **cleans up** / **makes** street art.

3 Graffiti Life also **teaches painting** / **buys street art**.

5 **Video Watch again. Complete the sentences.**

> advertising   art gallery   a company   London
> personality   street art   ~~vandalism~~   warehouse

1 In the past, most people thought that graffiti was __vandalism_____.

2 Nowadays, _____ sells for a lot of money.

3 A city street can now be a type of _____.

4 _____ is a great place to see street art.

5 Graffiti Life sometimes makes graffiti for _____.

6 _____ may send its employees to Graffiti Life to learn about team work.

7 Young adults work on their art in a _____.

8 Painting may help you discover a new part of your _____.

After you watch

6 **Answer the questions.**

1 Would you like your class to have a Graffiti Life workshop? Why? / Why not?

2 Do you think more street art would improve your town or city? Why? / Why not?

3 Is there graffiti or street art in your town or city that you would like to remove? Why? / Why not?

7 **Work in small groups. Imagine you are going to create a piece of street art.**

• Decide where in your area the street art could go.

• Work together to come up with an idea for the piece of art.

• Make some drawings.

• Explain your ideas to the class.

Online Homework      Challenge

Review

V Vocabulary

1 Complete the sentences about positive actions.

1 There are a lot of dirty dishes here. Can
I g _ive_____ you a h_and_____?

2 The floods in India are awful. We're going to
r_____ some money and d_____ it to
an aid organization.

3 "Can you come home now?"
"Sure. I'm at the beach. We had a cookout. We need
to p_____ u_____ our litter and then
I can go."

4 My uncle needs to go out so I'm going to
l_____ a_____ my baby cousin.

5 If the school asks for help with sports day, will you
v_____?

6 There was a problem with traffic in our street, so the
residents' association decided to s_____ a
campaign to make it safer.

2 Read the sentences. The words for people or places you might help are in the wrong places. Write the correct words.

1 I like ~~thrift stores~~ that campaign against nuclear
power. _environmental organizations_____

2 My mom borrowed an umbrella from our
animal shelters who live next door. _____

3 I didn't score, but one of my strangers, Sara, scored
three goals. _____

4 Mr. Lee told the children not to talk to environmental
organizations. _____

5 Do you like my jacket? I bought it in one of the
neighbors for 99¢! _____

6 My sister found a lost dog so she called a few
teammates. _____

3 Complete the texts with the creativity adjectives.

~~ancient~~   delicate   strange

This is an ¹ _ancient_____ wall
painting from the tomb of
Nebamun in Thebes, Egypt. When
they removed it from the tomb, it broke around the
edges because it is very ² _____. The painting
shows men with horses and two-wheeled "chariots".
The ³ _____ letters are "hieroglyphs", a writing
system used in Egypt 2,000–4,000 years ago.

clever   enormous   tiny

In 2016, *Solar Impulse 2*
became the first solar-powered
plane to fly around the world. It has ⁴ _____
wings of 72 m, only a little smaller than the wings of an
Airbus A380! Its ⁵ _____ technology uses 17,000
⁶ _____ solar cells to power four engines.

4 Complete the sentences with the simple past form of the creativity verbs.

build   compose   ~~discover~~   invent   paint   set up

1 Isaac Newton _discovered___ gravity in the 1680s,
after he watched an apple fall from a tree.

2 The ancient Egyptians _____ the Great
Pyramid at Giza 4,500 years ago.

3 Taylor Swift _____ *We Are Never Ever Getting
Back Together* in just 25 minutes!

4 Google _____ driverless cars in 2012.

5 Picasso _____ and drew over 13,500 pictures.

6 The international community _____ the
United Nations in 1945.

G Grammar

1 Read the imaginary situations. Write questions with *would*. Then write your own answers.

1 There's a lot of litter in the yard at your school.
what / you / do?
Q: _What would you do?_____
A: _I'd pick up the litter at break times._____

2 You see a homeless woman outside a food store.
you / give her some money?
Q:_____
A: _____

3 Your friend has just lost his wallet.
what / say?
Q:_____
A: _____

4 You see an old man trying to open a store door.
you / offer to open it for him?
Q:_____
A: _____

5 Congratulations! You've won $500.
how / spend it?
Q:_____
A: _____

2 Complete the second conditional sentences with the correct form of the verbs.

1 What _would you take_ if you _had to_ live on a desert island with just ten possessions? (take, have to)

2 You _____ it if people _____ at you. (not like, laugh)

3 If we _____ an argument, _____ you _____? (have, sulk)

4 If you _____ an app, I _____ so proud of you! (design, be)

5 Where _____ you _____ if you _____ live anywhere? (choose, can)

6 I _____ very upset if my boyfriend and I _____. (feel, break up)

7 I _____ a joke on someone if they _____ well. (not play, not be)

8 If you _____ a superpower, what _____ it _____? (have, be)

3 Make relative clauses using *are people who*, *are places where*, or *are things that*, and a–f.

1 Banks _are places_ _where_

2 Professors _____ _____

3 Phobias _____ _____

4 Bullies _____ _____

5 Kitchens _____ _____

6 Umbrellas _____ _____

    a people are scared of.
    b you can cook.
    c teach at a college.
    d keep you dry.
    e you save money.
    f threaten or fight with you.

4 Read about the invention of the car. Write subject or object questions for each answer.

Karl Benz and his wife, Bertha, set up Benz & Co. in 1883. In 1885, Karl designed and made the world's first car. His invention, the Motorwagen, only had three wheels. Benz & Co. made its first four-wheeled car in 1894.

1 Who _set up Benz & Co._ ?
Karl and Bertha Benz.

2 What _did Karl and Bertha Benz set up_ ?
They set up Benz & Co.

3 What _____ ?
He designed and made the first car.

4 Who _____ ?
Karl Benz invented the first car.

5 When _____ ?
In 1885.

6 How many wheels _____ ?
Three.

7 What _____ ?
Its first four-wheeled car.

Consolidation

Read the conversation.
Choose the correct words.

Isabel: I'm thinking of ¹ _volunteering_ this summer. Any ideas?

Sadie: What about helping at the Dogs' Home?

Isabel: At the ² _____? That's a good idea.

Sadie: Yeah. I ³ _____ the puppies there last year! They were cute, and so ⁴ _____!

Isabel: What did you have to do?

Sadie: We ⁵ _____ kennels. They looked just like little houses with doors and windows.

Isabel: Wow! Who ⁶ _____ to make them?

Sadie: They have staff ⁷ _____ help the volunteers. If you volunteered, you ⁸ _____ need to do anything too hard.

Isabel: Would you come with me if I ⁹ _____ to see the place?

Sadie: Yeah, sure, I'd go with you. Why not?

1 **a** donating   **b** raising   **c** volunteering

2 **a** animal shelter   **b** food bank   **c** homeless shelter

3 **a** looked after   **b** picked up   **c** set up

4 **a** clever   **b** enormous   **c** tiny

5 **a** composed   **b** built   **c** discovered

6 **a** helped you   **b** you helped   **c** did help you

7 **a** who   **b** where   **c** that

8 **a** weren't   **b** wouldn't   **c** didn't

9 **a** go   **b** gone   **c** went

A story about a memorable experience

1 Read the story. Which statement do you think is true?

a Jamie expected to win a prize.   **b** Jamie is a hard-working student.   **c** Jamie doesn't do well in exams.

At the end of every year, there is an awards day at our school. There are awards for students with the highest grades and for different sports. And sometimes there are some more unusual awards, too.

I never win anything. I'm not a bad student. I enjoy school, I always do my homework, study for tests, and I get good grades. I just don't get the top grades.

So I was sitting quietly at the ceremony this year and I was thinking about my vacation. Suddenly I heard my name, and everyone started clapping. "Congratulations!" my best friend shouted proudly. But I was confused. Did I win an award? What for?

I stood up and walked slowly to the front of the room. The principal gave me a certificate. "Would you like to make a speech?" he asked. I shook my head anxiously.

When I sat down, I read the certificate quickly. "This award is for Jamie Price because he always listens to people."

2 Read the story again. Answer the questions.

1 What was the event?

   It was an awards day at school.

2 Why was Jamie thinking about something different?

   _____

3 How did Jamie know he won an award? Give three reasons.

   _____

   _____

   _____

4 How do you think he felt when the principal asked him to make a speech? Why?

   _____

   _____

5 Did he make a speech? How do you know?

   _____

   _____

6 When did he discover the reason for his award?

   _____

3 Read the tip. Then <u>underline</u> the adverbs of manner in the story.

Tip **Good writers** use adverbs of manner to make their writing more interesting.

4 Complete the sentences with the adverbs.

carefully   confidently   easily   ~~happily~~   quietly

1 "We won!" he shouted __happily__.

2 I put her phone on the table _____. I didn't want to break it.

3 "I'm here to see Mr. Taylor," she said loudly and _____.

4 I passed the test _____ with the best grade in the class.

5 I opened the door _____ because I didn't want anyone to hear me.

5 Complete the chart with information about an experience you remember.

What was the event?	
What happened?	
Why do you remember it very well?	
How did you feel during the experience?	

6 Write about your experience.

- Use the chart in exercise 5.
- Use Jamie's text as a model.
- Add some adverbs of manner to make your writing more interesting.

Writing 2

School rules

1 Read the e-mail. Apart from appropriate clothes, what else should Beatriz bring?

_____

✉   ✕

To: Beatriz

From: Sophia Henderson

Subject: Re: FW: Beatriz's exchange student week

Dear Beatriz,

Your exchange student visit is in three weeks! I'm so excited! I'm writing to tell you about our school rules so that you know what to bring with you.

First, we don't have a uniform, but clothes have to be clean and appropriate for school. We have to wear shoes, not sneakers, and we aren't allowed to wear jeans. You can't wear a hat, and jewelry isn't allowed.

Second, students have to have a picture ID card in order to get into school and to use the cafeteria. If you want a nice picture on your card, bring one from home!

There are rules about electronic devices, for example, we aren't allowed phones in class. And there are other rules, but I can explain them later so you don't get confused!

This all sounds pretty serious, but don't worry. We're going to have so much fun!

See you soon,

Sophia xxx

2 Read the e-mail again and complete the chart.

When the exchange starts	¹ in three weeks
First rule	² _____
Second rule	³ _____
Other rules	⁴ _____

3 Read the tip.

Tip **Good writers** use expressions of purpose to give reasons.

Read the e-mail again and <u>underline</u> the expressions of purpose in the e-mail.

in order to   so   so that   to

4 Match the sentence halves.

1 I'm sending some information **to**   a get you an ID card.

2 I wanted to tell you now **so that**   b we can get your visa?

3 I'm going to need your picture **in order to**   c help you prepare for your visit.

4 Can you tell me your passport number **so**   d you aren't surprised when you get here.

5 Imagine that an exchange student is going to visit your school soon. Copy and complete the chart in exercise 2 with information about your school. The rules can be about:

behavior   clothes / uniforms   devices food / drinks   running   schedules studying / homework   talking in class

6 Write an e-mail to the exchange student.

• Use the chart in exercise 5.

• Use Sophia's e-mail as a model.

• Use the expressions of purpose in exercise 3.

Online Homework

1 Read Jack's essay. Write the correct numbers.

a Paragraphs <u>2</u>, _____, and _____ make suggestions to help with the problem.

b Paragraph _____ describes the problem.

c Paragraph _____ is the conclusion to the essay.

1 Between 7:30 and 8:00 every morning, over 500 students arrive at our school. Some arrive on foot, and some take the bus, but a lot of students arrive in their parents' cars. The entrance to the school is crowded and dangerous. **Personally, I think** cars are the main problem. **The way I see it**, there are three things we can do.

2 First, we should encourage students to take the bus or walk to school. Driving in cars causes a lot of air pollution in our city, and walking is healthier, too.

3 Second, if students have to come to school by car, **I feel** their parents should park their cars at the end of the street and not near the school entrance.

4 Finally, **in my opinion**, when parents park dangerously in front of the school entrance, they should have to pay some money to the school – a fine.

5 To sum up, cars are making it dangerous for students to enter the school safely in the morning. However, encouraging students to walk to school, or asking parents to park away from the school gates could solve this problem.

by Jack Barker

2 Read the essay again. Answer the questions.

1 Which group of students does Jack think are the problem?

<u>Students in their parents' cars.</u>

2 Why is walking to school better than driving?

_____

_____

3 What is the writer's second suggestion?

_____

_____

_____

4 Which is the worst place that some parents park?

_____

5 What phrase does Jack use to start his conclusion?

_____

3 Read the tip. Then read the text again and complete the four phrases.

> **Tip**
>
> **Good writers** express their opinions with a variety of phrases.
> In my _____, …
> The way _____ it …
> _____ feel …
> _____, I think …

4 Order the words to complete the sentences.

a feel / be / there / I / should

<u>I feel there should be</u> enough space for every student to sit down.

b there / Personally, / think / should / I

_____ be more places for students to recycle paper.

c can't / we / The / it, / see / I / way

_____ make people pick up their trash.

d we / should / opinion, / my / In

_____ encourage young people to do healthy activities.

5 Match the local problems 1–4 with the sentences a–d in exercise 4.

1 There aren't many places to play sports in your area. <u>d</u>

2 After the weekend, there is a lot of litter on the beach. _____

3 Our school should think more about the environment. _____

4 The buses to school are too crowded. _____

6 Plan an essay about a local problem. Use an idea in exercise 5 or one of your own.

Describe the problem.	_____ _____ _____ _____ _____
What are your suggestions to change the situation?	_____ _____ _____ _____

7 Write an essay about your local problem.

- Use your plan in exercise 6.
- Use Jack's essay as a model.
- Include a variety of phrases to express your opinion.

Describing pictures

1 Read the texts and match them with the pictures.

1 A street scene __

In this picture, tourists are watching a parade of people in costumes. It's sunny and the tourists are wearing shorts and sunglasses, so it can't be very cold. Some of them are taking pictures and they look like they're having fun. It might be in Brazil or Portugal because the shop's name is in Portuguese. Some people are looking down the street, so there must be something really interesting in the distance. What might happen next? I think that the parade might continue for a while.

Alfie, London

2 A beach scene __

This is a picture of a woman at the beach. She's walking or running by the beach, and her arms are in the air. The birds are flying away, so they might be a bit scared of her, but I don't think she's chasing them. She's smiling, so she must be <u>fairly</u> cheerful. The picture is quite bright so it must be sunny. The woman has long sleeves so it might not be summer yet. What might happen next? I think she's going to meet someone. Maybe they'll have lunch.

Polly, Toronto

2 Answer the questions.

1 What's the weather like in picture D?
<u>It must be warm and sunny because the people</u>
<u>are wearing shorts and sunglasses.</u>

2 Where is picture D? How do you know?
_____
_____

3 What's the weather like in picture B? How do you know?
_____

4 How does the woman in picture B feel?
_____

5 In both pictures, what do you think is going to happen next? Why? _____

3 Read the tip.

> **Tip** **Good writers** use modifiers to add detail to a description.

Read the texts again and <u>underline</u> the modifiers.

a bit   ~~fairly~~   not very   quite   really

4 Order the modifiers from 1 (weak) to 5 (strong).

1 > 2 > 3 > 4 > 5
_____ _____ fairly _____ _____

5 Choose the correct words.

1 I love your dress! It's **really** / **a bit** beautiful.

2 Can I open the window? It **'s a bit** / **isn't very** hot in here.

3 The movie wasn't amazing, but it was **fairly** / **really** good.

4 Let's get some food. I'm **quite** / **not very** hungry.

6 Plan a description of the other two pictures. Answer the questions for both pictures.

1 Where is the picture? How do you know?
2 Who can you see in the picture?
3 What is the weather like?
4 What is happening in the picture?
5 What do you think might happen next?

7 Write your descriptions.

• Use the descriptions in exercise 1 as a model.
• Use your notes from exercise 6.
• Use modifiers and modals of certainty and possibility.
• Say what you think is going to happen next.

Online Homework

A description of a relationship

1 Read Callum's description of someone he gets along with. What is similar (*S*) and different (*D*) about the boys?

1 their families   <u> D </u>

2 their personalities   _____

3 their ability to play video games   _____

4 their plans for college   _____

Joshua is my best friend and he's like a brother to me. I trust him with everything. We met in school, in the 6th grade. Our moms became good friends so we sometimes used to go to Joshua's apartment after classes. We're in 10th grade now.

One reason we get along is our personalities. We're very similar to each other – easygoing, cheerful, and hard-working.

We didn't always get along so well. Unlike me, Joshua has an older brother, and they often used to play video games together. I wasn't as good as him at gaming, and I used to feel really jealous. He used to tease me and we often fell out. That never happens now – but he still wins all the time!

And the future? We haven't decided about college yet. We probably won't go to the same one as Joshua's plans are completely different from mine. He wants to be a doctor and I want to be a software developer. But I think we'll be good friends for a long time.

2 Complete the answers with one word.

1	When and where did you and your friend meet?	We met <u>four</u> years ago at school.
2	Why do you get along?	Our _____ are very similar. We're both _____, cheerful, and hard-working.
3	How is your relationship different now from in the past?	Joshua used to _____ me and we used to _____ out.
4	What about the future?	We will probably go to different _____, but I think we will _____ good friends for a long time.

3 Read the tip. Then read the description again and <u>underline</u> the sentences with these phrases.

> **Tip**   **Good writers** talk about similarities and differences with phrases like:
>
> | similarities | differences |
> |---|---|
> | (*be*) like … | Unlike me, … |
> | (*be*) similar to … | (*be*) not as … as … |
> | | (*be*) completely different from … |

4 Rewrite the sentences with the words.

1 His hobbies aren't similar to mine. (different)
His hobbies are <u>completely different from mine</u>.

2 I'm better at sports than he is. (as)
He isn't _____.

3 Natalie's and my grades are almost the same. (similar)
Natalie's grades _____.

4 Luis is always cheerful. I am not. (unlike)
_____ is always cheerful.

5 Ruby and I have similar imaginations. (like)
Ruby's imagination _____.

5 Plan a description of your relationship with someone you get along with. Copy and complete the chart in exercise 2 for you.

6 Write your description.

- Use your plan in exercise 5.
- Use phrases to describe similarities and differences.
- Add a picture if possible.

A for and against essay

1 Read the essay quickly. What is Alicia's answer to the idea in the essay task?

Essay task:

According to research, teenagers need more sleep than adults and they naturally wake up later. So should high school classes start later? Write an essay discussing the advantages and disadvantages of starting classes at 10 a.m.

Should high school classes start later?

Parents and teachers complain that teenagers are always tired. However, it's not our fault. Teenagers need to sleep for longer than adults because of our body clocks, not because we're lazy! So should we change school schedules to make them better for teenagers?

On the one hand, this might be difficult for everyone else. If high schools start later, then teachers will finish work later, too. Teenagers' parents will also have to change their schedules. Some parents with two or more children might need to take one child to elementary school at 8 a.m. and another child to high school at 10 a.m. Students would finish at different times, too. What about parents who work?

On the other hand, if teenagers can get up later, then we won't be tired all day. We'll be able to concentrate and we'll get better grades. It will be better for our health. And there might be less traffic on the roads from 7 to 9 a.m., when the roads are busiest.

In conclusion, I think high school classes should start later because of the advantages for teenagers' health and education, although it will mean some changes for teachers and parents.

Alicia Harvey, WA

2 Read the essay again and complete the chart.

The problem	teenagers are too tired
The cause of the problem	_____
The idea	_____
Against the idea	_____
For the idea	_____
Conclusion	_____

3 Read the tip.

> **Tip** **Good writers** use expressions of contrast to explain differences.

Underline the expressions of contrast in the essay.

> although ~~however~~
> on the one hand   on the other hand

4 Complete the essay with expressions of contrast.

Most teenagers are against school uniforms.
¹ However___, there are arguments for school uniforms as well. ²_____, it's boring if everyone has to wear the same clothes. People should be allowed to wear what they like.
³_____, there are advantages to everyone looking the same. ⁴_____ people like to choose their own clothes, what students wear can cause bullying. Uniforms help students to feel proud of their school. Some schools say uniforms help students to behave better, too.

5 Read the essay task. Copy and complete the chart in exercise 2 to make a plan for your essay.

According to studies, teenagers feel stressed about how much they have to study at home, and they complain that they never have enough free time. Write an essay discussing the advantages and disadvantages of teenagers studying less and having more free time.

6 Write your essay.
- Use your ideas from exercise 5.
- Use Alicia's essay as a model.
- Use the expressions of contrast in exercise 3.

Online Homework

A persuasive post

1 Read Kate's post. Why is she writing?

a She wants to be president of the Student Council at Valley High.

b She wants to start a Student Council at Valley High.

c She wants to be a class representative on the Student Council.

○○○

HOME | ABOUT US | STUDENTS | | POSTS | NEWS

My name is Kate Samuels and I've just joined the 11th grade at Valley High. I'm really excited to be part of this school and to have the opportunity to join the Student Council.

I've been a member of student councils since the 8th grade. Although I'm new to Valley High, I was a council member at my last school for three years, and last year I was the council president as well.

I feel it is important that a class representative on the Student Council has the right personality. I am friendly and hard-working. In addition, I have excellent communication skills and I am confident about speaking in public.

As class representative, I would start a campaign for more after-school clubs. At the moment, we have lots of sports clubs, but not everyone is interested in sports.

Furthermore, I think we should have more school events such as concerts or fashion shows. Besides building the school community, this would also raise money for a charity or a school project.

Do you agree with my ideas?

If you do, vote for Kate Samuels as our class representative on October 12. Valley High is an awesome school. But we can make it better!

---

2 Read Kate's post again. Complete the chart for Kate.

	Kate	You
1 What is your previous experience?	member of Student Councils since the 8th grade, president in 10th grade	
2 What adjectives describe your personality?	_____, _____, _____	
3 What would you do as class representative?	_____ _____ _____	

3 Kate tries to make her writing persuasive. Complete the sentences.

1 She uses the pronouns I and _we_____ to make the text more personal.

2 She asks a _____, like "Do you agree with my ideas?" It makes the reader think.

3 She uses positive phrases like "_____ communication skills" and "confident about _____ in public."

4 Read the tip. Then read the post again and <u>underline</u> the sentences with these phrases.

> **Tip**
> **Good writers** link extra information with phrases like:
> *In addition, … / Furthermore, …*
> *… as well.*
> *Besides …*

5 Choose the correct words.

1 **In addition / (Besides)** being good at speaking in public, I am excellent at listening to people.

2 I work hard and I get good grades **as well / furthermore.**

3 There are twelve class representatives on Student Council. **As well / In addition,** there is a president.

4 I have the right personality. **Besides / Furthermore,** I have the experience.

6 Imagine you want to be a class representative on the Student Council. Now complete the chart in exercise 2 for you.

7 Write your post.

- Use your plan in exercise 6.
- Use the tips in exercise 3 to make your writing persuasive.
- Use some phrases in exercise 4 to link extra information in your post.

A biography

1 Read the biography. (Ignore the five highlighted mistakes.) What important prize did Einstein win?

ALBERT EINSTEIN

Albert Einstein is one of the most important figures in modern history. Everyone have heard of his famous formula "$E=mc^2$", but what else ∧ we know about this amazing man? He was born in 1879 in Ulm, Germany, and he has grown up in Munich. As a child, he loved math, physics, and music – he wanted playing the violin all day. Einstein once said: "If I were not a physicist, I will probably be a musician. I often think in music. I live my daydreams in music."

He went to college in Bern, Switzerland, in 1894 to study physics. He was married twice and he had three children. While he was working in an office in Bern, he produced his most original theories, including "$E=mc^2$". In 1909, he found a job at the University of Zurich, and in 1913, he moved to the University of Berlin where he wrote his famous "general theory of relativity." He won the Nobel Prize for physics in 1923.

In 1932, he moved to the U.S. He worked at Princeton University, and he lived in the U.S. for the rest of his life. Although he died in 1955, scientists are still fascinated by his incredible theories.

Maria da Sousa, Florianopolis

2 Read the biography again and answer the questions.

1 What is Einstein best known for?
   His $E=mc^2$ formula.

2 When and where was he born?
   _____

3 Where did he grow up? _____

4 What do we know about his childhood?
   _____
   _____

5 Did he go to college? If so, what did he study?
   _____
   _____

6 Did he get married or have children?
   _____
   _____

7 Why did he become famous?
   _____
   _____

8 When did he die? _____

3 Read the tip.

> **Tip**
>
> **Good writers** check their grammar. Here are five common mistakes:
> a subject–verb agreement
> b question forms
> c confusion of simple past and present perfect
> d use of gerund or infinitive forms
> e verb forms in conditional sentences

Correct the highlighted mistakes in the first paragraph of the biography.

a Everyone ~~have~~ heard → Everyone has heard

b _____
   _____

c _____
   _____

d _____
   _____

e _____

4 Read the task and plan a biography.

Task: You are going to write a biography of a creative person. They can be living or dead.

1 Choose one of the people below or any other creative person who you would like to write about.

> Adele   Beyoncé Knowles   Frida Kahlo
> John Lennon   Leonardo da Vinci
> Marie Curie   Maya Angelou   Oscar Niemeyer
> Steve Jobs   Tim Berners-Lee

2 Go online and find out about his / her life.
3 Answer the questions in exercise 2 about the person.
4 Find a few pictures of him / her.

5 Write your biography.

• Use your notes from exercise 4.
• Use Maria's biography as a model.
• Check your grammar and correct it.

Online Homework

Puzzles

1 Read the sentences. Write adjectives with letters of the same color.

> ed arra fus ~~oy~~ ed ght con ex ous ess je ed ~~ann~~ ed
> fri lax st hau str al re ss ed en emb ~~ed~~ ed

1 Jake's brother borrowed his phone without asking. Jake feels _annoyed_ .

2 Sue fell over in front of the whole school. She feels _____.

3 Robert's sister got a new phone from their parents. Robert feels _____.

4 Sara has three tests this week. She feels _____.

5 Marco is lying on the beach and reading a good book. He feels _____.

6 Macy hates spiders, and there's one in her bedroom. She feels _____.

7 Gustavo doesn't understand any of his math homework. He feels _____.

8 Luisa played soccer, basketball, and tennis today. She feels _____.

2 Read the sentences and complete the puzzle.

1 Some people cross their … when they are annoyed.

2 Many people … their head to say "No".

3 Some people bite their … when they are anxious.

4 We … fast when we do exercise.

5 Many people … their head to say "Yes".

6 Some people raise their … when they are surprised.

7 Some people … when they are embarrassed.

8 People … when they feel happy, or to be friendly.

Puzzle grid: 1 A R M S

Extra vocabulary

Parts of the face

1 Match the parts of the face with the pictures.

1 _forehead_

2 _____

3 _____

4 _____

5 _____

6 _____

7 _____

8 _____

9 _____

cheek chin eyebrow eyelashes eyelid ~~forehead~~ lips teeth tongue

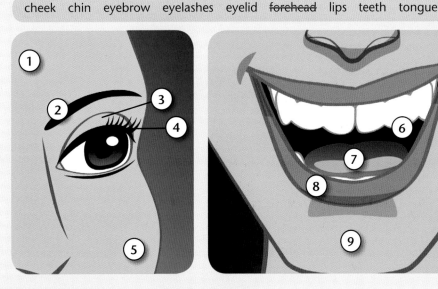

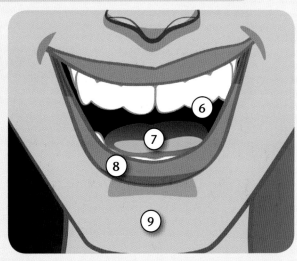

2 Which words in exercise 1 are plural? Which are singular? Use your dictionary to check the plural and singular forms for these words.

METRO EXPRESS

2 Puzzles

1 Read the code message from a teacher. What subject does the teacher teach? _____

A	●	B	◁	C	≡	D	▪	E	▽	F	⊢•
G	◗	H	△	I	◱	J	⁝⁝	K	◆	L	⬟
M	⊕	N	□	O	⊖	P	▶	Q	♡	R	⁝⁝⁝
S	⬟	T	▷	U	○	V	⠒	W	◈	X	▭
Y	◎	Z	⬠

◎⊖⊖ / ▪◱▪ / ● / ◗⁝⁝▽●▷ / ⁝⁝⊖◁ / ◎⊖⊖ / ▪◱▪□▷ / ⊕●◆▽ / ●□◎

Y O U / D I D / A / _____ / _____ / _____ / _____ / _____ /

⊕◱⬟▷●◆▽⬟ / ◁○▷   ◎⊖⊖ / ●⁝⁝▽□▷ / ●⬟⬟●◈▽▪▷ / ▷⊖   ○●▽ /

_____ / _____ / _____ / _____ / _____ / ___ / _____ / __

≡●⬟⬟≡○⬟●▷⊖⁝⁝

_____

2 Read the text and complete the puzzle. Use the orange letters to answer the question.

Tina and Clare **¹** <u>fight with</u> me all the time. I can't **²**_____ them because then they **³**_____ on me and they **⁴**_____ to take my stuff. They **⁵**_____ me … What should I do? Sara

¹f	i	g	h	t	w	i	t	h
²i								
³p				j				
⁴t								
⁵g					a			

What's Sara's problem? __ __ __ l __ __ __ __ __

Extra vocabulary

Uses of *get*

1 Look at the pictures and read the sentences. Match them with the meanings.

I **got** a hoodie for my birthday.

I **get** home at about six o'clock.

I want to **get** some new sneakers.

It's **getting** cold.

Mom, can you **get** my keys?

I **get** the bus to school.

a buy / obtain ___3___
b receive _____
c travel on transportation _____
d start to be _____
e bring _____
f arrive somewhere _____

2 Answer the questions for you.

1 How do you get to school? What time do you get there?
2 What did you get on your last birthday?
3 What new clothes would you like to get?

1 Find eight man-made and natural problems in the puzzle. (↑ ↓ ↗ ↘ → ←)

X	N	O	E	O	W	E	P	W	M
R	Y	V	V	Q	P	G	O	G	O
W	V	E	A	C	T	N	L	S	M
W	P	R	W	T	Q	A	L	R	F
T	Y	P	T	W	E	H	U	T	H
H	E	O	A	I	N	C	T	H	M
G	M	P	E	L	Z	E	I	S	S
U	H	U	H	D	K	T	O	H	U
O	D	L	U	F	M	A	N	J	D
R	G	A	J	I	G	M	Y	O	A
D	U	T	B	R	L	I	O	U	T
L	T	I	B	E	T	L	M	P	P
A	D	O	S	J	F	C	U	C	G
X	Y	N	E	S	A	E	S	I	D

STOP
THINK

recycle

In the U.S, people throw away $165 billion in food every year.

_____
food waste now.

Say NO to plastic bags. Buy bags you can

_____

Take shorter showers.

_____

water.

Plant a tree.

_____
the environment.

2 Unscramble the words and complete the posters.

vase   cuered   ereus   creptto   ~~celyere~~

Natural disasters

1 Match the natural disasters with the pictures.

avalanche   earthquake   ~~hurricane~~
landslide   tsunami   volcanic eruption

1 hurricane

2 _____

3 _____

4 _____

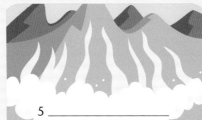

5 _____

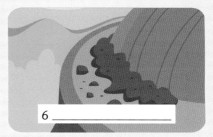

6 _____

2 Which of the natural disasters in exercise 1 happen in your country?

Puzzles

1 Read the Pigpen Code message about truth and lies.

A	B	C		J	K	L
D	E	F		M	N	O
G	H	I		P	Q	R

(code grid with S T U V and W X Y Z in diagonal sections)

[Pigpen code message]

Simon is pretending to be …

_____

_____

_____

_____

_____

2 Choose the correct ending for the message:

a Tell Simon the truth.   **c** Don't believe Simon.

b You can trust Simon.

3 Now write a message using the code.

4 Find the noun forms of the verbs in the puzzle. Look ↕ and ↔. ONE isn't in the puzzle. Which is missing?

act   collect   communicate   connect
decide   describe   discuss   explain
imagine   invent   ~~invite~~   prepare

I	I	N	V	E	N	T	I	O	N	N
N	C	O	N	Q	O	N	I	I	O	O
V	O	I	O	J	I	B	R	N	I	I
I	N	T	I	U	T	X	N	O	T	T
T	N	A	T	F	A	Z	O	I	A	P
A	E	R	C	P	N	V	I	S	N	I
T	C	A	E	E	I	Z	S	S	A	R
I	T	P	L	P	G	R	I	U	L	C
O	I	E	L	P	A	L	C	C	P	S
N	O	R	O	D	M	G	E	S	X	E
L	N	P	C	N	I	D	D	I	E	D
M	M	N	O	I	T	C	A	D	S	D

The missing noun is: _____.

Extra vocabulary

Prefixes: *un-* and *im-*

1 Find the negative forms of the adjectives in the wordsnake. Then copy and complete the chart.

comfortable   ~~friendly~~   happy   lucky   polite   possible

depoliteunfriendlyinhappyimpoliteuncomfortableimpossibleexhappyunluckyinpossibleunhappy

un-	im-
unfriendly	

2 Label the pictures.

1 impolite

2 _____

3 _____

4 _____

5 _____

6 _____

Puzzles

1 Read the situation. Lucas is on a date with one of the six girls. Who is she?

Lucas has six friends named Lara, Laura, Luisa, Lorena, Leticia, and Livia. Laura and her old boyfriend made up recently. Lara asked Lucas out. Luisa has fallen in love with a boy in another class. Lorena and Lucas don't get along. Leticia went on a date with Lucas a few weeks ago, but they didn't get along. Livia broke up with her boyfriend recently and doesn't want another one at the moment. Lucas gets along really well with Lara, but he isn't attracted to her.

2 Do the quiz.

Are you argumentative?

1 You want to sleep at a friend's house after a party, but your parents say "no."

  a I don't talk to them, I don't look at them, and I **sulk**!
  b I understand their reasons.

2 Your older brother teases you about your clothes.

  a I pretend to **cry** and tell my parents.
  b I ask him for fashion advice.

3 Your little sister is singing your favorite song, but she's making up the lyrics and they're all wrong.

  a I **shout** at her. She's so annoying!
  b I **laugh** and **hug** her. She's so cute, and funny!

4 You had an argument with a friend and they're ignoring you.

  a You tell them you don't care and **ignore** them, too.
  b You apologize and try to make up.

a: 1 point   **b:** 0 points

K E Y		
0–1	Great job! You must get along with almost everyone.
2	Try to be more relaxed. Having arguments is never the best solution.
3–4	You are argumentative! Does *anyone* talk to you?

Extra vocabulary

Things we do with our hands

Label the pictures with the verbs.

clap   ~~hold hands~~   knock   point   pull   push   wave

4 _____   5 _____

1 <u>hold hands</u>   2 _____   3 _____   6 _____   7 _____

Puzzles

1 **Read the descriptions. Find the pictures – you only have 40 seconds!**

1 It looks shiny, smooth, and hard. It isn't colorful. Find it! What is it?

2 It's colorful, and it looks soft but rough. Find it! What is it?

2 **Can you name the other things? Describe them!**

3 **Find the sentences about sleep. Then match them with the pictures.**

1 s i h t u e ' s i o s o m p o p t h o i t n s g s

It's ___snoring_____ ! ___d___

2 t h t e ' s s l y p i n t g f r o g a s w a r k t e

He's _____. _____

3 s e h t e s h e a d e d a s n k i h g h s t o i m s a i t r s e

She _____. _____

4 h t s i t h r t e ' s s w y w n a w n i o s i r s n s g s

She's _____. _____

5 t h s e s g h f e i e r t l o s o s o l o e p e r s p t h y

He _____. _____

Extra vocabulary

Adjectives for describing food

1 **Label the pictures.**

| bitter | ~~bland~~ | chewy | creamy | crunchy | juicy |

1 ___bland_____ 2 _____ 3 _____

4 _____ 5 _____ 6 _____

2 **How many types of food can you think of for each adjective?**

Puzzles

1 **Read the resolutions. The verbs are in the wrong places. Write the correct verbs.**

1 I'm going to ~~pick up~~ _donate_ some money to a charity.

2 I'm going to **raise** _____ the litter outside my apartment building.

3 I'm going to **look after** _____ my neighbor a hand with her shopping.

4 I'm going to **give** _____ my sister's baby so she can stay in bed for a few hours.

5 I'm going to **start** _____ money for a charity.

6 I'm going to **donate** _____ a campaign for more after-school clubs.

2 **Read the sentences and complete the puzzle.**

1 You might find a new pet at an _animal_ shelter.

2 Someone you play sport with is a _____.

3 People without a home sometimes stay at a _____ shelter.

4 Someone who is a lot older than you is a _____ citizen.

5 You might help stop climate change at an _____ organization.

6 Someone you don't know is a _____.

7 You can usually buy old clothes at a _____ store.

8 Someone you live very near is a _____.

Puzzle grid:
- C, L, S down (spelling CL...S)
- 1 ACROSS: A N I M A L

3 **Complete the statement with the mystery words and a correct answer for you.**

Two of my _____ are _____ and _____.

Extra vocabulary

Compound adjectives

Complete the sentences with the words.

brand new ~~second-hand~~ two-year-old well-organized world-famous

1 We love shopping in thrift stores for _second-hand_ clothes.

2 Unicef is a _____ charity.

3 I have a _____ niece and I love looking after her.

4 Charlotte is a really _____ person. Check out her closet!

5 This is a _____ T-shirt and I've already gotten coffee on it.

Stop Compound adjectives are formed from two or more words.

NETRO EXPRESS

Puzzles

1 Find eight more adjectives. Complete the puzzle and find the hidden word.

CLE	FASH	TI	RECY	INAL
ENOR	CLED	CATE	NGE	OLD-
IENT	STRA	ANC	MOUS	VER
DELI	ORIG	ION	NY	ED

The hidden word is: _____.

			C					
E	N	O	R	M	O	U	S	
			D					
O								
			S					
	O							
C							
A							
R						

2 Find seven more creativity verbs. Complete the questions.

When did ... ?

1 the French __build__ the Eiffel Tower?
2 The Beatles _____ *Yesterday*?
3 Bell _____ the telephone?
4 Sikorsky _____ the first helicopter that could fly?
5 Gates and Allen _____ _____ Microsoft?
6 Fleming _____ penicillin?
7 da Vinci _____ the Mona Lisa?
8 Satoshi Tajiri _____ Pokémon?

t	t	e	e	p	v	v	g	n	n	p	e
d	c	a	s	e	e	s	d	e	i	a	d
o	m	n	r	i	c	b	s	c	s	r	o
e	p	o	t	u	t	n	i	u	i	i	t

3 Answer the questions. You have one minute!

| 1510 | 1876 | 1889 | 1928 |
| 1939 | 1965 | 1975 | 1995 |

Extra vocabulary

Materials

1 Label the pictures.

brick   cardboard   ~~concrete~~   glass
leather   metal   plastic   wood

1 _concrete_   2 _____   3 _____   4 _____

5 _____   6 _____   7 _____   8 _____

2 What are the things made from?

bike   book
boots   desk
jacket   laptop
sidewalk   sneakers
tablet   wall

Boots are made from leather.

3 Read the riddle. What is the answer?

There is an ancient invention that people still use to see through walls. What is it?

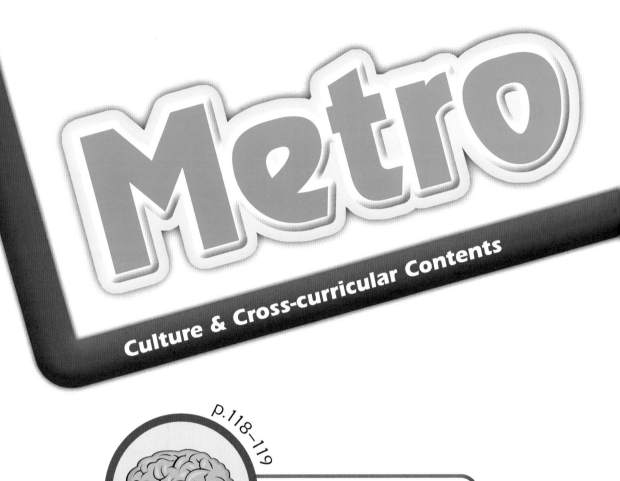

Metro

Culture & Cross-curricular Contents

 **Psychology: Memory**

Reading

1 🔊 100 What do the brain and muscles have in common? Read the short text and check.

The Brain: Use It or Lose It

We exercise our body to make our muscles stronger and healthier. Although the brain is an organ, not a muscle, the brain is *like* a muscle. It needs exercise and it gets stronger with practice. When people study hard and learn new things, their brains change and new neural connections grow. On the other hand, if you don't use your brain enough, it doesn't grow new connections. As the phrase says: "Use it or lose it."

2 In groups, discuss how you remember things. Then read the long text quickly. How many of the ideas in the text did you discuss?

3 🔊 101 Match the headings 1–5 with the gaps a–e in the text. Read, listen, and check.

1 Chunk numbers
2 Make a fist
3 Say it to remember it
4 How do we form memories?
5 Connect memories with images

4 Choose the best definition of *memory*.

a remembering things very easily
b the ability to remember things
c being able to remember a lot of facts
d something you did in the past

5 Complete the diagram of the multi-store memory model.

> don't pay attention and lose it
> long-term memory   rehearsal   remember
> ~~sensory store~~   short-term memory

6 Discuss the questions.

1 How long do memories last? How many can we have?
2 What does the brain do with information to form memories?
3 What is "rehearsal" and why does it matter?
4 What happens when we remember something?

7 Discuss the memory techniques in the text.

1 Have you ever tried any of the memory techniques?
2 Which do you think is the best? Why?

HOW MEMORY WORKS

Memory is an important function of the brain. There are two types of memory:

Short-term memory: memories last about 30 seconds. Your brain can only keep about seven short-term memories at once.

Long-term memory: memories can last all of your life. There is no limit to the number of long-term memories that your brain can store!

a _____

The **multi-store memory model** is a popular description of how the brain makes memories.

First, your **sensory store** receives information from your senses, especially sight, hearing, and touch. If you **don't pay attention** to this information, you **lose it** completely. If you **pay attention** to it, the information enters your **short-term memory**. It lasts for about 30 seconds in your short-term memory and then you **lose it**, unless you rehearse the information. Examples of **rehearsal** are repeating the information to yourself, or you seeing, hearing, or feeling it again. Rehearsal helps the information to last longer in the short-term memory. Information that lasts for longer periods in the short-term memory passes to the long-term memory. Information in the long-term memory lasts more or less forever. When you remember something, it passes from the long-term to the short-term memory while you are using it.

Multi-store memory model

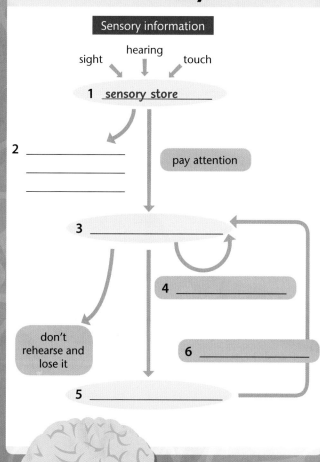

Sensory information
sight   hearing   touch
1   sensory store
2 _____
pay attention
3 _____
4 _____
don't rehearse and lose it
6 _____
5 _____

TRAIN YOUR BRAIN!

Anyone can train their brain to remember more. Here are four ways:

b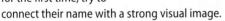

Our visual memory is powerful. When you connect a memory to an image, it makes the memory stronger:

- When you try to remember something, picture yourself where you were when you formed the memory.
- To remember a person's name when you meet them for the first time, try to connect their name with a strong visual image.

c _____

To remember things like phone numbers or shopping lists, make a fist with your right hand for 90 seconds. When you need to remember that information later, make a fist with your left hand for 90 seconds. Why? Because the right hand affects the left side of the brain, where we form memories. The left hand affects the right side of the brain, where we recall memories.

d _____

If you read something out loud, it's easier to remember it than if you read it silently. This is because you form a visual memory _and_ a hearing memory of the information.

e Chunk numbers _____

Don't try to remember a long number like 4657869705 as ten individual numbers. Divide it into pairs: 46 57 86 97 05. It is easier to remember five "chunks" than ten individual numbers because our short-term memory has a limit of about seven items.

Listening
Memory palaces

8 🔊 102 **Listen to the conversation. What is a memory palace?**

a something you enjoy remembering

b a way of remembering things

c a place where you can see people's memories

9 🔊 102 **How do you make a memory palace? Listen again and order the stages.**

a Use humor, or connect a word with an image. ____

b Picture somewhere you know well, for example, your home, street, or route to school. __1__

c In each location, picture something you need to remember. ____

d Notice large things in the journey – these are the locations in your memory palace. ____

e Imagine a journey around your memory palace. ____

10 🔊 102 **Listen again and answer the questions.**

1 What kind of information can you use a memory palace to remember?
   things that happen one after the other

2 What does Susan Bushell use a memory palace to remember? _____

3 How many locations are there in Susan's memory palace? _____

4 Do you think memory palaces are a good idea? Why? / Why not? _____

Project

1 You are going to compare two memory techniques and write a report.

1 Use two techniques from the reading text and listening text to remember information in order. Choose from:

> a poem / song
> a process in science or geography
> events in history   phone numbers

2 Work with a partner. Use each technique to remember equivalent information.

3 Make sure each test lasts the same amount of time.

4 Which technique worked best? Did you remember everything? Why?

2 Write your report.

1 Write a paragraph about each technique. Describe how you used the technique and what the results were.

2 Write a final paragraph to explain your conclusion about which technique was the best for you.

New York: Culture and immigration

Reading

1 In pairs, answer the questions.

1 Do you know what *immigration* means?

2 What are the most common nationalities of *immigrants* to your country?

2 🔊 103 Read the text. Match 1–6 to the information a–f.

1 8.5 million
2 7
3 about 3 million
4 2 million
5 80 million
6 800

a the number of languages you can hear in New York

b people at the St. Patrick's Day Parade in New York

c the number of immigrants to the U.S in the last 200 years

d the New York Subway line called the "International Express"

e the number of immigrants in New York now

f the population of New York

3 Read the text again and answer the questions.

1 What reasons does the text give for people leaving their home countries?

  Political, religious, and economic reasons.

2 Why was New York a popular place in the U.S. for Europeans?

  _____

  _____

3 What was one of the immigrants' problems in the early 20th century?

  _____

4 How did the number 7 subway line help?

  _____

  _____

5 What do you think you can find in, for example, Little India or Chinatown?

  _____

  _____

6 Who gets a holiday at the Chinese Lunar New Year?

  _____

7 When is St. Patrick's Day?

  _____

The World in New York City

Over the past 200 years, over 80 million people have left the countries they were born in and moved to the U.S. In the 19th century, many were Northern Europeans. Their reasons were varied: political, religious, and economic. But most of all, people were simply looking for a better life. At that time, European immigrants arrived by ship on the East Coast. Many chose New York because it was the cheapest place to travel to. And without money to travel across the U.S., many of them stayed in the city.

Now, there are immigrants from all over the world in New York, and over 35% of the city's 8.5 million population were born outside of the U.S. Experts believe it's possible to hear over 800 different languages in the city. The perfect place to experience this is on the number 7 subway line, or "International Express." In the early 1900s, large numbers of immigrants lived in crowded conditions in the center of New York. The city built the number 7 line to encourage them to move to better homes away from the center. The train line meant that they could live further away from the city center, but travel in easily for work. The plan was successful, and now each stop on this line is a community of people from different countries, with their own restaurants, businesses, and homes. Signs on the subway are in seven different languages!

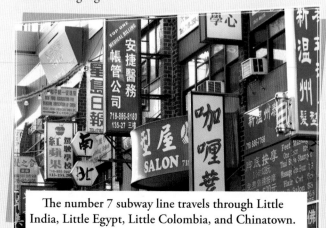

The number 7 subway line travels through Little India, Little Egypt, Little Colombia, and Chinatown.

St. Patrick's Day: Green is the national color of Ireland.

The cultural mix of New York means the city has festivals from all over the world throughout the year. For example in January or February each year, many New Yorkers celebrate the Chinese Lunar New Year – and every student gets a day off school! In March, more than 2 million people, from all over the world, watch the St. Patrick's Day Parade – a celebration from Ireland. It began in New York in 1762, and it's the biggest St. Patrick's Day parade in the world. Thousands celebrate smaller festivals, too – from Hong Kong Dragon Boat races to Brazilian Day in "Little Brazil" in the center of New York.

Listening
Sergey's story

4 Look at the picture and answer the questions.

1 Do you recognize the person?

2 Do you know where he was born?

3 Why do you think he and his family moved to the U.S.?

5 (104) Listen to the first part of the story and check your answers to the questions in exercise 4.

6 (105) Read the sentences. Then listen to the complete story and put the events in the correct order.

a The Brins flew to New York. _____

b Sergey had his ninth birthday. _____

c Sergey met Larry Page. _____

d Sergey's parents left their jobs. _____

e Mikhail Brin suggested moving to the U.S. __1__

f Sergey's parents got jobs. _____

7 (106) Complete the summary. Then listen and check.

> better computer father good job
> parents ~~Russian~~ son the U.S. well

Sergey Brin and his family are ¹ Russian immigrants. They went to ² _____ in 1979 because Sergey's ³ _____ wanted to find a better ⁴ _____. Sergey's mother didn't want to move, but she wanted a good future for her ⁵ _____.

After arriving, the family moved to Washington, D.C., and Sergey's ⁶ _____ got jobs. Sergey didn't speak English ⁷ _____ at first, and he found school difficult. But he got ⁸ _____ grades, and in college he studied math and ⁹ _____ science. In 1995, he met Larry Page and started a project to find ¹⁰ _____ ways to search the Internet. In 1997, that project became google.com.

Project

1 Use the Internet to find some famous immigrants to your country or the U.S. Choose one and complete the chart.

Who is it?	
Where is he / she from?	
Why did he / she move?	
What happened after he / she arrived?	
How did he / she become successful?	

2 Write the story of the person you chose. Include:

• information from the table in exercise 1.

• other interesting information you can find online or in books.

• some interesting pictures.

Weddings

Reading

1 Read the texts quickly. Check (✓) the topics that both Takeshi and Tara mention.

1 the food ☐ 4 the bride's clothes ☐

2 the drink ☐ 5 the music ☐

3 gift traditions ☐

2 🔊 **107** Read Takeshi's experience again. Match the Japanese words with their meanings.

1 kimono
2 kekkon hirōen
3 daifuku
4 goshūgi
5 hikidemono
6 nijikai

a Japanese cakes
b gifts for wedding guests
c a wedding party with friends and family
d a wedding party with friends only
e money gift from wedding guests
f a Japanese traditional oufit

3 🔊 **108** Read Tara's experience of her cousin's wedding. Choose *T* (True) or *F* (False). Correct the false sentences.

1 During her wedding ceremony, Tara's cousin wore a white dress. **T** ☑ **F** ☐

_____

2 Only Tara's close family came to the wedding ceremony. **T** ☐ **F** ☐

_____

3 The reception is the name for the party after the ceremony. **T** ☐ **F** ☐

_____

4 Tara's aunt made some of the food for the wedding. **T** ☐ **F** ☐

_____

5 The reception finished late on Saturday. **T** ☐ **F** ☐

_____

6 Tara's cousin and her husband didn't want any gifts from their guests. **T** ☐ **F** ☐

_____

4 In pairs, answer the questions.

1 Which events do you think are the most interesting or unusual?

2 Which of the two weddings would you prefer to go to? Why?

A Japanese wedding

My sister, Hanako, got married to her fiancé Satoshi last year. The first part of the ceremony, the *Shinto* ceremony, was very traditional, and only close family were there. My sister wore a traditional white dress, called a *kimono*. At the end, everyone had a small drink of *sake* – a type of Japanese wine.

Then there was a wedding celebration, called *kekkon hirōen*, at a hotel for family and some friends. Brides traditionally wear a red *kimono* at this party, but my sister wore a red dress. The groom wore a black suit. At the meal, we ate sushi, and we had a sushi cake – it's like normal sushi, but bigger! We also ate *daifuku* – traditional sweet rice cakes with beans and fruit inside.

In Japan, both the guests and the couple give wedding gifts. Guests give the couple *goshūgi* (money), while couples give *hikidemono* (small gifts) to the guests. We got some cake and some Japanese tea.

Nijikai means "second party" in Japanese. It's common in Japan for couples to have the *nijikai* a week or two after the wedding – just for friends. It isn't as formal as a *kekkon hirōen*, and guests pay to go. My sister and Satoshi had their *nijikai* in a restaurant. They really love music, so many of the guests sang or played a song at the party.

Takeshi

A JAMAICAN WEDDING

Tara

Before a wedding, it's traditional in Jamaica for everyone to go out into the street to see the bride. On Saturday morning, my cousin had to walk down her street, in her white wedding dress. Hundreds of people were shouting and clapping. She was a bit embarrassed, but happy!

Later that day, there was a ceremony in our church. There were a lot of guests. That isn't unusual in Jamaica. Anyone can come to a wedding!

After the ceremony, there was a huge party with family and friends – called the reception. There was a lot of food – goat and chicken curries are very common at Jamaican weddings. We also make special fruit cakes. My aunt started making my cousin's cake a year ago. My cousin's reception didn't finish until the next morning, and many people had a breakfast of fish and *ackee*, a type of fruit, before they left. I was exhausted!

In Jamaica, wedding gifts are common – but my cousin and her husband did something different. They both work for an environmental charity, so they asked for donations to their charity. Everyone thought it was a really cool idea!

Listening
Western wedding traditions

5 Read the list of past traditions at weddings in western countries. Were or are any of these traditions common in your country?

1 Men always used to ask the father of the bride for permission to marry – before asking their girlfriend.

2 The bride's family always used to pay for the wedding.

3 The bride and groom weren't allowed to see each other before the wedding.

4 Brides always used to throw their flowers to the unmarried women.

6 🔊 109 Listen and match 1–4 in exercise 5 to a–d.

1 _____   2 _____   3 _a_   4 _____

7 🔊 109 Listen again. Complete each sentence with one word.

a The bride and groom didn't use to be allowed to see each other before the wedding because one of them might change their _mind_.

b Nowadays, some men talk to the father of the bride before marriage because it is a _____ thing to do. However, they often do it after _____ their girlfriend to marry them.

c In the past, guests used to take a piece of the bride's _____ for luck. Nowadays, the tradition of _____ and catching the bride's flowers is common.

d Nowadays, the couple's families usually _____ the cost of the wedding. Many couples _____ for the wedding themselves.

Project

1 You are going to describe a typical wedding in your country. Make notes in the chart.

Ceremony	
Party	
Clothes	
Food / drink	
Other traditions	

2 Write your description. Use your chart in exercise 1 and include:
- information about past tradition.
- pictures of unusual food / drink, clothes, etc.

Literature

Reading

1 **Read the blurb and discuss the questions.**

1 Do you agree with Lord Henry?

2 Do you think it's better to be beautiful than to be good?

The Picture of Dorian Gray
by Oscar Wilde

"When we are happy, we are always good," says Lord Henry, "but when we are good, we are not always happy." Lord Henry's lazy, clever words lead the young Dorian Gray into a world where it is better to be beautiful than to be good; a world where anything can be forgiven – even murder – if it can make people laugh at a dinner party.

2 🔊 **110** **Read Extract 1. Complete the sentences with the names.**

Basil Hallward   Dorian Gray   Lord Henry

1 The picture is of _Dorian Gray_____.

2 _____ painted the picture for _____.

3 Harry is _____'s first name.

4 _____ feels afraid after he looks at the picture.

5 _____ wants to own the painting.

6 _____ never wants to get old.

3 🔊 **111** **Read the introduction and Extract 2 on page 125. Do you think Sybil and Dorian will get married? Why? / Why not?**

4 **Discuss the questions about Extract 2. Give reasons for your answers.**

1 How does Sybil Vane feel about Dorian Gray at the beginning of Extract 2?

2 Why do you think Dorian turns his face away from Sybil?

3 How would you describe how Dorian treats Sybil?

4 How do you think Sybil feels after Dorian leaves?

5 What is happening to the portrait of Dorian Gray? What is happening to Dorian Gray himself?

The Picture of
DORIAN GRAY

EXTRACT 1

In the house Basil Hallward stood in front of the portrait of Dorian Gray. "It's finished," he said. He wrote his name in the corner of the picture.

Lord Henry studied the picture carefully. "Yes," he said. "It's your best work. It's excellent. Mr. Gray, come and look at yourself."

Dorian looked at the picture for a long time. He smiled as he saw the beautiful face in front of him, and for a moment he felt happy. But then he remembered Lord Henry's words. "How long," he thought, "will I look like the picture? Time will steal my beauty from me. I will grow old, but the picture will always be young." And his heart grew cold with fear.

"Don't you like it, Dorian?' asked Basil at last.

"Of course he likes it," said Lord Henry. "It's a very fine work of art. I'd like to buy it myself."

"It's not mine to sell, Harry. The picture is Dorian's."

"I wish," cried Dorian suddenly, "I wish that I could always stay young, and that the picture could grow old."

Dorian Gray decided to marry a young actor named Sybil Vane. He went to see Sybil play Juliet in *Romeo and Juliet*. She normally acted very well, but today her acting was terrible. Dorian sees her after the play.

EXTRACT 2

"How can I pretend to be Juliet – to feel Juliet's love, when I now know what true love is?" asked Sybil.

Dorian turned his face away from her. "But I loved you for your art – because you were a wonderful actress," he said. His voice was hard. "You have killed my love. Without your art, you are nothing, I never want to see you again." Sybil's face was white with fear. "You're not serious, are you, Dorian?" she asked. She touched his arm with her small, gentle hand.

"Don't touch me!" he shouted angrily. He pushed her away, and she fell to the floor and lay there like a broken bird.

"Dorian, please don't leave me," she cried. "I love you better than anything in the world. Don't leave me!"

Dorian Gray looked down at her with his beautiful eyes. There was no love or gentleness in his face.

"I'm going," he said at last. "I don't wish to be unkind, but I don't want to see you again." Without another word, he left her.

All night he walked through the streets of London. When morning came, he went home. When he entered his house, he saw the portrait of himself that Basil Hallward had painted. There was something different about it, he thought. The face had changed – there was something unkind, and cruel about the mouth. It was very strange.

He picked up a mirror and looked at his own face, and then looked again at the face in the portrait. Yes, it was different. What did this change mean?

Suddenly he remembered his wish in Basil Hallward's house … his wish that he could stay young but the picture could grow old. The idea was impossible, of course. But why did the face in the picture have that cruel, unkind mouth?

Listening

5 🔊 112 **You are going to hear two more extracts from *The Picture of Dorian Gray*. Look at the picture. What do you think is going to happen to Dorian Gray? What do you think will happen to the painting? Listen to Extracts 3 and 4, and check your ideas.**

6 🔊 113 **Complete the sentences from Extract 3. Listen again and check.**

> beautiful   dangerous
> ~~fashionable~~   ~~rich~~   secret   strange

1 He enjoyed the life of a __rich__ and __fashionable__ young man.

2 He studied art and music, and filled his house with _____ things from every corner of the world.

3 After a while, _____ stories were heard about him – stories of a _____, more _____ life.

> cruel   famous   heavy   real   yellow

4 And they still came to the _____ dinners at his house.

5 The _____ mouth, the _____ skin, the _____ eyes – these told the _____ story.

7 🔊 114 **Read the questions. Then listen to Extract 4 and discuss your answers.**

1 Why does Dorian say, "Uncover that picture, Basil, and you will see my soul"?
2 How does Basil feel when he first sees the picture?
3 How does Basil know it's *his* portrait of Dorian Gray?
4 Why is Basil surprised by the picture?
5 Why does Dorian say, "I was wrong. It has destroyed me"?

Project

1 You are going to write a letter from Basil to Dorian. Think about:
• Basil's relationship with Dorian.
• how Dorian has changed.
• what Basil might think about Dorian's behavior.
• how Dorian's behavior could be better, and what advice Basil might give to Dorian.

2 Write your letter.

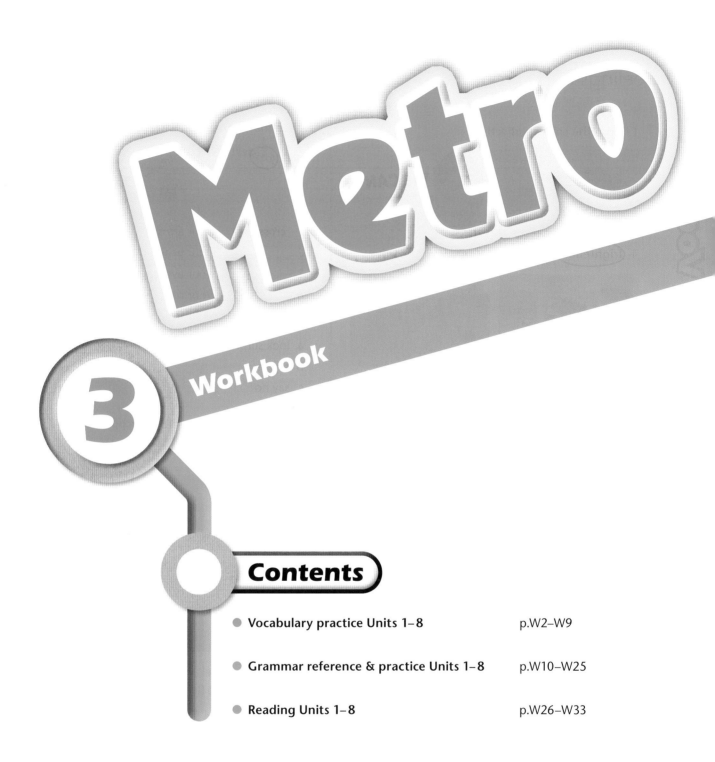

Metro

Workbook

3

Contents

James Styring & Nicholas Tims
Alexandra Paramour • Aírton Pozo de Mattos

OXFORD
UNIVERSITY PRESS

Vocabulary

Feelings and emotions

← Student Book p.14

1 Choose the correct adjectives.

1 (frightened) / relaxed

2 annoyed / positive

3 exhausted / jealous

4 stressed / shocked

5 exhausted / confused

6 frightened / embarrassed

2 Complete the conversations with -ed or -ing adjectives formed from the verbs.

annoy confuse frighten

Jack: Did you enjoy the movie?

Kyle: Not really. It was very ¹ _confusing_. I didn't understand what was happening!

Jack: Was it ² _____?

Kyle: No. I'm ³ _____ I paid to see it!

embarrass relax shock

Nina: Did your presentation go well today?

Liza: It was OK. But it was almost a disaster.

Nina: Why?

Liza: I forgot my notes. I was ⁴ _____ when I realized they weren't in my bag.

Nina: Oh no! What did you do?

Liza: At first, I didn't know what to say. It was really ⁵ _____. But then I stopped trying to remember the exact words and just spoke naturally. I felt more ⁶ _____ after that.

Body: actions ← Student Book p.18

3 Find four more verbs to complete the phrases 1–5. Then match them with a–e.

dshenvcrossfvyrnvebitewbhkvraisehgoakshakebiesshfdknodheieb

1 _cross_____ your arms _d_

2 _____ your head up and down _____

3 _____ your eyebrows _____

4 _____ your nails _____

5 _____ your head from side to side _____

a look surprised ~~d look annoyed~~

b say yes e look anxious

c say no

4 Complete the article with appropriate verbs.

FIVE TIPS FOR MEETING NEW PEOPLE

It's normal to feel anxious when you meet new people. Here are five ways to make a good impression.

1 Listen. N _od_____ your head to show that you understand what the other person is saying. Just don't do it too much!

2 S_____! When you look happy, it makes other people feel happier, too.

3 Use open, friendly body language. Don't c_____ your arms or look at the floor.

4 Don't worry if you b_____. Remember that the other person probably feels as shy as you.

5 Don't talk too fast. Speak in a slow, relaxed voice and don't forget to b_____!

✓ **I can** use ten adjectives for feelings and emotions.

☺ ◯ ☺ ◯ ☹ ◯

✓ **I can** use eight verbs and verb phrases related to body actions.

☺ ◯ ☺ ◯ ☹ ◯

do and make ← Student Book P.24

1 Complete the sentences with *do* or *make*.

1 I asked you not to __make__ a mess!

2 I'm going to _____ a complaint!

3 Just _____ your best and be positive.

4 _____ your chores first, please.

5 Please don't _____ so much noise. It's late!

6 Don't worry. We all _____ mistakes.

2 Complete the conversations with the correct form of *do* or *make*, and complete the missing words.

1 "Who's _making_ all that n_oise_?"
"It's my brother and his metal band."

2 "Did you enjoy the school play?"
"It was awesome! You all _____ a really great j_____!"

3 "Who _____ the m_____ here?"
"I did, sorry. I made a cake, but it fell on the floor."

4 "I was late because I was wearing the wrong shoes and I couldn't walk very fast."
"Don't _____ e_____! Next time, wear sneakers or leave home earlier!"

5 "Have you paid for that T-shirt?"
"Yes, I have. Here's the receipt. I haven't _____ anything w_____."

6 "Why do I have to make my bed?"
"Because I _____ the r_____ in this house and I say so!"

Bullying ← Student Book P.28

3 Match the sentences a–f with the verbs 1–6.

1 play a joke on someone ___f___
2 threaten someone _____
3 ignore someone _____
4 tease someone _____
5 gossip about someone _____
6 fight with someone _____

a Someone told me that Emily was at the movie theater with Aaron last night.
b Did your grandma make that sweater for you?
c I'm going to post this picture online if you don't do what I say.
d Joe kicked me!
e I'm not listening to you. Go away.
f Oh, no! There's an enormous spider in your hair!

4 Complete the problems with the correct form of the verbs.

fight gossip ignore play ~~tease~~ threaten

Your problems

Post your problems here and get advice from our readers.

Some girls in my class often ¹ _tease_ me about my clothes. My friends say I should ² _____ them, but it's really difficult not to react. I feel really upset all the time.

A boy at school has a really embarrassing picture of me and he and his friends are ³ _____ to post it online. I don't want everyone in the school to see it and ⁴ _____ about me. What should I do?

Last week, I ⁵ _____ a joke on a friend and he got really mad. Now he says he's going to hit me. I don't want to ⁶ _____ with him. What's the best way to say I'm sorry?

I can use ten phrases with *do* and *make*.

I can use six phrases related to bullying.

Vocabulary

Man-made and natural problems

← Student Book P.36

1 Match the issues 1–6 with the headlines A–F.

1 flood _____D_____   4 disease _____

2 heat wave _____   5 pollution _____

3 overpopulation _____   6 drought _____

(A) **Eating nuts possibly protects against cancer, say scientists**

(B) **Experts predict that there won't be enough homes, schools, or hospitals in 2025**

(C) CO₂ EMISSIONS LOWEST SINCE THE 1920S

(D) WATER LEVELS RISING AS HEAVY RAIN CONTINUES

(E) **Take only one shower a day to save water**

(F) TEMPERATURES IN PHOENIX, ARIZONA, TO REACH 42°C BY THURSDAY

2 Complete the words in the article.

Humans vs. Trees

We have lost about half of the world's original forests and we lose more every year. Here are two very important reasons to save our trees.

🍂 Trees keep our planet at a safe temperature. As we lose our forests, the Earth gets hotter and there are more ¹h _eat_____ w _aves_____. Hot weather sometimes causes ²w_____ and then we lose even more trees. Therefore, losing forests is both a cause and an effect of ³c_____ c_____.

🍂 When there aren't enough trees to absorb water, rain quickly causes ⁴f_____. This is a serious issue in Haiti in the Caribbean, which has lost large numbers of trees. It becomes difficult to grow food, and people are at risk of ⁵d_____ like cholera and malaria.

Environmental problems and solutions ← Student Book P.40

3 Choose the correct verbs to complete the sentences.

1 In the U.S., people **protect / recycle** about 34% of their trash.

2 It's possible that the world will **run out / throw away** of chocolate because more people are eating it.

3 The Sumatran orangutan is at risk of **recycling / becoming extinct**. The population is only about 7,500.

4 To **reuse / save** electricity, put your desk in a place with a lot of natural light.

5 Use less plastic to help **protect / reduce** fish and other ocean species.

4 Complete the poster with the verbs.

protect   recycle   reduce   reuse   ~~save~~   throw away

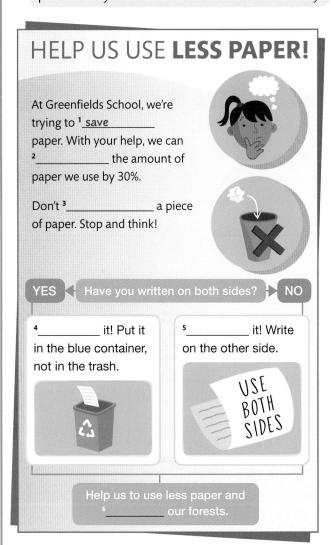

HELP US USE **LESS PAPER!**

At Greenfields School, we're trying to ¹ _save_____ paper. With your help, we can ²_____ the amount of paper we use by 30%.

Don't ³_____ a piece of paper. Stop and think!

YES ◄ Have you written on both sides? ► NO

⁴_____ it! Put it in the blue container, not in the trash.

⁵_____ it! Write on the other side.

USE BOTH SIDES

Help us to use less paper and ⁶_____ our forests.

 I **can** use vocabulary for man-made and natural problems.

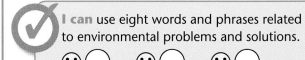 I **can** use eight words and phrases related to environmental problems and solutions.

Truth and lies ← Student Book P.46

1 Match the verbs 1–5 with the definitions a–e.

1 make up ___a___
2 promise _____
3 believe _____
4 admit _____
5 pretend _____

a invent (a story, etc.)
b behave in a way that makes people believe something that isn't true
c say you'll do something
d confess, say you did something
e think (someone) is telling the truth

2 Complete the story with the verbs.

admits   believe   lying   made up
pretends   promises   tell the truth   trust

The Boy Who Cried Wolf

The Boy Who Cried Wolf is a story about a boy who looks after sheep near his village. One day, the boy is bored, so he ¹_pretends___ to see a wolf. "Help! Wolf!" he shouts. The people in the village ²_____ that the boy and the sheep are in danger, so they run to help. When the boy ³_____ that he was playing a joke on them, the villagers are very annoyed.

The boy ⁴_____ not to do it again, but a few days later, he shouts "Wolf!" The villagers come running, and again, the boy says he ⁵_____ the story. Now the villagers are really mad.

The next day, the boy sees a real wolf. "Help!" he shouts. "Wolf!" Everyone thinks the boy is ⁶_____. "Ignore him," the villagers say. No one comes to help and the boy loses all his sheep.

The story teaches an important lesson: ⁷_____ if you want people to ⁸_____ you.

Nouns ending with -ion
← Student Book P.50

3 Complete the chart with the noun form of the verbs.

act   connect   explain   decide
discuss   imagine   invent   prepare

-tion	-sion	-ation
action	_____	_____
_____	_____	_____
_____	_____	_____

4 Complete the second sentence so that it has a similar meaning to the first. Use a noun formed from the bold verbs and the words in parentheses.

1 We **discussed** climate change for a long time.
   We had a long
   _discussion about climate change_____. (about)

2 You **described** the book really well.
   You gave a really good
   _____. (of)

3 Did Rob **invite** you to his party?
   Did you get an
   _____? (to)

4 Messaging is my favorite way to **communicate**.
   My favorite form
   _____. (of)

5 My brother has **collected** a lot of soccer magazines.
   My brother has a big
   _____. (of)

6 I like both flavors of ice cream, so it isn't easy to **decide**!
   I like both flavors of ice cream, so it's a
   _____! (difficult)

 I can use eight words and phrases related to truth and lies.

 **I can** use twelve nouns ending with -ion.

Getting along

Vocabulary

Relationship verbs ← Student Book P.58

1 Read the definitions and complete the puzzle with the missing words. What is the mystery word in the orange squares?

```
1 A T T R A C T E D
        2
    3
      4
  5
      6
```

1 be … to someone: think someone is good-looking
2 ask someone …: invite someone to go on a date
3 have an …: have an angry conversation
4 make …: end a disagreement
5 … in love: start having very strong feelings for someone
6 … up: end a relationship

2 Complete the missing words in the conversation with the correct form of the verbs.

Gina: What happened after school? Did you
¹a_s__k_ Lara o_u__t_?

Toby: Yes, I did, and she wants to ²g____
o____ a d____ ____ ____ with me.

Gina: That's awesome!

Toby: I guess. But now I'm not sure. I'm
³a____ ____ ____ ____ ____ ____ ____ ____
to Lara, but I ⁴m____ ____ ____ Emily. I think
I should ⁵m____ ____ ____ u____ with her.

Gina: But your relationship with Emily was a disaster.
You ⁶h____ ____ an
a____ ____ ____ ____ ____ ____ ____
nearly every day when you were together.

Toby: I know Emily and I didn't always ⁷g____ ____
a____ ____ ____ ____, but I love her. I made
a big mistake when I ⁸b____ ____ ____ ____
u____ with her.

Gina: Oh, Toby! Why didn't you decide this
yesterday? Poor Lara!

Expressing emotions ← Student Book P.62

3 What are the people doing? Look at the pictures and complete the sentences with the verbs.

> crying   hugging   laughing
> ~~shouting~~   staring   sulking

1 The man in the blue jacket is _shouting____.
2 The other customers are _____ at him.

3 The girl is _____.
4 Her mom is _____ her.

5 The boy is _____.
6 His parents are _____.

4 Complete the text messages. Use the correct forms of four of the verbs in exercise 3.

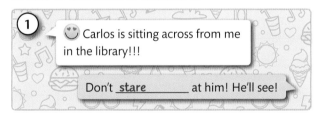

① Carlos is sitting across from me in the library!!!

Don't _stare____ at him! He'll see!

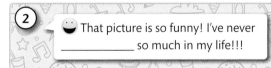

② That picture is so funny! I've never _____ so much in my life!!!

③ That was NOT A GOAL! I want to _____ at my TV!

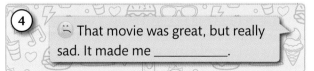

④ That movie was great, but really sad. It made me _____.

Vocabulary

Sense verbs and adjectives

← Student Book P.68

1 ~~Cross out~~ the adjective that *isn't* possible.

1 The milk smells **disgusting** / ~~smooth~~ / **fresh**.

2 This curry tastes very **soft** / **sweet** / **spicy**.

3 This chair isn't very comfortable. It feels **hard** / **colorful** / **rough**.

4 Your hair looks really **shiny** / **smooth** / **sour** today.

5 There's too much sugar in this tea. It tastes **hard** / **disgusting** / **sweet**.

6 I love this scarf because it feels really **soft** / **smooth** / **salty** against my skin.

2 Complete the tips with the words.

> disgusting feel feel fresh
> ~~look~~ rough smell taste

Your favorite life hacks

Life hacks are little tips that make life easier. Do you have a useful life hack to share?

If you want your hair to ¹ _look_____ really shiny, put yoghurt on it. Wait until the yoghurt is dry and then wash your hair. I admit that it feels a bit ² _____, but it works!

Tallulah, 15

Try making pancakes with just bananas and eggs. They ³ _____ sweet and you don't have to add sugar. They ⁴ _____ pretty good when they're cooking, too.

Louise, 15

Put your jeans in the freezer before you go to bed. They'll ⁵ _____ a bit cold when you put them on in the morning, but they'll smell really ⁶ _____. It's easier than washing them!

Jayden, 16

If you add coconut oil to your bath, your skin will ⁷ _____ really smooth. I used to have ⁸ _____ skin on my feet, but not anymore!

Sam, 17

Sleep ← Student Book P.72

3 Complete the sentences 1–6 with the words and match them with the sentences a–f.

> awake bed ~~dreams~~ nightmare
> snores yawn

1 I often have _dreams_____ about soccer. _c_

2 I lay _____ for hours last night. ____

3 My brother _____. ____

4 I had a _____ last night. ____

5 Don't _____ when people are talking to you. ____

6 Don't lie in _____ all morning. ____

a All my teeth fell out. It was horrible.

b Get up and do something useful.

c ~~They're usually about winning the World Cup.~~

d I was feeling anxious about my exams.

e Luckily, we don't share a room.

f They'll think you're bored.

4 Complete the missing words in the article. Use the correct forms of the verbs.

Why do we yawn?

We ¹y _awn_____ about eight times a day. But why? A common explanation is that it helps us to breathe in more oxygen and ²f_____ less s_____. However, this is probably a myth.

Scientists now think that yawning stops our brains getting too hot – like an electric fan. Our body temperature is highest just before we ³f_____ a_____. It goes down during the night and increases again when we ⁴w_____ u_____. That might explain why we yawn the most when we're ⁵l_____ i_____ b_____ at night and just after getting up in the morning.

 I can use four verbs and twelve adjectives related to the senses.

 I can use nine verbs and phrases related to sleep.

Vocabulary

Positive actions ← Student Book P.80

1 Match the sentence halves.

1 If you don't want this old sofa, donate ___f___

2 Let's start _____

3 We spent all day picking up _____

4 I'm looking after _____

5 If you're bored, you can give _____

6 We raised _____

a a campaign to save the park.

b litter at the beach.

c me a hand in the kitchen.

d my little sister this evening.

e over $100 by selling cookies.

f ~~it to charity.~~

2 Complete the missing words in the poster.

SAVE ALBANY LIBRARY!

Albany Library is a place for people of all ages in the community to read, learn, and meet each other. We've started a ¹c_ampaign___ to save it.

PLEASE JOIN US!

How can I help?

- ²D_____ books. If you have any books or DVDs that you don't want anymore, please give them to us!

- ³V_____. If you have time, please come and give us a ⁴h_____. You'll help people and get useful work experience at the same time.

- Organize an event to ⁵r_____ money. If you have an idea, we'd love to hear it!

Helping: people and places
← Student Book P.84

3 Find five more words and phrases to complete the chart.

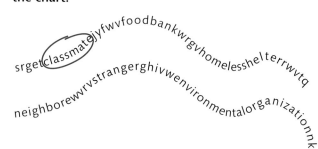

srget(classmate)jyfwvfoodbankwrgvhomelessshelterrwvtq
neighborewwrvstrangerghivwenvironmentalorganizationnk

People	Places
classmate	

4 Complete the sentences with the words.

animal shelters   senior citizens
~~strangers~~   teammates   thrift stores

1 Try to help everyone, not just your friends.
___Strangers_____ are just friends you haven't met yet!

2 _____ have more life experience than you do. Listen to them and you might learn something!

3 People should get their pets from _____. There are a lot of abandoned cats and dogs that need new homes.

4 It's important for _____ to help each other. If we work together, we all win.

5 Shopping at _____ is good for the environment. Why buy new clothes when you can reuse old ones?

 I can use seven verbs and phrases for positive actions.

 **I can** use ten nouns related to helping.

Creativity: adjectives ← Student Book P.90

1 Choose the best adjectives to complete the sentences.

1 Don't put the dress in the washing machine. It's very …

  a original.   (**b**) delicate.   **c** clever.

2 This designer makes jewelry from parts of old computers and other … materials.

  a old-fashioned   **b** enormous   **c** recycled

3 I don't like modern art. It's … and I don't understand it.

  a strange   **b** original   **c** ancient

4 We don't have space in the living room for that sculpture. It's …

  a delicate!   **b** tiny!   **c** enormous!

5 That's a very … idea! Let's include it in our project.

  a clever   **b** recycled   **c** old-fashioned

6 The … microchip in this toothbrush allows it to play music through your teeth.

  a ancient   **b** strange   **c** tiny

2 Replace the green words with the adjectives.

> ~~ancient~~ delicate enormous
> old-fashioned original

The Metropolitan Museum of Art

At the Metropolitan Museum in New York City's famous Fifth Avenue, you can experience 5,000 years of art, from ¹really old _ancient_ civilizations to the present day.

There are thousands of beautiful things, from ²new and different _____ modern paintings and sculptures to ³not modern _____ furniture and ⁴small and intricate _____ jewelry.

With a total area of more than 1,800,000 square meters, the museum is ⁵really big _____ and you can easily spend all day here.

Creativity: verbs ← Student Book P.94

3 Complete the phrases with the verbs.

> build compose ~~design~~ discover invent set up

1 _design_ a poster
2 _____ a song
3 _____ a cure for a disease
4 _____ a house
5 _____ a company
6 _____ a new product

4 Complete the timeline with the simple past form of appropriate verbs.

2000s: NASA ¹d _iscovered_ water on Mars.

1900s: Tim Berners-Lee ²c_____ the first web page.

1800s: Gustave Eiffel ³d_____ the Eiffel Tower in Paris.

1700s: Mozart ⁴c_____ his Requiem.

1600s: The artist Velázquez ⁵p_____ *Las Meninas*.

1500s: Galileo Galilei ⁶i_____ the first thermometer.

1400s: The Inca ⁷b_____ Machu Picchu.

 I can use nine adjectives related to creativity.

 **I can** use eight verbs related to creativity.

Vocabulary

Grammar

1 Body and mind

Use of gerund (-ing form)

The gerund is the -ing form of the verb. We use a gerund:

- like a noun, as the subject of a sentence.

  Speaking in public makes a lot of people feel anxious.

- after some verbs, for example: *enjoy, finish, hate, like, love, practice, start,* and *suggest.*

  *My friend **suggested going** to the movie theater.*

- after a preposition, for example, *about, after, at, before, by, for, in, of, on, to,* and *with.*

  *He's upset **about losing** the soccer game.*

 The gerund has the same form as the -ing verbs we use in the present progressive: base form + -ing.

- consonant + -e: take off the -e

  ride ➜ *riding* (NOT ~~rideing~~)

- stressed vowel + consonant (except *y*): double the final consonant

  run ➜ *running*

1 Find and correct four more spelling mistakes in the green gerund forms. One form is correct.

1 ~~Shareing~~ personal information online isn't a good idea.

   Sharing _____

2 Buy your ticket before geting on the bus. _____

3 I need to practice speakking in public. _____

4 Can you finish cleaning your room, please? _____

5 I'm frightened of loseing my wallet. _____

6 Visitting the Grand Canyon is an amazing experience. _____

2 Complete the sentences with the gerund form of the verbs.

1 I love _playing_____ (play) the guitar.

2 We wanted to have a cookout, but it started _____ (rain).

3 _____ (run) is exhausting. I prefer soccer.

4 I'm embarrassed about _____ (forget) his name.

5 _____ (ride) my bike on a sunny day makes me happy.

6 Always brush your teeth before _____ (go) to bed.

3 Complete the article with the gerund form of the verbs. Then match the gerunds 1–6 with the uses a–c.

¹ _Visiting_____ (visit) Australia was Eric's dream. There was just one problem: he was really frightened of ² _____ (fly). ³ _____ (take) a boat wasn't an option because the journey took 40 days and cost $4,000!

Eric's teacher suggested ⁴ _____ (learn) more about planes to help with his phobia, and gave him a book. After ⁵ _____ (study) the science of flying, Eric understood how planes work and why they're safe.

Eric flew to Australia a year later and now he loves ⁶ _____ (travel) by plane. "We're often frightened of things that we don't understand," he says. "All I needed was the right information."

a Gerund as a subject _____1_____ _____

b Gerund after some verbs _____ _____

c Gerund after a preposition _____ _____

I can use gerunds (-ing forms).

😊◯ 🙂◯ ☹◯

Use of infinitives; Gerund or infinitive?

The infinitive is *to* + the base form of the verb.
We use an infinitive:

- to talk about purpose.

  *I'm going to Denver **to visit** my cousins.*

  *She didn't offer **to help**.*

- after some verbs, for example: *decide, expect, learn, need, offer, plan,* and *want.*

  *We **decided to see** a science fiction movie.*

- after adjectives.

  *It's **rude to use** your cell phone at the table.*

4 Complete the chart with the infinitives 1–6 in the text message conversation.

> Why did you go to the mall?

> ¹**To buy** some new sneakers. I also needed ²**to look for** a birthday present for my sister.

> Did you get anything?

> No! It's impossible ³**to find** things that she likes. What did you do?

> I went to the beach ⁴**to have** a surfing lesson.

> Awesome! Was it fun?

> Yes, it was. It was difficult ⁵**to stand up** on the board, but I did it.

> I can't believe you learned ⁶**to do** that in your first lesson! That's amazing!

Infinitive of purpose	Infinitive after a verb	Infinitive after an adjective
_1_ ____	____ ____	____ ____

5 Complete the questions and answers with the pairs of verbs. Use the correct tense for the first verb.

> decide / go out   learn / drive   need / earn
> ~~offer / cook~~   plan / study   want / be

1 "Did you _offer to cook_____ dinner for your parents?"

"Yes, I did, but they _____ for a meal."

2 "What are you _____ in college next year?"

"Medicine. I _____ a doctor."

3 "Is your sister going to _____?"

"She wants to, but she _____ a lot of money first so that she can buy a car and pay for driving lessons."

6 Complete the article with the gerund or infinitive form of the verbs.

How to STRESS less

Talk to someone

¹ _Sharing_____ (share) our problems often makes them seem less important. It's always useful ² _____ (get) another person's opinion, too.

Sleep

³ _____ (sleep) is often difficult when we're stressed, but it's very important. We all need ⁴ _____ (have) about eight hours' sleep to feel good the next day. Plan ⁵ _____ (go) to bed at the same time every night and read a book ⁶ _____ (help) you relax.

Breathe

⁷ _____ (breathe) too quickly is both a cause and an effect of stress. Learn ⁸ _____ (think) about the way you breathe.

Think positive

When times are difficult, it's easy ⁹ _____ (forget) about the good things in our lives. Every evening, write down the things that you enjoyed ¹⁰ _____ (do) that day and the moments that made you smile. There are probably more than you realize!

I can use infinitives and gerunds.

Follow the rules

be allowed to, let, and make

We use *be allowed to* and *let* to talk about permission.

Be allowed to do something means "have permission to do something."

> **I'm allowed to use** my mom's laptop.
> (= I have permission to use my mom's laptop.)

Let someone do something means "give someone permission to do something."

> My mom **lets me use** her laptop.
> (= My mom gives me permission to use her laptop.)

We use *make someone do something* to talk about obligation.

> My parents **make me wash** the dishes.
> (= My parents say I have to wash the dishes.)

---

1 Complete the sentences with *let* or *allowed*.

1 I'm not _allowed_ to go to the party.

2 Do your teachers _____ you use cell phones in class?

3 We don't _____ people eat their own food in our coffee shop.

4 You aren't _____ to use calculators in the exam.

5 My brothers _____ me go mountain biking with them.

6 We're _____ to have a cookout this weekend!

2 Replace the green words with the correct form of *make* and any other necessary words.

1 My mom **says I have to clean** my room.
   makes me clean

2 Do your teachers **tell you to do** a lot of homework?
   _____

3 Grandma **doesn't tell us to go** to bed at 11 p.m.!
   _____

4 Joe's parents never **tell him to do** chores.
   _____

5 The soccer coach **says the players have to get up** at 6 a.m.
   _____

6 Does your school **say that you have to wear** a uniform?
   _____

3 Complete the message with the correct form of *allow*, *let*, or *make*.

How are you? I'm staying with my Uncle Pete and I'm having a great time! He's much more relaxed than my parents and he **¹** _lets_ me do what I want!

My parents always **²** _____ me start my homework at 5 p.m., but Uncle Pete **³** _____ me relax first. And I'm **⁴** _____ to have my dinner on the sofa. Mom always **⁵** _____ us eat at the table and she doesn't **⁶** _____ us watch TV when we're eating.

I'm **⁷** _____ to invite friends over this weekend, so do you want to come here on Saturday evening to play computer games? Uncle Pete **⁸** _____ me borrow his Xbox!

I can use *be allowed to*, *let*, and *make*.

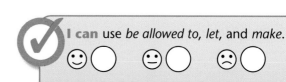

Zero conditional; Conditional imperative

We use the zero conditional to talk about things that always happen.

If you score the most goals, you win the game.

(The second action is always the result of the first action.)

We use the conditional imperative to give instructions and advice.

If you go to the supermarket, buy some milk.

A conditional sentence has two parts, or *clauses*: an *if* clause and a main clause.

We can change the order of the two clauses. When the *if* clause comes first, we put a comma after it.

If + simple present	simple present
If we talk in the library,	we **get** into trouble.

Simple present	*if* + simple present
We **get** into trouble	**if** we talk in the library.

If + simple present	imperative
If you go out,	**wear** a jacket.

Imperative	*if* + simple present
Wear a jacket	**if** you go out.

4 Write *if* in the correct place in the sentences.

1 __If__ you see a bear, _____ don't give it any food.

2 _____ Sam gets upset _____ nobody posts comments on his blog.

3 _____ you go by bus, _____ the trip takes three hours.

4 _____ you burn your finger, _____ put it under cold water.

5 _____ hot chocolate is delicious _____ you add chili.

6 _____ I feel tired _____ I don't sleep for eight hours.

5 Write instructions. Use *if* and add a comma if necessary.

1 you / have / a coffee / please / wash / your cup

   If you have a coffee, please wash your cup.
   _____

2 not wear / flip-flops / you / hike / in the mountains

   _____
   _____

3 you / have / any old clothes / put / them / in this box

   _____
   _____

4 you / have / a picnic / not leave / trash / on the beach

   _____
   _____

5 take / this medicine / you / have / a headache

   _____
   _____

6 you / take / pictures / please / not use / a flash

   _____
   _____

6 Add *five* words to the second sentence so that it has a similar meaning to the first. Add a comma if necessary. (Contracted forms count as one word.)

1 I don't eat tomatoes because they make me feel sick.

   If I _eat tomatoes, I feel sick_____.

2 Do you like jazz? Then come to our concert!

   Come to _____ jazz!

3 Smile! It helps people to feel more relaxed.

   If you _____ feel more relaxed.

4 Don't take the subway without buying a ticket.

   Buy _____ the subway.

5 I don't add extra sugar to cereal.

   If I eat _____ sugar.

6 Don't worry about making mistakes. It's normal!

   If _____.
   It's normal!

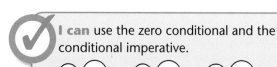 **I can** use the zero conditional and the conditional imperative.

3

Grammar

will / won't: future predictions

We use *will / won't* + base form to make predictions about the future based on our opinion, not on evidence.

We often use *will* after *I think* and *I don't think*.

> **I think** electric cars **will be** very popular.
>
> **I don't think** people **will live** in space.
> (NOT ~~I think people won't live in space.~~)

We can contract *will* with subject pronouns.

> *In 20 years, we'll (= will) go on vacation in space.*

Won't is the contracted form of *will not*.

> *We probably **won't** (= will not) find life on other planets.*

Affirmative

I / You / He / She / It / We / You / They	**will**	win	a Nobel Prize.

Negative

I / You / He / She / It / We / You / They	**won't**	live	on Earth in 2050.

Questions

Will	I / you / he / she / it / we / you / they	be	famous?

Short answers

Yes,	I / you / he / she / it / we / you / they	**will.**
No,		**won't.**

1 Complete the sentences with *will* / *'ll* or *won't*.

1 I think we **'ll** see more floods in the next ten years. They're a big problem in a lot of places.

2 I don't think people _____ stop buying books. People will always enjoy reading.

3 Malls _____ exist in 2025. We'll buy everything online.

4 I'm not worried about climate change. I think scientists _____ find a solution.

5 Overpopulation _____ be a big problem in the future. There are already too many people.

6 Teenagers _____ go to school in 2030. It won't be necessary for humans to learn anything.

2 Complete the questions. Then write short answers with your predictions for 2050.

In 2050 …

1 **Will people work** _____
(people / work)?
No, they won't. _____

2 _____
(the cell phone / exist)?
_____

3 _____
(humans / live) on Mars?
_____

4 _____
(robots / be) more intelligent than humans?
_____

5 _____
(climate change / continue) to be a problem?
_____

3 Complete the conversation with *will* / *'ll* or *won't* and the verbs.

be   be   be   cost   ~~go~~   happen   return   see

Joe: An organization in Europe wants to send 24 people to live on Mars in the next ten years.

Ali: Yes, I read about it. But [1] **will** people really **go** to Mars in 2026? It's hard to believe.

Joe: I agree. I can't imagine going! It's a one-way trip, so the astronauts [2] _____ to Earth. They [3] _____ their friends or families again.

Ali: [4] _____ it _____ possible to use Skype on Mars?

Joe: No, it won't. It's too far.

Ali: That's terrible!

Joe: I know. But a lot of people don't think the mission [5] _____. Some scientists think it [6] _____ too much money. Others don't think the technology [7] _____ safe. They say it [8] _____ possible to live on Mars for more than two or three months.

Ali: Well, I definitely don't want to go, then!

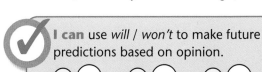
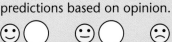

I can use *will* / *won't* to make future predictions based on opinion.

be going to: future predictions

We use subject + *be* + *going to* + base form to make predictions when we have concrete evidence – for example, something we know or can see helps us make that prediction.

> The other team is winning 8–0. **We're going to lose** the game.

Remember!

We can also use *be going to* to talk about plans and intentions.

> **We're going to visit** my cousins this weekend. (We've decided to visit my cousins.)

Affirmative			
I'm / You're / He's / She's / It's / We're / You're / They're	**going to**	**be**	late.

Negative		
I'm **not** / You **aren't** / He **isn't** / She **isn't** / It **isn't** / We **aren't** / You **aren't** / They **aren't**	**going to**	win.

Questions			
Am I / **Are** you / **Is** he / **Is** she / **Is** it / **Are** we / **Are** you / **Are** they	**going to**	miss	the bus?

Short answers	
Yes,	I **am** / you **are** / he **is** / she **is** / it **is** / we **are** / you **are** / they **are**.
No,	I'm **not** / you **aren't** / he **isn't** / she **isn't** / it **isn't** / we **aren't** / you **aren't** / they **aren't**.

4 Match 1–5 with a–e and complete the sentences with the correct form of *be going to*.

1 There's a heat wave in Miami right now. ___a___
2 Henry has eaten seven chocolate cookies. _____
3 It's 5 a.m. and I haven't slept at all. _____
4 It's sunny and the sky is blue. _____
5 Stop fighting with your brother! _____

a We _aren't going to need_____ (not need) our coats.
b You _____ (hurt) him!
c I _____ (be) exhausted tomorrow.
d He _____ (feel) sick.
e It _____ (not rain) today.

5 Write questions with *be going to*. Then write short answers.

1 I / fall / ?
   _Am I going to fall?_____
   _No___, you _aren't_. Don't worry!

2 they / run out / of / pizza / ?
   _____
   _____, they _____. There's only one piece left.

3 we / miss / the plane / ?
   _____
   _____, we _____. This traffic isn't moving at all.

4 Jones / win / ?
   _____
   _____, he _____. He's behind all the other runners.

5 it / snow / ?
   _____
   _____, it _____. This trip is a disaster!

6 Complete the sentences with the correct form of *will* or *be going to* and the verbs.

> not arrive   be   not enjoy   love   shoot   ~~steal~~

1 Leave your laptop here. I don't think anyone _will steal_____ it.

2 The train left 30 minutes late, so it _____ on time.

3 Kim's only 6, but she loves performing on stage. I think she _____ a famous actor when she's older.

4 The book was OK, but I probably _____ the movie.

5 Look! Gómez has the ball. He _____!

6 Be positive! Everyone _____ your music!

I can use *be going to* to make future predictions based on present evidence.

 ☺ ○   ☺ ○   ☹ ○

Grammar

First conditional

We use the first conditional to talk about possible or probable future events.

*If we **miss** the bus, we**'ll be** late for school.*

(The second action will be the future result of the first action.)

A conditional sentence has two parts, or *clauses*: an *if* clause and a main clause.

We can change the order of the two clauses. When the *if* clause comes first, we put a comma after it.

If + simple present	will / won't
If you lie all the time,	people **won't** trust you.

will / won't	if + simple present
People **won't** trust you	**if** you lie all the time.

1 Match 1–6 with a–f to make sentences and questions.

1 If you have a birthday party, ___f___

2 If I wear this sweater to school, _____

3 No one will understand you _____

4 She'll never make new friends _____

5 If I show you my new dress, _____

6 Zac's mom won't let him go out _____

a if you don't speak more clearly.

b will you give me your honest opinion?

c if she doesn't talk to anyone.

d if he doesn't do his chores.

e everyone will tease me.

f ~~who will you invite?~~

2 Find and correct one mistake in each sentence.

1 My parents (are) mad if I spend all my money this weekend.

  will be

2 What will happen if I'll click on this link?

  _____

3 If we'll score one more goal, we'll win the game.

  _____

4 If I get some money for my birthday, I buy a skateboard.

  _____

5 I don't go to Erica's party if you don't come with me.

  _____

6 We need to leave now. If we arrive late, they don't let us see the play.

  _____

3 Write first conditional sentences with *if* in the correct position. Check (✓) the ideas you agree with.

Hallo! **Hi!** **Ciao!** **Hola!** **Salut!**

Language learning: truth or myth?

Here are some ideas that people have about learning English. In your opinion, which are true and which are myths?

1 you / learn / more quickly / you / not be / frightened of making mistakes

  You'll learn more quickly if you aren't frightened of

  making mistakes. ☐

2 you / read / in English / you / learn / a lot of vocabulary

  _____

  _____ ☐

3 you / never speak / English / well / you / not live / in an English-speaking country

  _____

  _____ ☐

4 you / practice / speaking / with other students / you / learn / from their mistakes

  _____

  _____ ☐

5 you / not be / naturally good at languages / it / not be / possible to learn English

  _____

  _____ ☐

6 you / forget / the language / quickly / you / not use / it

  _____

  _____ ☐

I can use the first conditional.

😊 ◯ 🙂 ◯ ☹ ◯

Grammar

Modals: *might, must,* and *can't*

might (not)

We use *might* and *might not* to talk about actions or events that are possible in the present.

> The information **might not be** true.

We also use *might* and *might not* to talk about possible events in the future.

> It **might snow** tomorrow.

must

We use *must* to talk about something that we are certain is true in the present.

> Congratulations – you won the game! You **must be** very pleased.

can't

We use *can't* to talk about something that we are certain *isn't* true in the present.

> Kim lives 2,000 km from her grandparents. She **can't see** them very often.

Remember!

Can't and *must* also have other meanings.

can't = not able to; not allowed to

> I **can't** swim.
>
> You **can't** eat hot food on the bus.

must = have to

> You **must** finish exercise 7 for homework.

---

4 Choose the correct words. Does each sentence refer to the present or the future? Write *P* or *F*.

1 "Do you know that boy?"
   "No, but he **might** / **might not** be Emily's
   brother. They have the same color hair."   __P__

2 "Should we make a cake for Grandma's birthday?"
   "I don't think so. Grandma never eats sweet
   food, so she **might** / **might not** like it."   _____

3 "Why aren't the other students here?"
   "They **might** / **might not** know which
   classroom we're in. We aren't usually in this
   room on Tuesdays."   _____

4 "Do we need to buy more burgers for the cookout?"
   "Yes, we do. A lot of people are coming and
   we **might** / **might not** run out of meat."   _____

5 "I think Tim is annoyed with me, but I don't know why."
   "You probably didn't do anything wrong.
   He **might** / **might not** be stressed about his exams."   _____

5 Complete the sentences with *must* or *can't* and the verbs.

> be   clean   enjoy   have   serve   ~~sleep~~

1 Max drinks coffee all day. He _can't sleep_____ well.

2 I can't believe you ran 20 km! You _____
   exhausted.

3 Look at the mess in this room! You _____
   it very often.

4 Her house has seven bedrooms. She _____
   a lot of money.

5 That pizzeria is always crowded. It _____
   good pizza.

6 The presenter looks very anxious. He _____
   speaking in public.

6 Complete the conversation with *might, might not, must,* or *can't,* and the verbs.

Leah: I found a cell phone at
        my house after the
        sleepover. It's dark
        pink. Is it yours?

Emma: It [1] _can't be_____
        (be) mine. I'm
        talking to you on
        my phone right
        now!

Leah: Yes, that's true! I
        [2] _____ (be) tired!

Emma: Andrea's favorite color is pink. She
        [3] _____ (have) a
        pink cell phone case.

Leah: Andrea sent me a text earlier, so it
        [4] _____ (be) hers.

Emma: Hmm. Zara and Libby also sent
        texts after the sleepover, so they
        [5] _____
        (have) their phones. The only
        other person there was Ruby, so it
        [6] _____ (be) hers.

Leah: But why hasn't Ruby called me?

Emma: She [7] _____
        (know) your number – it's probably in
        her phone. Or maybe she's busy. She
        [8] _____ (call) you
        later. Who knows?

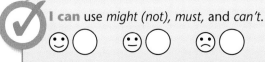

I can use *might (not), must,* and *can't.*

Present perfect: *just, already,* and *yet*

We use *just, already,* and *yet* with the present perfect.

We use *just* in affirmative present perfect sentences to say that something has happened very recently.

> *Peter **has just** called.*
> (= Peter called a moment ago.)

We use *already* in affirmative present perfect sentences to say that something has happened early, or earlier than expected.

> *"Can you set the table?" "I**'ve already done** it."*

We use *yet* in negative present perfect sentences to say that something hasn't happened, but that we expect it to happen.

> *Nick and Ben **haven't arrived yet**.*
> (= They haven't arrived, but they will.)

We use *yet* in present perfect questions to ask if something has happened.

> *"**Have** you **eaten yet**?" "No, I haven't."*

Remember!

We form the present perfect with the verb *have* and a past participle.

The past participle form of regular verbs is the same as the simple past: base form + *-ed*.

Some verbs have irregular past participles. (See the Irregular verbs list at the back of the book.)

1 Complete the sentences. Use *just* and the present perfect form of the verbs. Then match them with the pictures A–F.

1 They _'ve just made up_
  (make up).   __D__

2 She _____
  (watch) a sad movie. ____

3 He _____
  (steal) a laptop. ____

4 They _____
  (run) a marathon. ____

5 It _____
  (take off). ____

6 They _____
  (get) married. ____

2 Look at Hunter's list and write sentences about the things he has and hasn't done. Use the present perfect and *already* or *yet*.

1   He's already learned
    to play the guitar.

2 _____
   _____

3 _____
   _____

4 _____

5 _____

6 _____

> **Things to do before my 16th birthday!**
>
> 1   learn to play the guitar ☑
> 2   start a blog ☑
> 3   paint my bedroom ☐
> 4   try surfing ☐
> 5   fall in love ☑
> 6   ask Lucia out ☐

3 Write sentences and questions. Use the present perfect and *just, already,* or *yet*.

1 "the train / leave / ?"
   _Has the train left yet?_____

   "No, it hasn't. You have two minutes, so run!"

2 "I'm sorry I'm late!"

   "Don't worry! I was late, too. I / arrive."

   _____

3 "I've come to help you clean the kitchen."

   "You don't need to. Look! we / do / it."

   _____

4 "Did you enjoy the article I sent you?"

   "Sorry. I / not read / it."

   _____

5 "Sophie / call / ?"

   _____

   "No, she hasn't. I hope everything's OK."

I can use the present perfect with *just, already,* and *yet*.

 ☺ ◯   ☺ ◯   ☹ ◯

used to

Affirmative			
I / You / He / She / It / We / You / They	used to	live	in Canada.
Negative			
I / You / He / She / It / We / You / They	didn't use to	like	jazz.
Questions			
Did	I / you / he / she / it / we / you / they	use to	play	soccer?
Short answers			
Yes,	I / you / he / she / it /		did.
No,	we / you / they		didn't.

We use *used to* + base form to talk about the past.

> *Where **did you use to live**?*

> *We **used to have** an apartment in San Diego.*

We use it to talk about things that happened regularly in the past, but don't happen now.

> *My grandparents **used to write** letters to each other.*

We also use it to talk about states and situations that were true in the past, but aren't true now.

> *We **didn't use to be** friends.*

 Stop To talk about regular actions in the present, we use the adverb *usually*.
*I **usually** get up early.* (NOT ~~I use to get up early.~~)

4 Complete the sentences and questions with *use* or *used*.

1 I _used_ to love playing games on my cell phone.

2 My parents didn't _____ to have a car.

3 Did you _____ to have long hair?

4 We _____ to visit my grandparents every summer.

5 My sister didn't _____ to eat meat.

6 This building _____ to be a movie theater.

5 Complete the questions with *used to* and the verbs. Then write affirmative (✓) or negative (✗) short answers.

1 " _Did you use to have_ (you / have) any pets when you were younger?"

" _Yes, we did._ (✓) We had a dog named Bob."

2 "_____ (your brother / tease) you?"

"_____ (✓) We get along much better now."

3 "_____ (your parents / let) you drink soda?"

"_____ (✗) They said it was bad for our teeth."

4 "_____ (your mom / go) to our school?"

"_____ (✗) She grew up in Colombia."

5 "_____ (you / have) a bike?"

"_____ (✓) I rode it every day."

6 Complete the questions and answers with the correct form of *used to*. Use the pairs of verbs and question words where necessary.

have / not be
listen / love
~~live / work~~
play / not enjoy

Amy: [1] _Where did_ _____ you _use to live_ _____ in the 1960s, Grandma?

Sue: In New York City. My parents [2] _used to work_ _____ there.

Amy: [3] _____ you _____ sports when you were my age?

Sue: No, I didn't. I [4] _____ sports. I preferred music.

Amy: [5] _____ teenagers _____ to in the 1960s?

Sue: My friends and I [6] _____ The Beatles. They were very popular.

Amy: [7] _____ you and your parents _____ arguments about chores?

Sue: Yes, we did. I [8] _____ very good at cleaning my room.

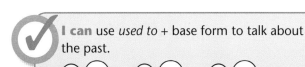 **I can** use *used to* + base form to talk about the past.

The senses

Grammar

Present perfect: *for / since*

We use the present perfect to talk about actions or states that started in the past and continue now. We use *for* and *since* to talk about the duration of these actions or states.

We use the present perfect + *for* + a period of time to talk about the length of time that an action or state has continued.

> *I've been here **for an hour**.*
>
> *Have you known your best friend **for a long time**?*

We use the present perfect + *since* + a point in time to talk about the moment when an action or state started.

> *I've had this coat **since 2015**.*
>
> *She hasn't done her chores **since last week**.*
>
> *Have they been in the library **since five o'clock**?*

We use questions with *How long … ?* to ask about the duration of an action or state.

> ***How long** have you liked spicy food?*

1 Complete the chart with the time expressions.

> ~~40 minutes~~   I was 4   lunchtime
> ten days   they got married
> 2 million years

Period of time
40 minutes
_____
_____
Point in time
_____
_____
_____

2 Complete the sentences with *for* or *since* and the best time expressions in exercise 1.

1 Why are these cookies still soft? I've baked them __for 40 minutes__ .

2 We're really hungry. We haven't eaten anything _____ .

3 Humans have existed on Earth _____ .

4 I'm pretty good at the guitar. I've played it _____ .

5 My grandparents have lived in the same house _____ .

6 I miss my best friend. He's been on vacation _____ .

3 Look at the timeline of Pierre's life. Complete the questions with the correct present perfect form of the verbs.

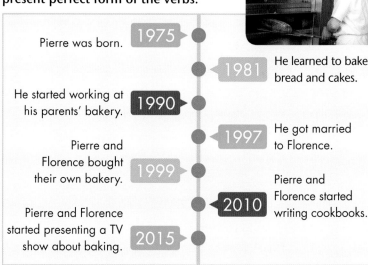

Pierre was born. **1975**

1981 He learned to bake bread and cakes.

He started working at his parents' bakery. **1990**

1997 He got married to Florence.

Pierre and Florence bought their own bakery. **1999**

2010 Pierre and Florence started writing cookbooks.

Pierre and Florence started presenting a TV show about baking. **2015**

1 How long __has Pierre baked__ (Pierre / bake) cakes?

2 _____ (Pierre / work) as a baker for a long time?

3 How long _____ (Pierre and Florence / be) married?

4 How long _____ (they / have) their bakery?

5 _____ (they / be) cookbook authors since 2000?

6 How long _____ (they / work) on TV?

4 Complete the answers to the questions in exercise 3. Use the correct present perfect forms of the verbs, *for* or *since*, and any other necessary words.

1 Pierre __has baked cakes since__ he was 6 years old.

2 Yes, he has. He _____ over 25 years.

3 They _____ 1997.

4 They _____ about 20 years.

5 No, they haven't. They_____ 2010.

6 They _____ a few years.

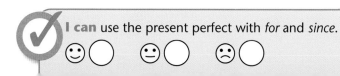

I can use the present perfect with *for* and *since*.

Simple past or present perfect?

We use the present perfect to talk about past experiences in our life. It isn't important when they happened, so we don't use past time phrases with the present perfect.

"Have you ever done anything really frightening?"

"Yes, I have. I've done a bungee jump."

We don't use the present perfect with past time phrases. We use the simple past to say when past events happened.

*I **did** a bungee jump **in 2016**.*

We can use the simple past to give more information about an experience.

*I've **done** a bungee jump. It **was** really frightening!*

5 Find and <u>underline</u> three more past time phrases. Which tense do these sentences all use?

1 He left school <u>two years ago</u>.

2 I've never seen a science fiction movie.

3 Last Sunday, we went to a Mexican restaurant.

4 In 2014, they bought their first home.

5 I finished my geography homework yesterday.

6 They've won the World Cup three times.

The underlined sentences all use the
<u>simple past</u>   .

6 Find and correct four verbs that are in the wrong tense. One sentence is correct.

1 ~~I've had~~ breakfast at 8 a.m. this morning.
   <u>I had</u>

2 Did you ever try Swedish food?
   _____

3 Oliver hasn't been at school yesterday.
   _____

4 I fell asleep on the sofa last night.
   _____

5 I've tried snowboarding. It's been fun.
   _____

6 I never rode a motorcycle. I'm 14!
   _____

7 Complete the conversation. Use the correct simple past or present perfect form of the verbs.

Meg: ¹ <u>Did you sleep</u>   (you / sleep) well last night?

Fay: No, I ² _____.
      I ³ _____ (have) a nightmare and
      ⁴ _____ (wake up) at 3 a.m.

Meg: ⁵ _____ (you / ever / have) the same nightmare more than once?

Fay: No, I ⁶ _____. How about you?

Meg: Yes, I ⁷ _____. It
      ⁸ _____ (be) horrible. Three years ago, I ⁹ _____ (dance) on stage for the first time. A few weeks before the show,
      I ¹⁰ _____ (dream) about falling off the stage. Then, the night before, I ¹¹ _____ (have) the same nightmare again.

Fay: And ¹² _____ (fall off) the stage on the night?

Meg: Of course not! It ¹³ _____ (be) fine.
      I ¹⁴ _____ (perform) on stage a lot of times since then and luckily I ¹⁵ _____ (never / feel) as anxious as that again.

I can use the simple past and the present perfect.

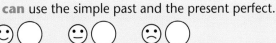
 ☺ ◯ ☺ ◯ ☹ ◯

7 Do the right thing

Grammar

would for imaginary situations

Affirmative			
I / You / He / She / It / We / You / They	'd / would	buy	a new car.

Negative			
I / You / He / She / It / We / You / They	wouldn't	live	in a city.

Questions			
Would	I / you / he / she / it / we / you / they	tell	anyone?

Short answers		
Yes,	I / you / he / she / it / we / you / they	**would.**
No,		**wouldn't.**

We use *would* and *wouldn't* + base form to talk about imaginary or hypothetical situations.

*Where **would** you **go** on your perfect vacation?*

*I'**d rent** a house next to the beach.*

*I **wouldn't stay** in a hotel.*

1 Complete the questions about Sadie's dream job. Use the correct form of *would* and the words.

1 What _would you do_____
   (you / do)?

2 What _____
   (the charity / do)?

3 _____ (it / be)
   a big charity?

4 _____ (you / work)
   in an office?

5 _____ (you / have)
   a lot of free time?

2 Match the questions 1–5 in exercise 1 with Sadie's answers a–e. Then complete the answers using the correct affirmative or negative form of *would*.

a I _'d_____ work for a charity.   __1__

b No, I _____. I _____
   work long hours, but I _____
   mind because I _____ enjoy
   my job!   ____

c It _____ help animals that
   are in danger of becoming extinct. ____

d Yes, I _____, but I _____
   be there all the time because I
   _____ travel a lot.   ____

e Yes it, _____. It _____
   be an international charity with
   offices all over the world.   ____

3 Complete the web forum with the correct form of *would* and the words.

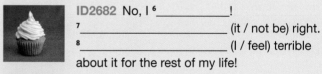

I work as a cleaner in a hotel, and today I found $200 in a guest's room after he left. I know this man is a millionaire.
¹ _What would you do_____ (what you / do) in my situation?
² _____ (you / keep) the money?

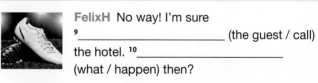

Chris_89 Yes, I ³_____. $200 isn't a lot of money if you're a millionaire. ⁴_____ (the man / not miss) it. ⁵_____ (I / spend) it on a party for my friends.

ID2682 No, I ⁶_____! ⁷_____ (it / not be) right. ⁸_____ (I / feel) terrible about it for the rest of my life!

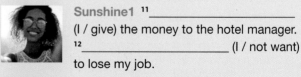

FelixH No way! I'm sure ⁹_____ (the guest / call) the hotel. ¹⁰_____ (what / happen) then?

Sunshine1 ¹¹_____ (I / give) the money to the hotel manager. ¹²_____ (I / not want) to lose my job.

L_Owen ¹³_____ (I / not say) anything, but ¹⁴_____ (I / not keep) it for me. ¹⁵_____ (I / donate) the money to charity.

 **I can** use *would* for imaginary situations.

Second conditional

We use the second conditional to talk about imaginary or hypothetical events and their results.

*If I **had** more time, I'**d help** you.*
(But I don't have a lot of time, so I can't help you.)

A conditional sentence has two parts, or *clauses*: an *if* clause and a main clause.

We can change the order of the two clauses. When the *if* clause comes first, we put a comma after it.

If + simple past	*would / wouldn't*
If I **knew** the answer,	**I'd tell** you.

would / wouldn't	*if + simple past*
I'd tell you	**if** I **knew** the answer.

Stop We can use *was* or *were* in the *if* clause after *I, he, she,* or *it*.
*If I **was** rich, I'd buy that car.*
*If I **were** rich, I'd buy that car.*

---

4 **Check (✓) the second conditional sentences that are correct.**

1 If we had some eggs, I'd make a cake. ☑
2 You'd feel better if you do more exercise. ☐
3 We'd have a party if our parents let us. ☐
4 If we sold 100 tickets, we'll raise $500. ☐
5 Mom would be mad if you lose your keys. ☐
6 If everyone donated money to charity,
 the world would be a better place. ☐

5 **Complete the sentences with the correct forms of the verbs.**

1 If they _weren't_ so sweet,
 I _'d have_ another one.
 (not be / have)

2 I _____ you if I
 _____ better at math.
 (help / be)

3 If he _____ on the Olympic
 team, he _____ a gold medal.
 (be / win)

4 If you _____ so much time on
 social media, you _____ your
 homework earlier. (not spend / finish)

5 If we _____ a bigger
 apartment, it _____ a problem.
 (have / not be)

6 I _____ pizza every day if
 I _____ in Italy. (eat / live)

6 **Add *five* words to the second sentence so that it has a similar meaning to the first. Use the second conditional. (Contracted forms count as one word.)**

1 Joey only talks to us because he's
 attracted to Kim.
 Joey _wouldn't talk to us if_
 he weren't attracted to Kim.

2 We aren't in Florida, so we can't go to
 the beach.
 _____,
 we'd go to the beach.

3 I can't call him because I don't know
 his number.
 I'd _____
 his number.

4 You're tired because you go to
 bed late.
 You _____
 went to bed earlier.

5 I want to volunteer at the food bank,
 but I don't have time.
 If _____
 at the food bank.

6 Our beaches are dirty because people
 drop litter.
 If people didn't
 _____
 be dirty.

I can use the second conditional.

Grammar

Relative clauses

We use a relative clause beginning with *who*, *that*, or *where* to give more information about a noun.

We use a relative clause beginning with …

- *who* to give more information about a person.

  A software developer is a person who creates computer programs.

- *that* to give more information about a thing.

  A 3-D printer is a machine that makes objects from plastic.

- *where* to give more information about a place.

  Salzburg, Austria, is the city where Mozart was born.

1 Match 1–5 with a–e and choose the correct relative pronoun.

1 A stylus is a thing   __c__

2 A chef is a person   _____

3 A gallery is a place   _____

4 Impressionism is a style of art   _____

5 Coyoacán is the place   _____

a **who** / **where** cooks meals in a restaurant.

b **who** / **where** the artist Frida Kahlo was born.

c **who** / **(that)** you use to write on a tablet.

d **where** / **that** you can see art exhibitions.

e **where** / **that** was popular in the 19th century.

2 Complete the relative clauses with relative pronouns and the correct form of the verbs.

🔍   + 2 items 🛒

ORIGINAL GIFT IDEAS FOR PEOPLE
WHO HAVE EVERYTHING

With this clever device, you can create your own movie theater! All you need is a room **¹** _where_ _there's_ (there / be) a big white wall. It's the perfect gift for a person **²**_____ _____ (love) movies.

This fun pink ball is a robot **³**_____ _____ (move) around your house and cleans the floor. It's great for people **⁴**_____ _____ (hate) chores. Cats love it, too!

Do you know someone **⁵**_____ _____ (enjoy) reading? Give them a reading tent and they'll always have a place **⁶**_____ _____ (they / can) relax.

3 Write answers to the questions. Use a relative clause and the words.

1 Who was David Bowie?

(a singer / was popular in the 1970s)

David Bowie was a singer who was _popular in the 1970s._

2 What is the Louvre?

(a museum / you can see the Mona Lisa)

_____

_____

3 What is Apple?

(a company / makes computers)

_____

_____

4 What is a vacuum cleaner?

(machine / cleans the floor)

_____

_____

5 Who is J.K. Rowling?

(the author / created Harry Potter)

_____

_____

6 What is Graceland?

(the house / Elvis Presley lived)

_____

_____

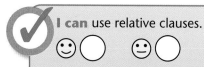 **I can** use relative clauses.

  ☺ ○   😐 ○   ☹ ○

Subject and object questions

In a subject question, the question word (*who, what,* etc.) refers to the person or thing that does the action.

> **Who** painted The Scream?
>
> **Edvard Munch** painted The Scream.

In subject questions, we don't use the auxiliary verb *do / does* in the simple present or *did* in the simple past.

In an object question, the question word (*who, what,* etc.) refers to the object of the action.

> **What** did Alexander Graham Bell invent?
>
> Alexander Graham Bell invented **the telephone**.

In object questions, we use the auxiliary verb *do / does* in the simple present and *did* in the simple past.

4 Are these subject or object questions? Write *S* or *O*.

1 Who invented the television?   <u>S</u>

2 Who did you meet at the party?   _____

3 What did you do last weekend?   _____

4 Who plays Batman in the new movie?   _____

5 What do you enjoy doing on weekends?   _____

5 Complete the questions in the interview with the correct form of the verbs.

What ¹ <u>do you do</u>_____ (you / do)?

I'm a pastry chef in a five-star hotel. I make desserts.

Who ²_____ (help) you in the kitchen?

I have a team of five chefs who help me.

What ³_____ (you / cook) last night?

Chocolate mousse and strawberry cheesecake.

Who ⁴_____ (eat) at your restaurant?

A lot of movie stars – although they don't all have dessert!

What ⁵_____ (you / enjoy) most about your job?

It's very creative. I love making desserts look beautiful.

Who ⁶_____ (you / admire)?

The French chef Gaston Lenôtre has always inspired me.

6 If the <u>underlined</u> words are the answers, what are the questions? Write questions with the correct form of the verbs.

1 <u>What does an interior designer do?</u>_____
(do)
An interior designer <u>chooses paint, furniture, carpets, etc. to decorate the inside of a building.</u>

2 _____
(write)
<u>Suzanne Collins</u> wrote *The Hunger Games.*

3 _____
(win)
Bob Dylan won <u>the Nobel Prize for Literature</u> in 2016.

4 _____
(design)
Commercial architects design <u>offices and stores.</u>

5 _____
(sing)
<u>Adele</u> sang the song for the movie *Skyfall.*

6 _____
(use)
Digital animators use <u>3-D animation software.</u>

I can use subject and object questions.

 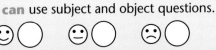

1 Read the article. Then match the summaries 1–3 with the paragraphs A–C.

1 How directors control our feelings _____
3 Why we feel emotions when we watch movies _____

2 Movies vs. real life _____

How HOLLYWOOD controls our minds

One moment we're laughing, and the next, we're biting our nails or jumping behind the sofa. We know movies aren't real, so why do we experience such strong emotions when we watch them?

A Psychologist Jeffrey Zacks answers this question in his book *Flicker: Your Brain on Movies*. According to Zacks, it's natural to copy emotions that we see. We smile when we see another person smile – even when that person is an actor in a movie. And because our bodies and minds are connected, our actions influence our feelings. When we smile, we feel happier. When we breathe fast, we start feeling stressed. When a character on screen does something embarrassing, *we* blush and feel a little embarrassed, too.

B In fact, the emotions we feel in a movie are sometimes stronger than the feelings we experience in real life. Why? In real life, Zacks explains, we can usually control our environment. We can choose what we look at or listen to. We can stop talking to someone or move to a different place. In a movie, it isn't possible to do that. The director controls everything that we see and hear.

C Just as chefs add sugar and salt to food, directors add emotional effects to their movies to make the experience more intense. They control the cameras so that we see through the eyes of one character. They use warm or cool colors to make us feel happy or sad. And, of course, music is very important. Think of any famous movie scene. Now imagine it without the music!

2 Read again. Answer the questions.

1 Who is Jeffrey Zacks?

   <u>He's a psychologist and the author of a book about movies and</u>
   <u>the brain.</u>

2 What usually happens when we see someone smile?

   _____

3 Why does smiling make us feel happier?

   _____
   _____

4 What difference between real life and movies does the article mention?

   _____
   _____
   _____

5 According to the article, in what way are directors like chefs?

   _____
   _____

6 How do directors produce emotional reactions? Write three techniques that the article mentions.

   _____
   _____

3 Find words 1–3 in the article and choose the most appropriate definitions, a or b.

   1 _____   2 _____   3 _____

1 copy /ˈkɑpi/
   a (verb) cheat by looking at someone else's work and writing what they have written
   b (verb) imitate; behave in the same way or do the same thing as somebody else

2 character /ˈkærəktər/
   a (noun) a person in a book, play, television show, or movie
   b (noun) the qualities that make someone or something different from other people or things

3 environment /ɛnˈvaɪərnmənt/
   a (noun) the air, water, land, animals, and plants around us
   b (noun) the conditions in which you live, work, etc.

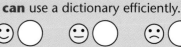 **I can** use a dictionary efficiently.

1 Read the question in the web page introduction. Then skim the responses quickly and complete A–D with *Yes* or *No*.

Strict teachers: your opinions

Strict teachers are good teachers. Do you agree?

A <u>Yes</u>

If teachers let students make a lot of noise in class, it's really difficult to concentrate. Some people in my science class are always talking really loudly and the teacher doesn't do anything. It's impossible to ignore them, but I can't say anything – in my school, people tease you if you say you enjoy studying. It's the teacher's job to make them be quiet.
Gemma, 16, U.S.

B _____

I think people learn well when they feel happy and relaxed, not when they're stressed or frightened of doing something wrong. Our math teacher is really strict and we aren't allowed to talk in class. If we make a mistake, she shouts at us. My English teacher is much more easygoing and I think I learn better in her classes.
Maxime, 15, France

C _____

Some people say that school rules are only appropriate for young children, but I don't agree. All groups of people need rules – including adults – and someone needs to make people follow those rules. That's why societies need police officers! If teachers are too easygoing, students start behaving badly. It's human nature!
Raúl, 17, Mexico

D _____

In my opinion, people are happier to follow rules if they're allowed to make them. Our geography teacher lets us make the class rules at the beginning of the school year. We agree what we should and shouldn't do and we make a contract, which the teacher puts on the wall. If someone breaks a rule, she just stands next to the contract and smiles. We usually behave well in her class, not because she's strict, but because she treats us like adults.
Holly, 16, South Africa

2 Read again. Who expresses these opinions? Write *G* (Gemma), *M* (Maxime), *R* (Raúl), or *H* (Holly).

1 It isn't easy for students to make other students follow the rules. _G_

2 Letting students make their own rules is a good idea. _____

3 It isn't easy to learn if you don't feel relaxed. _____

4 Everyone needs rules, even teenagers and adults. _____

5 Students can't work well when other students are chatting. _____

6 Treating students as equals is better than being really strict. _____

3 Complete the sentences with one word from the web page.

1 Gemma says that she can't <u>*ignore*</u> the noise in her science class.

2 She says that you can't say that you like school because people _____ you.

3 Maxime isn't _____ to talk in his math class.

4 He says that his math teacher _____ at students when they get an answer wrong.

5 Raúl says that we need strict teachers for the same reason that our societies need _____.

6 Holly's teacher lets them write their own rules and put them in a _____.

I can skim a text to get the general idea.
☺ ○   ☺ ○   ☹ ○

Reading

1 Read the article. What *won't* robots be good at in the future, according to Professor Domingos?

_____

Artificial intelligence: **three big questions**

When will we have artificial intelligence?

If you use computers, artificial intelligence (A.I.) is already part of your life. In the past, people needed to tell computers what to do. Now computers can learn new things independently. This is called machine learning. Web companies use it to study what we buy online and recommend products. Professor Pedro Domingos, a professor of computer science at the University of Washington, Seattle, says that one day we'll probably have super-intelligent computers that can learn *anything* without instructions. Domingos believes this will happen in the next 100 years and that it will change the world.

Will humans become extinct?

According to the scientist Professor Stephen Hawking, A.I. will be "the best or worst thing ever to happen to humanity." Right now, no one knows if A.I. will be good or bad, but Domingos thinks it will be mostly positive. It's possible that super-intelligent computers will find cures for diseases, help protect the environment, and predict – or even stop – natural disasters. So maybe future humans will live in a cleaner and safer world where no one gets sick and where there are no earthquakes, volcanoes, or floods.

Will robots steal people's jobs?

Domingos thinks they will. People often imagine that we won't need human cleaners or restaurant servers in the future. In fact, Domingos says, those jobs aren't at risk because robots won't be as good at carrying things and avoiding obstacles as humans. However, because robots will be extremely good at complex thinking, Domingos predicts that they'll do the jobs of doctors and lawyers better than humans.

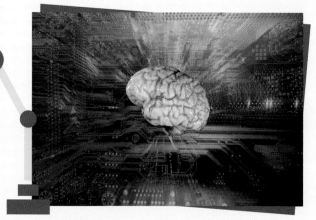

2 Read again. Choose the correct answers.

1 Domingos believes that in the next 100 years, computers …
   a won't change a lot.
   b will become super-intelligent.
   c will become less important than they are now.

2 Domingos predicts that A.I. will …
   a make the world a better place for people.
   b be dangerous for the planet.
   c be very bad news for humans.

3 According to Domingos, robots will do …
   a the jobs of cleaners and servers.
   b the jobs of doctors and lawyers.
   c all jobs.

3 Answer the questions. Use your own words where possible.

1 What can computers do now that they couldn't do in the past?
   In the past, computers couldn't learn new things on their own, but
   now they can.

2 Who uses machine learning right now and why?
   _____
   _____

3 What is Professor Stephen Hawking's prediction about A.I.?
   _____
   _____

4 Why is it possible that super-intelligent computers will make the world safer for humans?
   _____
   _____
   _____

5 In Professor Domingos's opinion, why will robots be a threat to doctors and lawyers?
   _____
   _____

I can find and understand opinions in a text.
☺○ ☺○ ☹○

1 **Scan the web forum quickly and find …**

1 the age of Casey's sister. __8__

2 a country where companies can't advertise to children. _____

3 the percentage of American children aged 3 to 14 who used the Internet in 2015. _____

4 the product that Paige saw an ad for. _____

5 the toy that Ryan wanted. _____

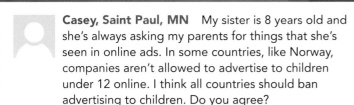

NO MORE ADS!

 Casey, Saint Paul, MN   My sister is 8 years old and she's always asking my parents for things that she's seen in online ads. In some countries, like Norway, companies aren't allowed to advertise to children under 12 online. I think all countries should ban advertising to children. Do you agree?

Tomás, Belmont, CA   Dishonest ads shouldn't be allowed, but I don't think you can stop companies advertising to children. In 2015, 66% of children aged 3 to 14 in the U.S. used the Internet. That's a lot of people! If companies stop selling products to children, they'll lose a fortune. The Internet is an amazing invention, but if you want websites to be free, you'll need to accept the ads.

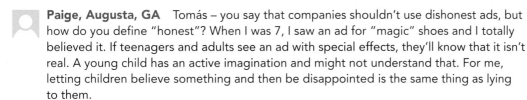

 Paige, Augusta, GA   Tomás – you say that companies shouldn't use dishonest ads, but how do you define "honest"? When I was 7, I saw an ad for "magic" shoes and I totally believed it. If teenagers and adults see an ad with special effects, they'll know that it isn't real. A young child has an active imagination and might not understand that. For me, letting children believe something and then be disappointed is the same thing as lying to them.

Ryan, Concord, NH   If children never see ads, how will they learn not to trust them? When I was about 5 or 6, I saw an ad on a cereal box for a "free" plastic dinosaur, and when Mom said I couldn't have it, I got really upset. Mom explained that it wasn't free because you needed to buy eight boxes of cereal and I didn't even like cereal – or dinosaurs! These situations can't be easy for parents, but it's important for children to learn about marketing techniques or they might make bigger mistakes when they're older.

2 **Read again. Complete the sentences with** *Tomás, Paige,* **or** *Ryan.*

1 __Ryan__ thinks it's important for people to see ads when they're young.

2 _____ doesn't think companies will stop advertising to children.

3 _____ says that children and adults respond to ads in different ways.

4 _____ says that it isn't always easy to say if an advertisement is telling the truth or not.

5 _____ thinks that advertisements for children sometimes create problems for adults.

6 _____ and _____ say they learned important lessons about advertisements when they were younger.

3 **Read again. Match the highlighted words and phrases in the web forum with the definitions.**

1 an enormous amount of money
__a fortune__

2 ways of advertising and selling products
_____

3 the use of computers or photography to show things that don't really exist
_____

4 not allow _____

5 the ability to create pictures in your mind
_____

 I can scan a text quickly for specific information.

Reading

1 **Read Eliana's blog post and check (✓) the ideas that she expresses.**

a Words aren't always enough on their own. ☐

b We probably won't need written words in the future. ☐

c Humans used pictures and symbols to communicate before there were emojis. ☐

Why I ♥ the emoji   Home | Blog | About me | Contact me

I've just read an article saying that language is at risk because young people are using emojis. I completely disagree! In today's post, I'm going to explain why.

Emojis are useful. When we speak, we don't only use words – we also use body language. We laugh, we cry, and we hug each other. In writing, especially in short messages, feelings are often more difficult to communicate. Emojis are like body language – they can show that we're teasing someone or laughing at a joke they've just made. Emojis help us get along better.

Using pictures and codes to communicate isn't new – people have already done it for thousands of years. In about 30,000 BC, people used to paint pictures on the walls of caves. When people started writing, in about 3,000 BC, they used symbols based on pictures – for example,

Ancient Egyptian hieroglyphics. Much later, in the 1800s and early 1900s, people used to send telegrams. Shorter telegrams were cheaper, so people invented codes and abbreviations in order to use fewer words.

In 1993, text messaging arrived. Text messages didn't use to be easy to type and there used to be a character limit, so people invented emoticons, like :-) and abbreviations, like LOL (laughing out loud). In 1998, Shigetaka Kurita, a Japanese designer, invented emojis. At first, you could only use emojis on a few devices, but most smartphones and tablets could read them by 2011, and they quickly became popular.

Of course, we need words to communicate exactly what we want to say. We haven't stopped using them yet and I don't believe we will. But when we use emojis and words together, we understand each other's feelings better. How can that be a bad thing? ☺

2 **Read again. What happened in these years? Complete the sentences.**

1 In about 30,000 BC,
people painted pictures in caves to
communicate with each other.

2 In about 3,000 BC,
_____

3 In the 1800s and early 1900s,
_____
_____

4 In 1993, _____
_____

5 In 1998, _____
_____

6 By 2011, _____
_____
_____

3 **Read again. Answer the questions in your own words.**

1 What has Eliana just read?
She's just read an article about emojis and their effect on language.

2 According to Eliana, in what way are emojis similar to body language?
_____
_____

3 How did people use to save money when they sent telegrams?
_____
_____

4 Why did people start using emoticons and abbreviations in text messages?
_____
_____

5 Why didn't emojis become popular immediately after Kurita invented them?
_____

I can identify the main events in a text.

1 Look at the title of the article and the pictures. Check (✓) the ideas that you think the article will mention.

1 Putting on new socks ☐   4 A food smell from the past ☐

2 Smelling fresh coffee ☐   5 Lying in bed when it's raining outside ☐

3 Walking in fresh snow ☐   6 Finding money you forgot you had ☐

2 Read again and check your answers in exercise 1. Label the pictures with the names.

Simple pleasures

When we're busy and stressed, we often forget to appreciate the little things in life. What are the simple pleasures that make you smile?

 A

 B

 C

 D

I've always loved putting on new socks because they feel really soft and smooth. I don't know why, but they never feel like that after you wash them. I also love it when I've just cleaned my room. It's easier to relax when everything is clean and fresh.

Darius, 15

Have you ever woken up, thought it was the morning, and then realized it wasn't? It happened to me last night. I woke up and heard rain outside. Then I realized it was only 3 a.m. and I could stay in bed for four more hours. There's nothing better than lying in a warm, comfortable bed when you don't have to get up!

Harry, 16

I like smelling things – usually food – that I haven't smelled since I was little. My family is from Buenos Aires, but we moved to the U.S. when I was 4 and I haven't been back to Argentina since then. Last week, I visited a street food market and someone was selling empanadas. They smelled exactly like the empanadas my grandma used to make.

Noelia, 14

Finding things that you think you've lost is a great feeling. A few months ago, I lost my favorite bracelet. I couldn't find it anywhere. Then I had a dream that it was under the sofa. The next morning, I went to look and there it was! Finding money you didn't know you had is awesome, too. Last week, I found $10 in some old jeans and used it to buy ice cream for my friends. That made me happy!

Tamsin, 15

3 Read again. Choose *T* (True), *F* (False), or *DS* (Doesn't say). Correct the false sentences.

1 Darius thinks socks feel softer after you wash them a few times. T☐ F☑ DS☐

   He thinks they're softer when they're new.

2 Darius says he feels less stressed when his room is clean. T☐ F☐ DS☐

_____

3 Noelia often goes to Argentina on vacation. T☐ F☐ DS☐

_____

4 Noelia used to make empanadas with her grandma in Argentina. T☐ F☐ DS☐

_____

5 Harry had to get up at 3 a.m. this morning. T☐ F☐ DS☐

_____

6 Tamsin found her bracelet under her bed after having a dream about it. T☐ F☐ DS☐

_____

 I can predict what a text is going to say.

☺ ◯   ☺ ◯   ☹ ◯

Do the right thing

Reading

1 Read the article and match the headings A–E with the tips 1–5.

A Think about what you have in common with people

~~B Be curious when you meet new people~~

C Have new experiences

D Try to understand, but be open, too

E Read books and watch movies

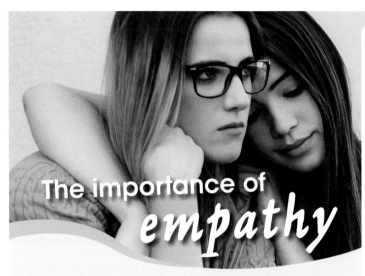

The importance of empathy

"What makes us happy?" Most psychologists agree that strong connections with the people around us are crucial for happiness. However, they say that it isn't only our relationships with our family and friends that matter: we also tend to be happier if we live in communities where people look after each other and give each other a hand.

The philosopher Roman Krznaric claims that in many countries, like the U.S., people are losing these connections. They might be richer than they used to be, but they don't know their neighbors' names. According to Krznaric, the well-being of all human societies depends on empathy – people's ability to understand each other's feelings and experiences. If people had more empathy, Krznaric says, they'd be happier and there would be fewer social problems.

So would we learn to be more empathetic if we practiced? Krznaric believes that we would, and suggests some ways that everyone can develop empathy:

1 __B Be curious when you meet new people__

We often spend our time with friends and classmates who are similar to us. Of course, we need to be careful when meeting strangers, but we can learn a lot from people with different experiences.

2 _____

These are great ways to imagine what the world would be like if we were older, came from another country, or lived in a different period in history.

3 _____

It's easy to look at someone or hear their accent and think we know who they are. We're usually wrong! Focus on what you share, not on the differences between you.

4 _____

If you never tried surfing, sushi, or samba, you'd never know if you liked it. Trying new things helps you understand other people's interests.

5 _____

Really listen to what other people say. However, also remember that a conversation needs two people. Express your feelings, too.

2 Read again. Choose the correct answers.

1 Many psychologists say that in the happiest societies, people …

   a have big families.
   b help each other.
   c live close to their family and friends.

2 Krznaric says that in the past, people in countries like the U.S. …

   a generally had more money.
   b had more neighbors.
   c knew more people in their community.

3 Krznaric believes that watching movies …

   a stops us communicating with our families.
   b helps us understand how other people might feel.
   c is more fun for people with high levels of empathy.

4 Krznaric says that if we try new things, we'll …

   a usually enjoy them.
   b meet people with similar interests to ours.
   c have more respect for things other people like.

3 Find words and phrases in the article with meanings 1–5.

1 extremely important   __crucial__

2 are often   _____

3 general health and happiness   _____

4 able to understand other people's feelings   _____

5 think about, concentrate on   _____

I can identify the meaning of unknown words.

1 Read the article quickly. When did Disney buy Pixar? _____

PIXAR: where science meets imagination

Computer animation is one of the world's newest and most exciting creative industries. It's also one of the best examples of art and science coming together to create something magical. There are now hundreds of computer animation studios, but none has been more important in the history of digital animation than Pixar.

The history of Pixar begins in the 1970s. George Lucas, the man who created the Star Wars movies, wanted to discover new ways to use computer graphics in animation. In 1979, he invited a group of top computer scientists to work for him and five years later, they presented their first movie, *The Adventures of André & Wally B.* It was only two minutes long, but its use of computer graphics was truly original.

The person who named the company "Pixar" was Steve Jobs, the man who set up Apple. Jobs bought the company in 1986 and in the next few years, the team made several short 3-D computer animated movies, including *Luxo Jr.*, *Red's Dream*, and *Tin Toy.* They continued to invent new animation technology and became famous for their clever and creative techniques.

In the early 1990s, The Walt Disney Studios knew that their 2-D animations were becoming old-fashioned, so in 1991, Disney and Pixar agreed to work together. The result was *Toy Story* in 1995. It was the world's first full-length computer-animated movie and it was extremely successful.

In the next ten years, Pixar and Disney produced more movies together, including *Toy Story 2*, *Monsters, Inc.*, *Finding Nemo*, and *Cars.* Pixar made an enormous amount of money and in 2006, Disney bought the company. Pixar has continued to make very popular films, such as *Up*, *Finding Dory*, and *Coco.* With more than 25 Oscars and billions of fans, it has earned its place in movie history forever.

2 Read at the questions and <u>underline</u> the key words.

1 <u>Why</u> did <u>Lucas</u> ask a group of <u>computer scientists</u> to work for him in <u>1979</u>?
   To help him invent new computer animation techniques.

2 Who gave Pixar its name?
   _____

3 What did the company do in the late 1980s?
   _____
   _____

4 Why did Disney decide to work with Pixar?
   _____
   _____

5 Why was *Toy Story* important in movie history?
   _____
   _____

6 What did Pixar do between 1996 and 2006?
   _____

3 Read again. Answer the questions in exercise 2 in your own words.

I can look at the questions before I read and underline useful words as I read.

ACKNOWLEDGEMENTS

Cover photographs reproduced with permission from: Alamy Stock Photos (couple/Ian Allenden); Getty Images (team/Blend Images – Moxie Productions), (painting/Hill street Studios); Oxford University Press DAM (laptop vector/Shutterstock/sabri deniz kizil).

Back cover photograph: Oxford University Press building/David Fisher.

STUDENT BOOK

Commissioned photography by: Benjamin Norman pp.12, 13 (Rob & Vicky), 14 (Vicky), 14 (Rob), 23, 24, 32 (Jack, Naomi, Ollie & Piper), 35, 45, 46, 57, 58, 67, 68 (Vicky & Tripp), 79, 80 (Vicky), 89, 113 (extra vocabulary); Mark Bassett pp.52 (folded paper), 53 (boy sniffing laptop), 115 (boy with coffee stained T-shirt).

Video stills by: Oxford University Press/People's TV pp.22 (Watch video), 22 (ex.4), 32 (Watch video), 44 (Watch video), 54 (Watch video), 66, 76 (Watch video), 76 (Professor Charles Spence), 88, 98 (Watch video).

Illustrations by: Nicolas Gremaud/Anna Goodson pp.10, 17, 28, 41 (ex1), 72, 74, 81, 85, 109, 114 (puzzles); Nick Harris pp.124, 125; Adam Horsepool/Advocate Art pp.5 (ex5), 16, 24, 33 (ex2), 39 (ex3), 61, 73, 112, 119; Joanna Kerr pp.5 (ex7), 49, 55, 68 (ex2 icons), 117, 118; Mona Meslier Menuau/Advocate Art pp.15, 19, 33 (ex4), 58, 83, 101, 114 (extra vocabulary); Simon Reid pp.48, 50, 60; Ben Scruton/Meiklejohn Illustration pp.4, 9, 25, 34, 40, 46, 47, 71, 77, 87, 110, 113; Tom Woolley/Astound US pp.6, 39 (ex4), 41 (ex3), 111.

The publisher would like to thank the following for permission to reproduce photographs: 123RF pp6 (coding on laptop/welcomia), 6 (hands and notebook/Dejchat Apichattham), 6 (preparing food/Anna Bizoń), 6 (architect plans/David Izquierdo Roger), 6 (stethoscope/Anton Samsonov), 6 (toy shop/vadim yerofeyev), 8 (tropical destination/ahfotobox), 10 (appetizer/Maksim Shebeko), 10 (skewers on grill/Lukas Gojda), 13 (football pitch/Chris Hill), 13 (blue sky/Phatthanit Roengsamran), 13 (colourful wall/saksan maneechay), 13 (friends/dolgachov), 13 (campsite/welcomia), 14 (cat/Eleonora Vatel), 14 (lavender field/Andrey Kotko), 14 (teen girl/Martin Novak), 14 (cat/Wichat Matisilp), 14 (trendy shoes/yayha), 14 (scary movie/Antonio Guillem), 17 (Japanese boy/ziggymars), 18 (shy man/studiograndouest), 18 (woman by coast/Antonio Guillem), 20 (students in library/Jasminko Ibrakovic), 22 (Mexican city street/Kobby Dagan), 28 (rehab group/Vadim Guzhva), 29 (father and daughter/Oleg Dudko), 32 (teen watching TV/daisydaisy), 35 (La Quinta California/welcomia), 36 (mosquito/maewshooter), 36 (forest fire/Dmytro Gilitukha), 36 (Japan street/pabkov), 38 (meteor/solarseven), 38 (overpopulation/Michael Rosskothen), 38 (volcano eruption/Patricio Hidalgo), 44 (Tribowl Building/panya khamtuy), 45 (school/Olga Volodina), 51 (handbag/Edward Olive), 52 (lipstick/picsfive), 52 (cockroach/Mr.Smith Chetanachan), 54 (girl and skateboard/lzflzf), 54 (girl and socks/Andras Gyula Csontos), 62 (angry businesswoman/Dean Drobot), 62 (funny movie/kzenon), 62 (senior friends hugging/diego cervo), 66 (city park/Mykhaylo Pelin), 68 (pretzels/Brent Hofacker), 68 (curry/Buthsakon Lojanaparb), 68 (sweets/5second), 68 (blanket/Andreja Donko), 68 (sandpaper/gavran333), 68 (pebbles/Maruna Skoropadska), 68 (tulips/andreadonetti), 68 (garbage/tainar), 68 (rambutan/somchai khunwiset), 69 (mango and rice/Suphakain Wongcompune), 69 (fruit/Auttachod Thaensila), 69 (market fruit/fedorkondratenko), 71 (New York skyline/Kan Khampanya), 73 (cinema/Wavebreak Media Ltd), 75 (clouds/Potapova Valeriya), 76 (human brain/nerthuz), 76 (laboratory/dotshock), 77 (coke/siraphol), 77 (multicolored houses/Anastasy Yarmolovich), 77 (sports car/Michal Bednarek), 77 (snake/Mihai Andritoiu), 77 (fruit market/Pablo Hidalgo), 77 (bed/Rakop tanyakam), 80 (donating charity items/Ian Allenden), 80 (election help/Lisa Young), 83 (student discussion/Cathy Yeulet), 84 (pensive girl/dolgachov), 88 (counselling/Cathy Yeulet), 88 (fishing boats/Jeremy Richards), 89 (graffiti/steve ball), 90 (old fashioned glasses/sergey ishkov), 90 (painted background/makingfaces), 94 (manicure/Aleksandr Khakimullin), 94 (science lab/Wavebreak Media Ltd), 94 (Sydney/Marco Saracco), 94 (radioactive sign/Aleksandar Levai), 94 (global technology concept/scanrail), 94 (music score sheets/scanrail), 98 (graffiti/ymgerman), 98 (graffiti/rumandawi), 100 (dog/mexitographer), 114 (golf ball/Anek Suwannaphoom), 114 (tennis ball/Tadeáš Skuhra), 114 (banana/Владимир Решетник), 114 (orange/wingedbull), 114 (sliced bread/lisa870), 114 (cleaning items/David Izquierdo Roger), 114 (ceramic tiles/homy_design), 115 (teens shopping/Mirko Vitali), 116 (concrete wall/Roman Tsubin), 116 (glasses/Wutichai Chaometeewut), 116 (leather shoes/aninna847), 116 (wood texture/keren woodgyer), 116 (brick wall/Alina Oleynik), 116 (cardboard/Le Moal Olivier), 116 (metal nuts/Yegor Larin), 116 (coloured bottles/khunaspix), 122 (Japanese wedding/Chih Hsien Hang), 122 (sushi/Dmitry Kalinovsky), 122 (Japanese desert/PaylessImages), 123 (wedding cake/Galyna Tymonko);

Affectiva p21 (child on ipad with Affdex score); Food Is Art Ltd. p92 (chocolate sofa/Prudence Staite); Alamy Stock Photo pp8 (Wimbledon/Greg Balfour Evans), 8 (volleyball/RosaIreneBetancourt 9), 10 (museum/RosaIreneBetancourt 3), 36 (welcome sign, Australia/imageBROKER), 43 (volcanologist/Biosphoto), 69 (Asian flower market/Fabio Nodari), 80 (SNP activists/Scott Campbell), 84 (food bank/RosaIreneBetancourt 4), 84 (serving the homeless/Jim West), 94 (ice cream van/Tony Watson), 100 (first practical car/nik wheeler), 102 (teen students/Zoonar GmbH), 104 (Dachshund dog/Jan Sochor), 104 (beach jump/incamerastock), 104 (Iberian Mask festival/robertharding), 111 (running shower/Image Source); Bridgeman Art Library Ltd pp52 (Mona Lisa, c.1503-6 (oil on panel), Vinci, Leonardo da (1452-1519) / Louvre, Paris, France), 63 (Cotton plant, as imagined by John Mandeville (engraving), English School, (14th century) / Private Collection), 90

(Germany: Duck-Rabbit optical illusion, Fliegende Blatte, Munich, 1892 / Pictures from History), 90 (Water jar depicting a warrior and a woman making a libation, Late Archaic Period (ceramic), Greek, (5th century BC) / Museum of Fine Arts, Boston, Massachusetts, USA / Henry Lillie Pierce Fund), 94 (design for a flying machine, c.1488 (pen & ink on paper), Vinci, Leonardo da (1452-1519) / Bibliotheque de l'Institut de France, Paris, France), 94 (The Kiss, 1907-08 (oil on canvas), Klimt, Gustav (1862-1918) / Osterreichische Galerie Belvedere, Vienna, Austria); Getty Images pp6 (police officer/Stephen Sisler), 8 (martial arts lesson/William West), 8 (200m race/Johannes Eisele), 8 (bungee jump/Matthew Micah Wright), 8 (snowboarder/Daniel Milchev), 8 (whitewater rafting/John & Lisa Merrill), 10 (teens doing makeup/sturti), 11 (Brazilian Capoeira/Yasuyoshi Chiba), 14 (teen on phone/Catherine Ledner), 14 (teen reading book/Anouk de Maar), 18 (woman on phone/JGI/Tom Grill), 18 (girl bites nail/JGI/Jamie Grill), 18 (trendy man/Roberto Westbrook), 18 (lady shaking hair/alfalfa126), 19 (mother and daughter/JGI/Jamie Grill), 21 (robot taking photograph/Toru Yamanaka), 23 (library/Stella), 26 (teens in class/Phil Boorman), 28 (peer discussion/asiseeit), 30 (father and daughter/Image Source), 31 (students/DUEL), 32 (teen hoovering/A. Chederros), 32 (teen doing washing/Peter Dazeley), 32 (girl playing drums/dlewis33), 32 (teen watering flowers/Rainer Elstermann), 32 (teen using laptop/Jim Craigmyle), 40 (Boyan Slat/Michel Porro), 42 (teens in library/Inti St Clair), 43 (colonised Mars/Victor Habbick Visions), 43 (girl in park/Oxana Denezhkina), 43 (young man/Hero Images), 43 (student/Hero Images), 46 (birthday decorations/Moodboard Stock Photography Ltd.), 47 (astronaut Buzz Aldrin/NASA), 47 (Buzz Aldrin/NASA - Apollo / digital version by Science Faction), 49 (girl with trophy/Hero Images), 51 (teen friends/Tetra Images), 52 (porphyrophora polonica/Paul Starosta), 53 (pasta harvesting/Keystone), 55 (girl using microscope/Cultura RM Exclusive/Nancy Honey), 59 (teens laughing/Hero Images), 61 (teen couple/Caiaimage/Trevor Adeline), 62 (anxious girl/JGI/Jamie Grill), 62 (football confrontation/JW Ltd), 62 (students on campus/Moxie Productions), 63 (one dimensional globe/George Diebold), 63 (young kids/Visage), 63 (man in woods/Jupiterimages), 64 (teen discussion/gawrav), 65 (Adolf Dassler/ullstein bild), 65 (football/Timm Schamberger), 67 (empty classroom/Image Source), 70 (Erik Weihenmayer/John Storey), 75 (sleeping teen/EMPPhotography), 75 (sleeping teen/Reza Estakhrian), 75 (student studying/elenaleonova), 75 (lonely teen/Matt_Brown), 80 (boys doing homework/Ronnie Kaufman/Larry Hirshowitz), 80 (volunteers litter picking/Hero Images), 84 (teen using tablet/Geri Lavrov), 84 (dog shelter/Camille Tokerud), 90 (pencil artwork/Barcroft), 90 (Banksy artwork/Fred Duval), 92 (chewing gum art/Antony Jones), 92 (chewing gum art/Antony Jones), 93 (little people artwork/Barcroft), 93 (3D street artist/Edgar Mueller), 94 (music app/Gary Burchell), 94 (amusement ride/Kyodo News), 94 (Google office/View Pictures), 95 (tamagotchi/Kimberly Butler), 97 (technology fair/Robyn Beck), 99 (Egyptian charioteers/Hulton Archive), 104 (chasing seagulls/Wander Women Collective), 105 (teen friends/Ben Pipe Photography), 106 (student asleep/Image Source), 111 (growing tree/Hero Images), 113 (fast food restaurant/Kevin Dodge), 115 (Unicef tent/Jawed Tanveer), 115 (girls with mobile/Westend61), 120 (Chinatown/Michael N. Paras), 121 (St. Patrick's Day Parade/Anadolu Agency), 121 (Sergey Brin/Steve Jennings), 122 (Japanese boy/Indeed), 123 (teen in park/Drazen Lovric), 123 (wedding/Rob Melnychuk), 124 (sophisticated man/Yuri_Arcurs); Heather Hulbert p98 (heart graffiti, New York); iStockphoto 14 (information sign/ftwitty); Oxford University Press pp69 (tropical fruit/Shi Yali), 91 (vintage telephone/erashov), 91 (graffiti/Stephen Birch), 91 (plastic elephant/Sergey Karpov), 91 (easter island heads/Thomas Barrat); OUP DAM pp8 (diver and turtle/Richard Whitcombe), 8 (skydiver/2happy), 8 (surfer/Getty), 11 (sewing/Monika Wisniewska), 11 (aeroplane/MC_PP), 22 (world map/Shutterstock), 25 (teen boy/Hello Lovely), 26 (white smartphone vector/Shutterstock/Aaron Amat), 26 (tablet and smartphone vector/Shutterstock/d3images), 26 (smartphone vectors/Shutterstock/LOVEgraphic), 26 (empty classroom/Shutterstock/Bernhard Lelle), 39 (the sun/Shutterstock/xfox01), 31 (bullying/wavebreakmedia), 36 (flooding/federicofoto), 36 (traffic/ssuaphotos), 36 (desolate landscape/Philip Lange), 56 (polar bears/FloridaStock), 62 (crying child/Getty), 70 (brain 3D illustration/Fedorov Oleksiy), 82 (girl and dog/Alamy), 82 (teen boy/Chris King), 82 (teen boy/Hello Lovely), 111 (traffic lights/AlinaStreltsova); Press Association Images pp65 (Rudolf Dassler/Karl Schnoerrer/DPA), 87 (Tristin Budzyn-Barker/Max Gersh/Rockford Register Star via AP), 87 (roommates/AP Photo/Mike Groll), 97 (Ann Makosinski/Matt Crossick/Empics Entertainment); Rex Shutterstock 10 (teen birthday/OJO Images), 10 (Japanese women/Blend Images), 11 (stage performance/Blend Images), 11 (Adele/Richard Isaac), 65 (Jesse Owens/Glasshouse Images), 70 ('brainport' device/REX/Shutterstock), 84 (volunteers planting trees/imageBROKER), 84 (charity shop/Alex Segre), 90 (recycled toy cars/Bruno Morandi/robertharding), 94 (Lord of the Rings/Pierre Vinet/New Line / Saul Zaentz / Wing Nut), 99 (Solar Impulse 2/Xinhua News Agency), 108 (Albert Einstein/Roger-Viollet), 120 (European migrants/Everett Collection); Science Photo Library p47 (moon landing/DON BAIDA); Shutterstock pp7 (dentist/Dreams Come True), 8 (skateboarder/goofyfoottaka), 8 (football match/Natursports), 13 (forest/N K), 13 (beach sunset/Andrew Shiels), 13 (teens playing video games/CandyBox Images), 13 (digital camera/Yen Hung), 18 (happy man/eurobanks), 18 (woman laughing/Aleksei Isachenko), 21 (pizza making/Africa Studio), 21 (technology concept/Titima Ongkantong), 25 (teen girl/AJR_photo), 25 (teen student/Monkey Business Images), 26 (Thumbs Up icon set/Yurlick), 27 (teens driving/digitalskillet), 31 (bullying/Syda Productions), 36 (crowd as world/Arthimedes), 37 (climate change/Bernhard Staehli), 43 (recycle vector/Bellovittorio), 43 (Earth from space/studio23), 44 (Seoul street/Vincent St. Thomas), 44 (San Francisco skyline/zhu difeng), 49 (cat/DavidTB), 49 (cat/Nailia Schwarz), 53 (kangaroo/Richard J Ashcroft), 53 (abstract background/NYS), 54 (decorated living room/MestoSveta), 55 (teen with football/Air Images), 57 (park/Jon Bilous), 63 (girl with teddy/ESB Professional), 65 (football game/Mikkel Bigandt), 68 (lemon and limes/Alena Haurylik), 68 (knocking on wood/cagi), 68 (hot air balloons/topseller), 68 (jewel beetles/aSuruwataRi), 69 (tropical fruit/kungverylucky), 75 (girl coughing/Stas Ponomarencko), 75 (acne skin/Ocskay Bence), 75 (unhealthy food/Lightspring), 78 (couple at the theatre/Goncharov_Artem), 79 (suburban neighborhood/rSnapshotPhotos), 80 (girl walking dog/Himchenko.E), 80 (desserts/Elena Elisseeva), 82 (student/Monkey Business Images), 82 (teen girl/Iakov Filimonov), 82 (teen boy/Monkey Business Images), 82 (teen student/Monkey Business Images), 84 (teen studying/CandyBox Images), 94 (interior designing/Naphat_Jorjee), 94 (handyman/Uber Images), 94 (girl on laptop/Solis Images), 98 (graffiti/ValeStock), 103 (school road sign/StacieStauffSmith Photos), 107 (student/Monkey Business Images), 111 (recycling/Lightspring), 111 (money in garbage/Romariolen), 111 (disposable bags/Richard P Long), 111 (towel/Vince Clements), 115 (clothing/Kostikova Natalia), 123 (Caribbean food/Rohit Seth), 124 (silver frame/Iakov Filimonov); Stephen Lund (Victoria, BC) p92 (Happy New Year doodle/GPSdoodles.com), 92 (giraffe doodle/GPSdoodles.com).

The authors and publisher are grateful to those who have given permission to reproduce the following extracts and adaptations of copyright material: p.92 Extract from 'Food is Art: How it all began' by Prudence Staite from http://www.foodisart.co.uk/FOOD_IS_ART/HOME.html. Reproduced by permission. pp.124–125 Extract from The Picture of Dorian Gray by Oscar Wilde, retold by Jill Nevile. This simplified edition © Oxford University Press 2008. Reproduced by permission of Oxford University Press. p.97 'Ann Makosinski: Teenage inventor uses TEDx Teen talk to call on young people to ditch their smartphones' by Susie Mesure, 16 January 2016, http://www.independent.co.uk. Reproduced by permission.

Special acknowledgement is due to Lewis Lansford for the Watch *pages.*

WORKBOOK

Illustrations by: Nicolas Gremaud/Anna Goodson pp.2, 6, 18; Andy Parker pp.9 (ex4), 24; Ben Scruton/Meiklejohn Illustration pp.3, 5, 23; Tom Woolley/Astound US p.4.

The publisher would like to thank the following for permission to reproduce photographs: 123RF pp13 (caution bears sign/welcomia), 22 (football boots/Alexander Makarov), 25 (pastry chefs/kzenon), 25 (interior designer/Wavebreak Media Ltd), 31 (money in jeans/miroslav110), 31 (taking off socks/nito500); Alamy Stock Photo pp31 (Spanish empanadas/4k-Clips); Getty Images pp2(college students/Compassionate Eye Foundation/Chris Ryan), 12 (teen watching TV/Paul Bradbury), 15 (girls rock climbing/Steve Coleman), 19 (women look at photo album/BURGER), 24 (David Bowie/Michael Putland), 29 (kids using tablets/Hero Images), 31 (teen sleeping/Tetra Images), 32 (consoling a friend/Westend61); iStockphoto pp7 (woman yawning/ariwasabi), 12 (clean your room/KLH49), 17 (using mobile/velvelvel); OUP DAM pp8(bake sale/Monkey Business Images), 10 (plane take off/Mehdi Photos), 20 (baker/racorn), 22 (motor cross-country/Crok Photography), 22 (cupcake/Pinkcandy), 22 (paint brushes/Tatiana Mihaliova), 26 (cinema audience/lev dolgachov), 26 (cinema reaction/Deklofenak); Rex Shutterstock pp33 (Toy Story/SNAP); Shutterstock pp5 (city climate change/kwest), 9 (museum, New York/Phototasty), 11 (positive attitude concept/marekuliasz), 14 (Mars/Vadim Sadovski), 16 (leaflet illustration/Goderuna), 22 (teen girl/mavo), 27 (teacher/Pressmaster), 28 (artificial intelligence concept/Christian Lagerek), 30 (sending emojis/Nicotombo).

Special acknowledgement is due to Alexandra Paramour for the Workbook, pages W1–W35.

The authors and publishers would like to thank all the teachers and schools whose feedback, comments, and suggestions have contributed to the development of Metro*. The authors would also like to thank all of those involved in the production of* Metro*. James Styring dedicates the series to Jude Robert Alver Styring.*